In *The reinvention of love* Anthony Low argues that cultural, economic and political change transformed the way poets from Sidney to Milton thought and wrote about love. Examining the interface between broad social, political and economic practices and individual psyches, as reflected in literary texts, Professor Low illuminates the connections between material circumstances, perceptions and ideals. In a series of well-informed readings of the work of Sidney, Donne, Herbert, Crashaw, Carew and Milton, he shows how from the late sixteenth century poets struggled to replace the older Petrarchan tradition with a form of love in harmony with a changing world, and to reconcile human love and sacred devotion. Donne fled the social world; Carew made new accommodations with it; Milton revised it. For Milton, sacred love, cut off from communal norms, verges on hatred, while married love takes on the burden of assuaging loneliness in a threatening world. Thus, under the pressures of psychosocial change, new cultures, new habits of perception, and new forms of poetry emerge.

THE REINVENTION OF LOVE

THE REINVENTION OF LOVE

Poetry, politics and culture from Sidney to Milton

ANTHONY LOW

New York University

CAMBRIDGE
UNIVERSITY PRESS

Published by the Press Syndicate of the University of Cambridge
The Pitt Building, Trumpington Street, Cambridge CB2 1RP
40 West 20th Street, New York, NY 10011-4211, USA
10 Stamford Road, Oakleigh, Melbourne 3166, Australia

First published 1993

Printed in Great Britain at the University Press, Cambridge

A catalogue record for this book is available from the British Library

Library of Congress cataloguing in publication data
Low, Anthony, 1935–
The reinvention of love: poetry, politics, and culture from Sidney to Milton /
Anthony Low.
p.   cm.
Includes index.
ISBN 0 521 45030 6
1. English poetry – Early modern, 1500–1700 – History and criticism. 2. Love
poetry, English – History and criticism. 3. Politics and literature – England. 4.
Language and culture – England. 5. Sidney. Philip, Sir 1554–1586 – Criticism and
interpretation. 6. Milton, John, 1608–1674 – Criticism and interpretation. I. Title.
PR535.L7L68 1993
821′.309354–dc20   93-18184 CIP

ISBN 0 521 45030 6 hardback

Publication of this book has been aided by a grant from the Abraham and Rebecca
Stein Faculty Publication Fund of New York University, Department of English.

TAG

*This one is for Peter, Liz,
Katie, Nick, Alex,
Michael, Frances, Jessie,
Edward, and Charlotte*

"We sat grown quiet at the name of love."
Yeats, "Adam's Curse"

Contents

Preface

I began working on this book in 1986, but, because of various obligations unconnected with it and the pressure of administrative duties, my ideas saw light only gradually, in the form of preliminary articles and talks. Completion was delayed until New York University granted me sabbatical leave in the fall of 1991. Perhaps that delay was as well, since the subject I had undertaken – the effect of cultural, political, and economic change on how people think about love, as seen in representative seventeenth-century poetry – was subtle and complicated. As far as possible, I have tried to let the poems and the other materials I have worked with dictate the kind of book that has emerged. One may be tempted, in exploring such a large area – much subject at this time to political passions – to begin with a set thesis, method, or ideology. My own biases will no doubt emerge and convict me. Still I have tried at every stage not only to interpret, which is the essence of the study, but to let the poetry guide that interpretation and speak for itself.

After having undertaken a previous investigation of poetry and cultural change, I have been confirmed by this new study in my faith that poets are far more sensitive than most of us to the broad cultural and political transformations in society that impact on our individual lives. Poets may usually be relied on to respond to religious, political, and economic forces of change in ways far more subtle and interesting than any theories that we, as critics, might retrospectively bring to bear. The critic's task is to tease out and to bring into comprehensible order what might not be evident to a casual reader. This is not to argue that theory is useless. Any theory worth its salt should open our eyes to things we would otherwise miss. My primary allegiance, however, has always been to the writer, to the individual text and the texts as they relate to one another, and to historical facts and social forces, so far as we can reasonably know or infer them. In these latter days, no one would venture to proclaim that fathoming any of these three – writer, poem, or history – is a matter of complete, transparent certitude or of undoubted factuality. But neither, most reasonable people would agree, are they matters of utter indeterminacy.

My other allegiance is to notional readers, who, I like to think, are persons – whatever their beliefs or desires – curious to learn something new. There is something oppressive in the thought of "interpretive communities" of like-minded readers, clubbing together to read only like-minded writers – and consigning all others to oblivion. What ennui, only to read what we already know.

I also write for non-notional friends and colleagues. I have been helped and encouraged in the course of writing by many such friends, including Ernest Gilman (who not only read the book with grace and efficiency but ran the department in my absence so I could write it), Harold Bloom, Denis Donoghue, Blanford Parker, Robert Raymo, Raphael Falco, Marshall Grossman, Michael C. Schoenfeldt, Robert V. Young, John R. Roberts, Arthur Kinney, Kirby Farrell, Deborah Shuger, Achsah Guibbory, and Judith Hertz, as well as by a dozen anonymous journal readers and two readers for the press, and by friendly or helpfully critical remarks from audiences at several scholarly conferences. John T. Shawcross and Jason P. Rosenblatt were among those who made helpful suggestions. I remember a frequent query from friends at such conferences: "What are you working on now?" "Well, actually, it's the same thing I told you about last year." (And the year before.) As usual, none of these persons is responsible for my perseverance in error, whether factual, political, or stylistic; but they have often cheered me up and faithfully pointed out omissions of citation, phrases needing disentanglement, points that readers might misunderstand, and embarrassing lapses and typographical errors that will never see print.

Early versions of parts of this book were presented as papers: at the MLA convention in 1986, at the NEMLA conference in Boston and the second annual conference of the John Donne Society in Gulfport in 1987, at the ninth Renaissance Conference at Dearborn in 1990, and at the Milton Seminar at Harvard in 1992. Versions of parts of the book have also appeared as articles: in *Studies in the Literary Imagination* (1989); as "Donne and the Reinvention of Love," *English Literary Renaissance* 20 (1990): 465–86; in *New Perspectives on the English Religious Lyric of the Seventeenth Century*, ed. John R. Roberts (University of Missouri Press, 1993); in *Culture and Cultivation in Early Modern England: Writing and the Land*, ed. Michael Leslie and Timothy Raylor (Leicester University Press, 1992); in *Discourses of Desire*, ed. Claude Summers and Ted-Larry Pebworth (University of Missouri Press, 1993); and in a special Herbert issue of *Renascence* edited by R. V. Young scheduled to appear in 1993. I thank the editors of these journals and presses for their courtesy, their frequent helpfulness, and for permission to reprint. I am also grateful for permission to quote as my epigraph a line from "Adam's Curse," in *The Poems of W. B. Yeats: A New Edition*, edited by Richard J. Finneran (New York: Macmillan, 1983).

Introduction

This is a book about ways of loving, under changing cultural, political, and economic circumstances, as expressed in poetry from Sir Philip Sidney to John Milton. I have chosen to begin it in the last decades of the sixteenth century and to end it a hundred years later, because this is an especially critical period of cultural transition – of transition in society generally and more particularly in prevailing attitudes toward love. When I began working on this book, I meant to limit it to secular love poetry in relation to cultural change. But poems, like facts, have a way of forcing their own terms on the reader. The result is a book that is somewhat less neat and orderly than I first intended, but hopefully truer to its subject. It ranges "downward" to consider such matters as the lovers' sexuality and material circumstances and "upward" to touch on their highest aspirations and ideals.

It proved simply too limiting not to consider the relations between secular and sacred love. Writers at the time thought there were important connections, as well as differences; indeed, it is hard to see how these two loves could fail to intersect in some way. Broadly defined, religious love is love to which people give – or believe they ought to give – the highest priority. Notionally, the highest allegiance of most men and women in the period was to the Christian God; actually (as in other times) their allegiances might vary considerably from the professed ideal. Whether or not a particular poet loved God first, or something else, nonetheless his subordinate loves, for persons and for things (or for himself) were bound to be colored by his ultimate allegiance.

I

As I worked with the poetry, it gradually became apparent that a system of biblical metaphors, which writers used to describe relations between men and women, between created beings and God, and between God and his Church, is especially revealing, helping us not only to understand literary works and their interrelationships but also some of the attached cultural and psychological attitudes. An ancient tradition, which includes the Song of Songs, the Pauline Epistles, and the Book of Revelation, as well as many succeeding commentaries, springs from the originating verse in Genesis: "Therefore shall a man leave his father and his mother, and shall cleave unto his wife: and they shall be one flesh" (Genesis 2:24).[1] An intricate system of imagery exfoliates from this earliest verse on love and marriage: a system that comments on it, interacts with it, and sometimes extends it into new areas of reference. In the Bible, from Genesis to Revelation, and in later theological, devotional, and literary traditions – as well as in the marriage service – this verse commenting on the marriage of Adam and Eve develops into a rich system of metaphors connected with human love, divine love, and Christian community, which I term the biblical marriage trope. This trope in turn proves, in Milton's case especially, to have revealing connections with the broad trend toward the secularization of western culture, which gained decisive momentum during the seventeenth century.

I have chosen to discuss the poets on which I draw sequentially, beginning with Sir Philip Sidney. So the book begins on a largely secular note. I take Sidney to be an important representative of older ways of thinking about love. In particular, he represents the central traditions of courtly and Petrarchan love, which converge and combine in the love poetry of the Elizabethan period. But he is also among the first poets to discover – much to his discomfort, if not his virtual self-destruction – that the older ways of loving were no longer satisfactory to a man in his historical situation. As Thomas Kuhn has shown with respect to scientific revolutions, discrepancies, dissatisfactions, and a general feeling that something is vaguely amiss, generally precede the working-out of a new set of explanations.[2] Much the same is true of other cultural systems and of inward psychological attitudes, which may gradually become incompatible with changing circumstances, until ones that work better are developed to replace them. With regard to love, Sidney was not only a last brilliant exemplar of the older, aristocratic Petrarchan tradition, but an important precursor of a century-long process of change and reinvention.

A pivotal figure in the reinvention of love is John Donne. Chapter 2 is devoted to his secular love poems, especially the *Songs and Sonets*. Donne began with attitudes molded by the Petrarchan tradition, with which he struggled for a good part of his life. Under great social and psychological pressures (partly attributable to his difficult personal situation in relation to society) he invented a new kind of private love: idealized, Romantic, mutual, and transcendent in feeling. This new love, however, was so far ahead of its time culturally that it is questionable whether even Donne himself could have understood all its potential implications. In his last years, his thoughts turned in other directions. It took two centuries for events (including the Industrial Revolution and the rise of Romanticism) to catch up with Donne – and more than three centuries before his love poems could be appreciated as they have been by readers in the modern period.

Donne also wrote some of the strongest devotional poems in the language. In chapter 3, I take up some of the difficulties he had in transforming his early loves for "profane mistresses" and for his wife into the sacred love of God. Some of the same personal characteristics and attitudes that made Donne so innovative as a lover of women – among them his active, insistent masculinity – proved impediments to his loving God, but also were sources for much of the conflicted, paradoxical, baroque power of his best divine poems.

In chapters 4 and 5, I consider the sacred love poems of George Herbert and Richard Crashaw. These two poets offer instructive contrasts with Donne. Herbert is unable, or unwilling, to carry the biblical marriage trope to its logical conclusion, with respect to either the Church or his own soul. Instead, at the point where courtship gives place to consummation and marriage he substitutes another human relationship, that of parent and child. The result is an influential unsexing of sacred verse. In contrast with both Donne and Herbert, Crashaw revels in assuming the role of the Bride, which the marriage trope necessarily imposes on poets who employ it. Donne's masculinity and Herbert's sense of patriarchal superiority contrast with Crashaw's willing "femininity." Crashaw happily uses women as intermediaries and resigns himself to their traditionally passive and self-sacrificial role. In all three writers, the love of God is expressed in terms of various human relationships, and is emotionally colored by them.

In chapter 6 I return to earth to examine the secular love poetry of Thomas Carew. Like Donne, Carew was subjected to heavy psychological pressures by his difficult family situation and by society. But, because he had the advantage of writing a generation later than Donne, he was better able to incorporate changing historical circumstances and social interactions into his vision of love, and to find a more practical solution. Where Donne invented a new kind of love that idealizes the privacy of the loving couple and rejects the material and social worlds, Carew invented a love that makes a place for itself in the daily transactions of society by imitating the new economic mobility just coming to the fore in England's agricultural marketplace. As Donne validates what would eventually become the Romantic ideal of the loving couple, who perforce retreat from the world and set up magical walls against it, Carew validates the more pragmatic, market-driven notion of the individual lover who serves his (or her) own freedom and happiness by replacing courtly loyalty with libertine mobility. Although libertinism was not new, Carew gave it a new kind of ethical justification, which he borrowed from the progressive thinking of such New-Scientific "improvers" in the field of agriculture as Samuel Hartlib.

As Donne provides the center of gravity for the earlier part of this study, Milton is the center of gravity of its last part. Chapter 7 considers the question of Milton's versions of the love of God and of the Church, especially as revealed by his handling of the marriage trope. For Milton, sacred love is so zealous and vehement that it may often appear in the form of hatred or rejection. Many readers have been disturbed by the violent "bigotry" of his writings. More recently, others have approved his revolutionary fervor. Milton was temperamentally unable to accept the tropes of the Church as a loving Bride and as a universal Mother. Instead, he provides his readers with a new model of sacred love, in which the Church and other cultural institutions have no part. His is a love always in danger of individuation and isolation. In Milton's prose and in *Paradise Lost*, divine love borrows from tradition but at the same time cuts itself loose from traditional and communal norms. In this regard, Milton is not only a late exponent of Christian love, bringing it down into the modern world and acclimating it to its new circumstances, but an early precursor of Modernist and – more notably – Postmodernist ideological zeal and political commitment.

In chapter 8, I discuss the paradox that Milton was famous throughout the eighteenth century and long afterward as the patron of loving, companionate marriage, but that he was equally widely known as the Great Divorcer. There is an intimate connection in his writings between love and divorce – as there is between divine love and divine hatred. Uniquely for his time, Milton proposed a doctrine of divorce on the grounds of incompatibility. His views of marital compatibility and incompatibility, which are carried over implicitly into *Paradise Lost*, prove difficult, perhaps impossible, to reconcile with his fundamentally Christian ideas concerning grace and freedom. Adam and Eve are an exemplary pair who represent a new ideal of love and marriage – an ideal remarkably similar to Donne's in some ways but far more influential – that is based on a kind of occult natural supernaturalism rather than on Christian or on rational principles. It aspires to its own version of eternal transcendence. In *Paradise Lost*, as in the *Songs and Sonets*, companionate love and marriage take on the heavy burden of assuaging loneliness, curing alienation, and sheltering the loving couple against the assaults of a hostile world. Society, the extended family, the patronage network, even God and the

Church, no longer have effective power to deal with the burgeoning psychosocial pressures of cultural change upon love.

Since my topic is large, I should begin by remarking on a few things this book is *not* about. Inevitably I touch on desire, sexuality, gender roles, dominance and submission, feminism, patriarchy, and other matters related to love of great topical interest. I do so only insofar as my argument takes me in these various directions. Love remains my central concern, not the varieties of "sexual politics." I should also say that my concern is almost entirely limited to the love of male poets for women and for God or the world. I have bounded my discussion in this way because the subject is broad enough, if not already too broad. I am confident that many other scholars, more capable than I in these areas, will continue to study women poets and various other questions related to feminism and to gender theory, with which I am only indirectly or intermittently concerned. I have often profited from reading such work – as I hope will be evident in the following chapters – but I am not primarily concerned to address these ongoing discourses directly.[3]

Because my focus is on a selection of love poets who were all men, and also because I sometimes speak in terms of seventeenth-century perceptions, I have often written "he" where it might have seemed more politic to have written the now generally preferred form, "he or she." I have done so deliberately – though not without considerable thought, frequent hesitation, and concern not to be misinterpreted – as a way of speaking more honestly and responsively to what this book is about than the mere pretense of "correct" usage. The question of whether men and women love or desire in just the same way is vexed and complicated. I have not attempted to enter into it. Certainly there are culturally induced differences between men and women – differences which in turn differ in various times and places – if not underlying biological differences. The peculiar psychological quirks and habits of male love poets, as expressed in their work, are often clearly different from those of female love poets. It would have been dishonest and confusing had I always written "she or he," in contexts where what I really mean is only or chiefly "he."[4] I hope, nonetheless, that women readers can profit from what I have to say about poet lovers who, from their point of view, represent the "other."

In the same way, I know there are "class" limitations in choosing to write about the particular poets I have chosen. They are by no means all courtiers, all equally well-born or privileged, all Protestants, or all similar in personality; but (I realize) they all are members of a privileged few who attended Oxford or Cambridge and formed the loosely knit group of lettered men who (if only because of their university degrees) called themselves nobles or gentry. We might wish that the seventeenth century were more like ours, but we cannot change it now. I have confined my study to these particular writers for several reasons. One is that I find major poets more satisfying to work with than minor ones, and these were among the major poets of their time. Another is that "major" poets are likely to be more than usually sensitive to cultural change. They are exceptionally good as poets, in part, not only because they are "universal" in some mystical sense, but because universality – which I take to be the ability to speak strongly to readers of other centuries and cultures – is likely to arise (paradoxically) from unusual responsiveness to particular personal and historical circumstances. Other significant markers of cultural change may, of course, be found in ballads and broadsides, as well as in the popular theater, but I leave those fields to others.

It is with particular regret that I have omitted consideration of Spenser, Shakespeare and Jonson, but no one can undertake to do everything in a book of decent proportions. C. S. Lewis has suggested that Spenser and Shakespeare played a critical role in turning love away from courtly origins toward a new ideal of mutual love and courtship leading to marriage.[5] Spenser was perhaps the sanest and most thorough poetic investigator into all the varieties of love.[6] Shakespeare, especially in his festive comedies, contributed equally to the new ideal of marriage, even though altogether his views about love were far more complicated and ambiguous than Spenser's. Love leading happily to marriage amounts to only a corner of what Shakespeare has to say on the subject, but, being Shakespeare, it is a very capacious corner.[7] I have chosen not to write in detail about Shakespeare or Spenser at this time for several reasons. First, because critics have already written so much that is to the point, and I hope readers will join me in preferring to avoid a long labor of summary. Second, because close rereading of either poet would require a book in itself, or at least several large chapters in this one. And third, because Spenser, despite his amazing complexity, predominantly represents what I would call the "official" position – that is, society's and Christianity's position – on love and marriage, a position with which most of us are already familiar. The curve of development that I undertake to describe would have been further complicated by including them, but I do not think that it would have been fundamentally altered.

I should add that this is not *primarily* a sociological or a historical study of love. I have used my knowledge of sociology and history, often tacitly, but I have not attempted to provide a study that is highly detailed in either area. Such work has been done by others, notably by Michel Foucault in such general works as *The Archeology of Language* (1972) and *The Order of Things* (1970), as well as in his unfinished study of human sexuality. Nearer to the present subject, Lawrence Stone, in *The Family, Sex and Marriage in England*, 1500–1800 (1977), has written a ground-breaking if controversial work, which has since been much built upon, disputed, and revised by others.[8] Of course I refer constantly to history, biography, and practice as well as to poetry. For that reason, a study of this kind would be impossible without reliance on the archival work of traditional historians and biographers and the provocations of recent cultural historians. My own hope, however, is to contribute to the ongoing multi-disciplinary conversation something new chiefly about what the poems themselves reveal concerning changing attitudes toward love. As Lauro Martines has argued, poems are also pieces of history, fragments of the past, although they are ordinarily "oblique and coded."[9] Much of this book is therefore a work of what some have called "decoding," in the light of cultural, historical, and political circumstances. I would prefer, however, to call it a work of interpretation.

As the last but most important of these preliminary caveats, I propose to offer no detailed theory to account for the precise mechanisms at work in what I consider to be the most interesting point of investigation for literary-cultural studies of a historical kind: examination of the interface between broad social, political, and economic practices and individual psychologies as reflected in literary texts. That culture, poetry, and the perceptions of individuals effect one another is obvious; but to my mind no one has yet given a full and satisfactory account of the mechanisms involved. Where many great thinkers have partly failed, it would be presumptuous of me to proffer a complete solution. But I hope this book may point toward further work that might be done to investigate how poetry can help us understand more clearly what goes on at the critical juncture of personal psychological processes with larger cultural forces. Out of the collision between the social and the psychological our future develops. In turn, such investigations throw new light on the poetry – not the least of a literary critic's concerns.

Marxists and New Historicists of various persuasions have proposed a number of theories, in recent years generally more sophisticated and workable than the old Marxist model (sometimes now called vulgar), which argued that all culture is merely a superstructure built on determining material economic events. Nevertheless an unexamined "materialism" usually continues to shape our newer models, with the resulting frequent conviction that culture shapes people but people cannot shape culture. Postmodernists of many kinds continue to fall into less obviously materialist yet similarly problematic assumptions: for example, that we are entirely the prisoners of our systems of discourse, or that it is only possible for a reader to read what he already knows how to read.[10] Such theses, like Zeno's paradox, are readily "proven" yet fly in the face of practical experience.

Many theories of this kind, fashionably "materialist" in their assumptions, continue to have the weakness that they allow insufficiently for the possibility that people can change "the world" just as "the world" changes people. In Samuel Hazo's elegant formulation:

> the world we dream
> is what the world becomes,
> and what the world's become
> is there for anyone's re-dreaming.[11]

If Milton had not existed, the world might have turned out to be just the same as it is – but then again, it might not have. To take the thought experiment further, if none of the poets in this study had existed – or if no poets at all had existed – things would surely have turned out differently. But the hypotheses become increasingly absurd. These writers were essential parts of the cultural fabric of their times. At the least, Donne and Milton and their fellows can help us to understand *how* things have turned out. Without consenting to the particulars of his final thesis, I would heartily agree with Owen Barfield's contention, well supported by modern science as well as by philosophical arguments, that those who see change in human history as "a formless process determined by the chance impact of events" are themselves victims of "the idolatry of the age of literalness" – that is, of the illusion that the phenomena we perceive are identical with the underlying physical reality, that they are purely objective, purely material, unchangeable "things."[12]

In place of one-way models of cause-and-effect, which assume that events determine consciousness and never the other way around, I shall rather propose what seems to me immediately evident, from common observation, that the interchange between material and psychological processes operates in both directions. We change our circumstances; our circumstances change us. Our changing perceptions or ways of seeing things, and in turn our changing language or discourse, determine how we behave, indeed they determine what it is easily possible for us to see and do. How we behave, what we see and do, in turn gradually change our perceptions, our language, our systems of discourse. I offer this simple two-way model as an assumption, as an obviously credible, if here unproven, axiom on which I intend to proceed. The following discussions are based on it. As they proceed, they will, I hope, reinforce the plausibility of the assumption with which we now begin.

CHAPTER I

Sir Philip Sidney: "huge desyre"

If one had to choose a single word to sum up Sir Philip Sidney, that word might well be "desire."[1] In his life, he was the very knight of desire; in his writing, the very poet of desire. In love and politics alike, desire was the pervasive driving force behind his thoughts and actions. The strong presence of this underlying truth of feeling was clear enough to David Kalstone in 1965, when he published what is still among the best close readings of *Astrophil and Stella* and of what he calls its "Petrarchan vision." "The sonnet sequence allows Sidney to dramatize from yet another point of view the lofty aims of the lover and the defeats imposed by desire."[2] A. C. Hamilton points out that before *Astrophil and Stella* courtly and Petrarchan love sequences typically end either in retraction or in transcendence. By persisting in desire to its fruitlessly bitter end, Sidney's Astrophil represents a radical departure "from the ending of any earlier sonnet sequence."[3] One may agree yet add that in his bleak ending Sidney simply takes the essence of Petrarchism to its logical conclusion, and so to destruction. Above all, Petrarchism is a strong poetics of desire, of terrible longing for the absent and unobtainable. At other times Sidney himself wrote poems of recantation – the two "Certain Sonnets" formerly attached to *Astrophil and Stella* and now generally thought to have been written earlier – and is said to have repented of his love for Penelope Rich on his deathbed.[4] But within the bounds of the sonnet sequence Astrophil is like a Petrarch who never repents, never assumes the persona of an Augustine to expose his own early errors.[5]

As a poet and figure of desire – of amatory desire, political desire, religious desire, masculine desire, and simply human desire – Sidney provided the perfect basis for the rapid invention of the mythical Sir Philip Sidney, who sprang into remarkable life immediately after the poet's death.[6] Knightly poet, chivalric lover, Protestant idealist, perfect gentleman, Sidney became the embodiment of all his admirers' desires, the focusing figure of a hopeful future increasingly less realizable and of a vanishing and now unobtainable past. Although Sidney was greatly admired as an exponent of a proud – but ever imperfectly realized and ever endangered – new Protestant civilization in England, and as a primary originator of a remarkable, prolific flowering of new poetry, it also became increasingly clear, beginning at the time of his death, that he represented the last truly vital flowering of an older ideal, which may be summed up in the words Petrarchan, courtly, and aristocratic.[7] Petrarchan love, the dominant mode in England from the days of Wyatt and Surrey, and courtly love, which had ruled men's minds since the days of Chaucer and Skelton, both now intertwined in a rich English Renaissance synthesis, and found in Sidney their last great exemplar and spokesman. No longer would it be possible to love nobly and to desire endlessly in quite the same fatally splendid way. Indeed *Astrophil and Stella* marks the crowning achievement of golden Petrarchan love poetry in England yet at the same time reveals the fissures of its forthcoming dissolution, as – under the pressure of accelerating change in the basic politics, economics, and culture of England – new desires, ideals, and anxieties begin to crowd in and displace it.

Of course, we know that Sidney puts the Petrarchan conventions into question in the opening sonnets of his sequence. Others poets have used conventional language and inventions; Sidney will take his muse's advice, look in his heart, and write. We also know that, in saying this, Sidney is performing one of the accepted rhetorical moves – indeed, that he is still thoroughly within the Petrarchan tradition. His protests of sincerity and of naturalness are a nice instance of courtly *sprezzatura*, of art concealing art yet allowing itself to be seen and to be admired for its skill. This is only a superficial or a pretended resistance to convention. The real signal that the tradition no longer suffices emerges only gradually, toward the close of the sequence, as Astrophil sinks into flat, hopeless despondency. He neither attains his desire nor repents of it – nor is he any longer even capable of sustaining it. He can find no outlet from his predicament. As we shall see, for Astrophil to escape the Petrarchan conventions would require of him a basic change of stance in his way of loving, a basic change of attitude, rather than a mere tinkering with rhetoric. Sidney finds, in *Astrophil and Stella*, that the courtly Petrarchan stance of endless desire without requital no longer works. But he is still too much immersed in an older, aristocratic culture to find a way out of this dead end. It will remain for other poets, over the course of the next century, to discover workable substitutes for Petrarchism – to reinvent the nature of love.

The question of where Sidney the poet stands in relation to Astrophil the fictive character has been endlessly debated. Those who think of Astrophil as a negative *exemplum*, as a perfect example of how *not* to behave, are usually also among those who stress his invented nature and emphasize the ironic distance between him and his creator.[8] James Scanlon takes a strongly Robertsonian view of *Astrophil and Stella* as a cautionary tale. Astrophil's fate is intended by Sidney to warn readers away from similarly foolish and sinful behavior.[9] Such a one-sided reading tends to reduce and to trivialize *Astrophil and Stella*, but there is far too much evidence in the sequence itself, as well as in our knowledge of Sidney's other works and of the norms of behavior in what was still predominantly a Christian society, for us simply to shrug it off. Astrophil *does* behave sinfully and foolishly; yet the effect of his tale is hardly trivial.

One reason why *Astrophil and Stella* cannot be reduced to a sermon in morality is that, as Alan Sinfield points out, however much we try to draw a sharp line between Astrophil and Sidney, Sidney chose to identify himself in some measure with his protagonist. "[I]f the poem is Sidney's dire warning of the dangers of the overthrow of reason and all Christian values by sexual passion ... then it is very strange that he should wish to identify himself at all with his protagonist."[10] It is not, however, entirely strange that Sidney should identify himself with a foolish sinner: he would hardly be the first or the last writer to do so. For another effect of this almost literal identification, as Sinfield recognizes, is to draw the reader into closer psychological "identification" with Sidney's poetic persona. We see things from Astrophil's point of view. We sympathize with him. In turn, we feel closer to the apparently self-revealing and self-accusatory Sidney. Our response becomes complex, uncertain, and ambivalent, although perhaps it may be partly explicable as "sympathetic involvement with and ethical detachment from the speaker."[11]

It may help us to keep in mind the audience for whom *Astrophil and Stella* was presumably intended. The sonnets were not written for publication, to expose Sidney to the gaze of any stranger who might buy and read his book. They were circulated in manuscript to his friends, to sympathizers and doubters, and perhaps even to covert underminers: to an audience, therefore, who presumably already knew about Sidney's various failings, including his proneness to desire, his impolitic rashness, and his dubious infatuation with Penelope Rich. This would be what Arthur Marotti has called a "coterie" audience – which is to say that it would be exclusive, and already to some degree "in the know."[12] Once he released it, however, Sidney could not be confident that the manuscript would be restricted to his friends alone. In this sense, to circulate it privately was to lose control over it – in effect to "publish" it, a word that Sidney himself uses in Sonnet 34. But it is highly unlikely that Sidney wrote *Astrophil and Stella* with the book-buying public or some unknown posterity as its primary, intended audience. Thus (to extend Ferguson's argument), the sonnet sequence may be viewed as a covert, indirect, and carefully crafted rhetorical "defense" or "apology," in which Sidney admits his known sins to a circle of courtly friends through the persona of Astrophil in order to excuse, mitigate, and reinterpret them.

But what do the sonnets themselves say about motive? Speaking through Astrophil, Sidney returns several times to ask Sinfield's very question: Why should he publish his foolishness to the world? In sonnet 34, Astrophil first offers one reason: "'Art not asham'd to publish thy disease?' / Nay, that may breed my fame, it is so rare" (lines 5–6). Does literary ambition drive the poet, or perhaps ambition to use poetry as a means to success in politics and love? Sidney's voice sounds too ironic here to accept such a reading. To be known to suffer from a disease, even a rare one, is a questionable distinction. Astrophil, more immersed in his quandary than Sidney, immediately wonders if there is any advantage in becoming famous for his "fond ware" (line 7). But the sonnet's close puts the possibility of finding an explicable motivation, even a foolish motivation, further into doubt:

> Peace, foolish wit, with wit my wit is mard.
> Thus write I while I doubt to write, and wreake
>   My harmes on Ink's poore losse, perhaps some find
>   *Stella's* great powrs, that so confuse my mind. (lines 11–14)

Anticipating Freud's "Relation of the Poet to Day-Dreaming," Astrophil – or Sidney – confesses to writing out of a state of mental civil-war or self-destruction, simply because he must.[13] His love for Stella drives him to various conflicted acts of self-revelation and self-annihilation. Much the same explanation appears in sonnet 50: "So that I cannot chuse but write my mind" (line 9). Then, when he thinks to cancel the self-revealing sonnet, he cannot. Half comically he offers another reason: because it begins with Stella's ineradicable name.

Sonnet 45 proposes a traditional, practical reason for the act of writing: to persuade Stella to return his love, to "pitie the tale of me" (line 14). That straightforward motive (though complicated by the presumption that she can be induced to pity the fictionalized tale of his woe more easily than she can pity him in person) might apply to the earlier sonnets, but not, apparently, to the whole sequence, which ends with Astrophil's recognition that he has no hope. If Astrophil has nothing practical to gain from Stella, did Sidney then write to educate a broad readership by his own sad example, accepting censure and ridicule for the benefit of others? Sonnet 104 rebukes such a response, attacking not only "Envious wits" (line 1), presumably

Sidney's rivals for recognition, power, and love, but also facile moralists:

> Your morall notes straight my hid meaning teare
> From out my ribs, and puffing prove that I
> Do *Stella* love. Fooles, who doth it deny? (lines 12–14)

The drawing of moral judgments based on Astrophil's story is vividly portrayed as an action that is killing and destructive. It tears its supposed "moral notes" "from out" the poet's "ribs," as if the would-be moralist were tearing out the lover's living heart.[14] Sonnet 107, the next to last in the sequence, makes a similar point: "O let not fooles in me thy workes reprove, / And scorning say, 'See what it is to love'" (lines 13–14). To say that Astrophil is a sinner or a fool is to say that Stella has made him one, which he declares to be inadmissable. We can, of course, judge the person who says this to be a self-defensive fool and condemn his plea as no better than wishful thinking, from which we should maintain an ironic distance – a distance we must then presume also to have been Sidney's. But who among us can feel himself wiser or wittier than Sidney – or even wiser or wittier than poor Astrophil? That surely is another sobering lesson of the sequence. To respond with unqualified reproach and scorn is to assume Sidney's label of fool. The sequence is so constructed as to categorize its audience as understanding and forgiving aristocrats, members of Sidney's circle, or as censorious and inhuman judges, who exclude themselves from that circle by their very posture of judgment. If those are the only two choices we are offered, no doubt most of us would prefer to number ourselves with the first group, and not the second.

Taking our example from Sidney, who on Ringler's evidence recanted in verse before he proceeded to commit his principal sin in that medium, let us go on to consider the apparent solution given by his well-known retractions before we further consider the problem of the desiring lover in *Astrophil and Stella*. The problem turns out to be far more intractable than either we or Astrophil might have wished, for, as even the retractions reveal, in Sidney desire is simply unquenchable:

Thou blind man's marke, thou foole's selfe chosen snare,
Fond fancie's scum, and dregs of scattred thought,
Band of all evils, cradle of causeless care,
Thou web of will, whose end is never wrought;

Desire, desire I have too dearely bought,
With price of mangled mind thy worthlesse ware,
Too long, too long asleepe thou hast me brought,
Who should my mind to higher things prepare.

But yet in vaine thou hast my ruine sought,
In vaine thou madest me to vaine things aspire,
In vaine thou kindlest all thy smokie fire;

For vertue hath this better lesson taught,
Within my selfe to seeke my onelie hire:
Desiring nought but how to kill desire.

In the octave the whole weight of Sidney's rhetoric comes down on the one repeated word: "Desire, desire." Desire is the "Band of all evils," the underlying connection between all other sins and errors. It is, in other words, that universal "concupiscence" about which St. Augustine and St. Thomas (among others) wrote so much. Concupiscent desire, a product of the Fall, is now a basic and inescapable constituent of human nature. Desire does not even need a specific object to work on. As a Lacanian or other Poststructuralist critic might put it (though of course in more current language than Sidney's), desire is a "cradle of causeless care." It is ever displaced from its secret origins. It is self-begetting. It seeks an unattainable object to project itself and fixate on. A "web of will," its "end is never wrought," its closure or satisfaction never found.

In the sestet the speaker forcefully declares, in the face of desire, that he has found a solution. "But yet in vaine thou hast my ruine sought, / In vaine … / In vaine … / For vertue hath this better lesson taught." Yet, after all, the lesson that virtue teaches proves less than comforting or definitive. The speaker as good as confesses that he has only determined to begin ridding himself of one form of desire by fiercely trying to displace it with another. At the close of the sonnet we still find him in a state of longing and of agitated internal conflict: "Desiring nought but how to kill desire." Unrequited sexual or worldly desire, to which he has long been subjected, gives place (if indeed it *has* yet given place) to unrequited religious desire. The basic paradox remains unresolved; the ending leaves the speaker only beginning to clutch at some hope of amendment. Although the other of the paired retractions, "Leave me ô Love," abandons the terminology of desire for that of love, it too represents a desperate longing for an assured spiritual life that the speaker has not yet attained. Sidney may hope for future resignation to the divine yoke, but at present he can do no more than "aspire to higher things" or seek "heav'n." In the final couplet he takes what amounts to a blind, almost suicidal, anticipatory leap into eternity: "Then farewell world, thy uttermost I see, / Eternall Love maintaine thy life in me." This hopeful resolution still must be put into practice. Truly for Sidney the end of desire "is never wrought" until the point of death. Nor do his other writings or the evidence we have about his ambitious but frustrated life suggest that, short of death, he ever freed himself of the restless stirrings and perpetual cravings of desire. If we can believe the anonymous report, he broke the thread of desire for Lady Rich only on his deathbed.[15]

If in his retraction Sidney can do no more than long for hope, and if religion itself offers him no present escape from desire, then we can hardly expect that the lesson of his secular poetry will be much more sanguine. The importance of desire in his early poems is suggested by the strongly emotional adjectives with which he couples the word. In the *Lady of May* desire is brave; in poems from the *Arcadia* it is hot, high, huge, unrefrained, long, deep, dull, and base.[16] Desire variously flatters, rules, enflames, clips wings, tosses on restless seas, and inflicts painful wounds. In *Certain Sonnet* 6, Sidney vividly pictures desire's insistent, irrational longing, its effect on its victim, in the image of a baby's demanding cry:

> Sleepe Babie mine, Desire, nurse Beautie singeth:
> Thy cries, ô Babie, set mine head on aking:
> The Babe cries "way, thy love doth keepe me waking."
>
> Lully, lully, my babe, hope cradle bringeth
> Unto my children alway good rest taking:
> The babe cries "way, thy love doth keepe me waking."

> Since babie mine, from me thy watching springeth,
> Sleepe then a litle, pap content is making:
> The babe cries "nay, for that abide I waking."

No promise of future "content" is sufficient to still the cravings and cryings of desire. Nor, we may extrapolate from the situation ("pap content is making"), has any prior moment of contentment sufficed to silence its present cries. Greedy inconsolable desire is ever waking, ever crying, for food and for satisfaction that it cannot have – now, at once, and always.

It is not entirely surprising that, apart from Shakespeare,[17] the greatest Renaissance poets of desire are all courtiers. For, in pursuing their profession, indeed in realizing their aristocratic identity, courtiers are inevitably caught between noble ambition and humiliating dependency, and find themselves in a situation only too apt to fan insatiable desire. As we shall see, cultural change worsened Sidney's predicament. Loss of a head to Henry VIII was almost pleasanter than loss of heart under Elizabeth. In that earlier generation, love might seem as unrequited as it later seemed to Sidney, yet fundamental differences may be discerned. For example, the Earl of Surrey, in his sonnet "When ragying love with extreme payne," finds his plight as a lover almost unendurable. When "wofull smart" has brought him to "the poynte of death," however, he likes to cheer himself by comparing his predicament to that of the Greeks at the siege of Troy. That war was bloody, protracted, nearly endless, at times seemingly hopeless, but – a fundamental point – it was at least honorable and indeed finally successful. Surrey is actually heartened by this bleak comparison of his love to the ten years of tribulation which the Greeks endured:

> Therefore I never will repent,
> But paynes contented stil endure:
> For like as when, rough winter spent,
> The pleasant spring straight draweth in ure,
> So after ragyng stormes of care
> Joyful at length may be my fare.[18]   (lines 25–30)

Satisfaction of his love is only a possible hope, never perhaps to be realized; yet that hope gives him essential satisfaction in his endless suffering.

Indeed Surrey can take satisfaction in his endless desire even if requital is impossible. In his sonnet "Love that doth raine and live within my thought," using another martial metaphor, he compares his situation to that of a conquered stronghold. In the face of his mistress's beauty, his "cowarde love" has retreated down into his heart, where it lurks and complains. Surrey presents himself as a vassal to lordly love. Like a good retainer, he vows to remain faithful in spite of all:

> Yet from my lorde shall not my foote remove.
> Sweet is the death that taketh end by love.   (lines 13–14)

These lines highlight one of the essential qualities of the love formed by the convergence of courtly and Petrarchan love in the earlier English Renaissance. This love intimately combines concepts of honor and of feudal obligation with endless internal longing. The feudal relationship implicit in this model of love obliges the lover, if he wishes to escape the stain of shameful recreancy, to remain loyal to his love and to his mistress until death, regardless of the length and intensity of his suffering or the small chance of success. The Petrarchan internalization tangles loyalty with desire, and fixes them both on the unobtainable object.

"Love that doth raine" is, of course, an imitation of Petrarch's *Rime* 109, "Lasso, quante fiate Amor m'assale." But as critics have observed, Surrey, like Wyatt before him, adds to Petrarch's inward longing the explicitly courtly theme of loyalty to a feudal superior in the face of death or of what amounts to self-destruction. As Surrey's contemporary Wyatt puts it:

> What may I do when my maister fereth
>   But in the feld with him to lyve and dye?
>   For goode is the liff, ending faithfully.[19]   (lines 12–14)

In both versions the master (love) is at fault, and the servant (the lover) is innocent. Nevertheless, a loyal servant must follow his master, right or wrong, or else he will lose the honor that gives him his very being.

The theme of honor is pervasive in *Astrophil and Stella*. It is also

deeply ambivalent. On the one hand, loving Stella so pre-
occupies Astrophil that it keeps him from performing his public
duties as he should. It robs him of rationality. On the other
hand, it inspires him to win tournaments and to distinguish
himself as a gentleman. It is the feather in his cap. In sonnet 13,
Jove, Mars, and Love dispute whose coat of arms is the fairest,
with Phoebus as judge. Jove represents government, and Mars
war, the two noblest pursuits a gentleman could follow. But
Cupid (curiously like an upstart Elizabethan inventing or
improving his pedigree)[20] produces the noblest arms of all:

> *Cupid* then smiles, for on his crest there lies
>   *Stella's* faire haire, her face he makes his shield,
>   Where roses gueuls are borne in silver field.
> *Phoebus* drew wide the curtaines of the skies
>   To blaze these last, and sware devoutly then,
>   The first, thus matcht, were scarcely Gentlemen.
>
> (lines 9–14)

To say that, compared to a lover, a ruler and a warrior are
scarcely gentlemen is a comical hyperbole, but it contains a
residuum of truth. Astrophil's love for Stella may be irrational
and shameful, insofar as a gentleman should be a Christian and
a public servant. Yet it would also be shameful, indeed far more
shameful, if he were to desert his love. Astrophil is confronted by
a division of conflicting duties. His commitment to be loyal,
once made, cannot be honorably withdrawn and must take
precedence over every other obligation, even at the cost of
ruining and damning himself.[21]

The English Renaissance saw a renewal both of chivalry and
of courtly love. The two are obviously connected and governed
by codes of aristocratic, quasi-feudal behavior and perception.[22]
As the Renaissance proceeded, especially under Queen Elizabeth, politics and patronage converged with love, and the two
kinds of "courting" became almost interchangeable.[23] This
near interchangeability came about largely because of the
convergence of two aspects of desire: desire for reward, and
desire for the unattainable ideal that gives life meaning. Desire
for reward has been amply noted by New Historical studies of

the last decade. Men court patrons and mistresses because they want some material return, financial or sexual, or both. They want to satisfy their lusts, to seek position, power, and social aggrandizement. Less noticed is another aspect of desire, which is less interested in a crude immediate return than in a kind of self-validation.[24] Men follow feudal superiors or worship ladies because they thus give meaning to their lives, confirm their worth, gain honor, prove their nobility, and establish their own inmost identity as persons. The idea that one gains worth by loving and serving what is worthy is a basic tenet inherited from the feudal past and approved by most writers of the time. If a man is faithful to the worthy object of his desire, even to the end, he wins victory from apparent defeat.

We find both kinds of desire in *Astrophil and Stella*. Part of the admired "realism" of the sequence comes from Sidney's frank admission of his mixed motives. Sonnet 71 devotes thirteen lines to one form of desire, and one to the other:

> Who will in fairest booke of Nature know,
>   How Vertue may best lodg'd in beautie be,
>   Let him but learne of *Love* to reade in thee,
> *Stella*, those faire lines, which true goodnesse show.
> There shall he find all vices' overthrow,
>   Not by rude force, but sweetest soveraigntie
>   Of reason, from whose light those night-birds flie;
> That inward sunne in thine eyes shineth so.
>   And not content to be Perfection's heire
> Thy selfe, doest strive all minds that way to move,
> Who marke in thee what is in thee most faire.
> So while thy beautie drawes the heart to love,
>   As fast thy Vertue bends that love to good:
>   "But ah," Desire still cries, "give me some food."

Kalstone, who pays this sonnet more attention than any other in the sequence, emphasizes both its capacity to balance differing visions and invite "multiple interpretations," and the force of the last line in overthrowing the previous thirteen. His emphasis is finally on the latter argument. "[T]he point of the poem is to show the power of desire to bring a carefully created structure toppling to the ground" (p. 119). That is an attractive reading for our century, but convincing as it is, it remains partial. It insufficiently recognizes the presence of desire throughout the body of the poem as well as in its explicit appearance at the turn.

After all, from a rational, Christian perspective, there is no excuse for Astrophil, or for Sidney, to continue to indulge himself in love for a married woman (an impediment the sequence emphasizes) either lustfully *or* idealistically. The conflict is not only between "reason" and "desire," as Kalstone and most interpreters since would have it, but between *two forms* of love and desire, ideal and sexual. Reason versus desire was the familiar form of the debate, which descends from medieval tradition. This partial reading is understandable, since Sidney himself obscures his situation by drawing on the old debate for his rhetorical structure. But Astrophil's situation subjects the debate to modifying tensions. The conflict is not only between Christian virtue and courtly love, reason and lust, but between one form of amorous desire and another. As Kalstone notes, the poem is an imitation, and in some ways a demolition, of a Petrarchan original, *Rime* 248, "Chi vuol veder quantunque po Natura." But Petrarch's original is not merely idealistically virtuous, as Kalstone suggests.[25] It aches with an idealized longing. That strong note of desire is much diminished in the early lines of Sidney's version – partly because Stella has not died and thereby shown that "cosa bella mortal passa et non dura" ("this beautiful mortal thing passes and does not endure").[26] Yet desire is a necessary part of a vision that includes "*Love*" combined with "reason" in the captivating bonds of "sweetest soveraigntie" – to another's wife and to whatever further aspirations Stella represents for him.

Almost always in *Astrophil and Stella* Sidney uses the actual word "desire" to mean desire for physical satisfaction, desire for solid "food" as he sometimes puts it. Yet, throughout the whole sequence and in the Sidney myth, Sidney is, after all, Astrophil, the star-lover. His desire is also fixed on an unattainable ideal. In the eighth song, in a scene of intense sensuality, he pleads for Stella's surrender. When she refuses, his "song is broken" (line 104). Rejection leads Astrophil into the bleak despair with which the sequence ends. Yet in this same song Astrophil also

speaks of an ideal beauty, which, although always inseparable
from his sexual longings even at its purest, is surely the epitome
of the high Petrarchan, unreachable ideal:

> "*Stella* soveraigne of my joy,
> Faire triumpher of annoy,
> *Stella* starre of heavenly fier,
> *Stella* loadstar of desier.
>
> "*Stella*, in whose shining eyes,
> Are the lights of *Cupid's* skies,
> Whose beames, where they once are darted,
> Love therewith is streight imparted.
>
> "*Stella*, whose voice when it speakes,
> Senses all asunder breakes;
> *Stella*, whose voice when it singeth,
> Angels to acquaintance bringeth.
>
> "*Stella*, in whose body is
> Writ each character of blisse,
> Whose face all, all beauty passeth,
> Save thy mind which yet surpasseth."   (lines 29–44)

This powerful combination of longings for a spiritual ideal and
a sexual object proves impossible for Astrophil to maintain – yet
equally impossible for him to relinquish. Indeed, the combination of motives and feelings represents the root conflict of
the Petrarchan vision, repeated in various forms by a thousand
other poets, from Petrarch to Sannazaro, from Surrey to Sidney
himself, but now, in combination with courtly love, drawing
toward a historical moment of unbearable and unsustainable
intensity.

As Marotti has argued in "'Love is Not Love,'" in order to
secure her throne despite the cultural disadvantage of being a
woman, Queen Elizabeth brought the language of amorous
desire strongly into the political arena and the patronage
system. Amatory desire, already linked internally in conventional thinking with other forms of worldly desire, became even
more closely identified with political ambition – with the
burning need of men like Sidney for recognition and preferment.
Another major exemplar of this terrible mixture of amatory and
political desire is Sidney's contemporary, Sir Walter Ralegh.

Ralegh rose far higher in the Queen's dangerous political
affections than Sidney ever did, but the outcome was similar.
He too found no resolution to his desire. He left as a late poetic
legacy the broken fragment of *The Ocean to Scinthia*, in which he
mourns the hopeless failure of all his worldly desires, which
centered on the figure of the Queen who has now rejected and
disgraced him:

> Shee is gonn, shee is lost! Shee is found, shee is ever faire!
> Sorrow drawes weakly, wher love drawes not too.
> Woes cries, sound nothinge, butt only in loves eare.
> Do then by Diinge, what life cannot doo.
> . . .
> Thus home I draw, as deaths longe night drawes onn.
> Yet every foot, olde thoughts turne back myne eyes,
> Constraynt mee guides as old age drawes a stonn
> Agaynst the hill, which over wayghtie lyes
>
> For feebell armes, or wasted strenght to move.
> My steapps are backwarde, gasinge on my loss,
> My minds affection, and my sowles sole love,
> Not mixte with fancies chafe, or fortunes dross.[27]

(lines 493–96, 509–16)

In the sharply nostalgic line, "My steapps are backwarde,
gasinge on my loss," Ralegh evokes the ritual of backing away
from the queen for the last time. Thus he recalls the presence
chamber and its central figure, with all that they evoke of love
and ambition, from a prison cell. His visionary ideal has now
retreated irrevocably into the past: both Ralegh's personal past
and also, I would argue, a cultural and poetic past that was to
prove equally irrecoverable. Sidney and Ralegh, coming at the
end of an age, desire endlessly but reach a new impasse in their
desires. *The Ocean to Scinthia* closes on the same note of bleak
disappointment and withering, unsatisfied desire as *Astrophil and
Stella*. Both poets have lost that essential confidence that
unrequited loyalty will eventually, as Surrey propounds in the
example of the Greeks at Troy, bring its just reward – or, as
Surrey and Wyatt find in the example of Love's defeated
soldier, simply *be* its own reward.[28]

Ralegh and Sidney found the Petrarchan stance of endless

desire inadequate to their situations, I would suggest, because they had the ill luck to be unsuccessfully ambitious at just the historical moment when political desire, which formerly had the cachet of noble ambition to justify it, was beginning to be viewed with increasing disillusionment. Preferment seemed ever less likely in men's eyes to be a confirmation of noble worth, and ever more likely to be a step up the ladder of manipulation, pretension, and greed, with figures like Lord Burghley, of little aristocratic mien, securely at the top. The Tudor policy of creating new nobles and gentry, to support a line of initially dubious legitimacy and with largely new political, economic, and religious ambitions, had already damaged the mystique of the patronage system, whose best justification was in its origins in the feudal ideal of loyalty and service.

Ambition to confirm one's aristocratic identity and serve the state was degenerating into social climbing and competition for spoils. "Honor," as several biting satires complained toward the close of the century, was gained by the purchase or gift of monastic lands, or of the lands of the old nobility. Political ambition, always open to suspicion in any age, was increasingly detached from validating aristocratic ideals. In the contest for honor and recognition the perpetual winners were not Sidney or Ralegh but the gray, Machiavellian Cecils, who knew what Queen Elizabeth really needed in a statesman. Given the Queen's aims, of keeping herself in power and securing the Protestant national order – not risking it in foreign adventures – such results were inevitable. Never again, as it proved, would the old ideals without renovating transformation serve the changing ends of English monarchy.

Courtly Petrarchan desire, which impelled the lover faithfully to serve his lady just as a feudal servant served his master, and which was thus consonant with the old order, proved no longer useful for an aspiring lover to employ. It was more than convenient for the Queen to keep the courtly love conventions alive, and thus to keep her jostling courtiers where she wanted them, but this manipulation of old ideals for new ends, with which they were finally incompatible, was bound to disappoint the poet-lovers who had the ill luck to serve under her in that role. While the ideal holds, as we have seen, the courtly lover can snatch victory from defeat by his faithfulness. But if it collapses, as it did in the later years of Elizabeth's reign, the defeat becomes a defeat indeed, and faithfulness has lost its fundamental purpose.

As Lawrence Stone has suggested, as well, the aristocracy was undergoing a major crisis at this time.[29] It survived, in a manner, but only by changing and by developing new modes of behavior, both political and amatory. We shall find that Thomas Carew, a courtier-poet who served his monarch two generations after Sidney, learned from hard experience quite a different style of loving from Sidney's: one that better suited the shifting demands of the patronage system. While Sidney's model for a lover's behavior remained nostalgically feudal, and Ralegh's steps were backward, gazing on his loss, Carew – though still a polished aristocrat – found a more useful and forward-looking model in the New-Scientific agricultural marketplace.

In some respects, Petrarchan desire is recognizably "modern." Indeed, two terms, "sexuality" and "desire," have almost entirely displaced "love" from what we like to call our "postmodern discourse." We can well understand and sympathize with Sidney's desire. It was a longing for sexual fulfillment and, related to that, for political and material success. But it also derived from an undifferentiated longing for something unobtainable. If one wants to translate it into current ways of thinking, it might be thought of as deriving from an impossible wish for transcendence, or for the recapture of an infant's unindividuated bliss, or for possession of Lacan's obscure "objet a." This recognition of common feelings between ourselves and Sidney is an important reason why *Astrophil and Stella* continues to speak to twentieth-century readers, modern and postmodern, to those who admire Sidney for his psychological "realism," perhaps even more strongly than it once spoke to earlier generations who admired him for his high romantic chivalry.

But, as we have seen, Sidney's desire also had recognizably courtly as well as Petrarchan components. This is the element that seems archaic in Sidney's style of loving, and that even in his own time ensured that his desire would fail. Above all – above God, above reason, above worldly success – he longed for honor and recognition of noble worth. To Sidney and his contemporaries it must have seemed that the aristocratic ideal was flowering anew. But it was actually about to fall into a long process of change and decay. As we have suggested, in matters of love and chivalry Sidney was among the last representatives of the old age and among the first of the new. The chief *raison d'être* of an aristocrat, after all, is to fight. Although that function continued to have some degree of currency in England for centuries to come, warfare in feudal terms and according to feudal ideals was already giving way before the advance of new political, social, and technological forces.

Sidney managed to die in battle. His legend endured. But *Don Quixote* (1605) was published within a generation of his death. Loyalty in a losing cause, dying bravely, would continue to be admired, but usually with mixed emotions and with increasing wonderment. Chivalric ideals would persist through many further revivals and transformations, but increasingly detached from a firm basis in politics, economics, and the broader culture. As the metaphors introduced by Wyatt and Surrey into their versions of Petrarch's original sonnet suggest, the English Renaissance love tradition rested for a while on a connection between Petrarchan longing and feudal loyalty. But the long devolution from the full aristocratic ideal toward the differing values of a market economy and then of an industrial society was bound to affect people's modes of thinking about love. True, there would later be significant returns to the chivalric ideal of love, among the Romantics, the Victorians, and, even later, among popular writers. But no longer would it seem credible to desire and to serve a lady endlessly, with unrewarded loyalty – at least without seeming more an oddity, an anachronism, or a pathological victim, than a worthy exemplar. Even Sidney found his commitment to Petrarchan love – although once entered into inescapable – in practice impossible.[30] As we shall see, his immediate successors, beginning with Donne, would try new variations on the Petrarchan ideal and find them, too, unworkable. Gradually, however, expanding cultural change, personal hardship, and individual psychological need would impel several of them to discover real alternatives. After a generation or two, the basic courtly-Petrarchan stance of an unrequited lover faithful unto death would become virtually unthinkable.

CHAPTER 2

John Donne: "Defects of lonelinesse"

The line of aristocratic love poetry from Wyatt and Surrey to Ralegh and Sidney reveals most clearly how Petrarchan love came to its unsustainable climax and inevitable breakdown in high Renaissance England, as it first merged with courtly ideals and internalized them, and then proved incapable of satisfying the intense desires that were unleashed by this combination of poetic traditions at just the moment that the broader culture was moving away from the feudal vision of worth and nobility. On the periphery of this courtly crisis in love poetry were such sonneteers as Daniel and Drayton, who, as paid observers of the aristocratic scene and as mediators between the court and the book-buying public, had less at stake personally, though more financially. Such semi-professional poets, often admirably competent, sometimes brilliant, could continue to work the old modes as long as there was a continuing demand for them among interested patrons or among book-buyers who coveted inside knowledge of how aristocrats should love.[1]

As I have suggested in the introduction, beginning with Shakespeare and Spenser a new kind of lover appears on the scene. Instead of courting endlessly and vainly in the Petrarchan manner, the new lovers will marry and live happily ever afterward – if they can ever straighten out their psychological problems, overcome the usual familial and social impediments, and discern and follow the true, virtuous path. In the event, for Spenser the impediments prove so difficult that (as recent critics point out in response to C. S. Lewis) none of his major heroes in *The Faerie Queene* as we have it ever actually manage to get married – which leaves *Epithalamion* (with *Amoretti* as its preface and *Prothalamion* as a kind of variant or pendant) as the only finished instance of the arduous journey to the altar.[2] In Shakespeare's comedies, by contrast, practical impediments are often resolved by arbitrary interventions and miraculous resolutions[3] – another way of suggesting, perhaps, that ordinary mortals cannot expect to reach ideal happiness without extraordinarily good luck.

Admitting that the ideal is not easily attained is not the same thing, however, as proving that it does not exist. The change in loving that Shakespeare and Spenser introduced was a significant and apparently simple change in the ideal at which real people as well as poets aimed. Interest shifted from the intricacies of endless aristocratic courtship to problem-solving courtship, that is, to incipiently middle-class courtship leading to marriage. But honor and nobility were not yet dead. And, as we may know from our reading of the poetry, if not from practical experience, love is seldom simple. Sexual desire pulls the lover one way, affection another, ambition a third, friends and family a fourth, society a fifth, religion a sixth, honor a seventh, idealism an eighth, and so on. At the same time, at the other end of the loving relationship is another person with feelings and motivations of her own, which (though sometimes opaque to the lover or even to the author) are presumed to be of equal complexity. Alignment of the forces is not easy. Spenser shows us the new official ideal in *Epithalamion*: shows us in his own marriage a love in which the forces align; a love both human and Christian, sexual and affectionate, private and public; a love approved by Church and society, which leads the lovers immediately from Church into bed and to the procreation of children, who will follow their virtuous parents into heaven. So, at least, Spenser hopes and prays.[4] But we shall find in Donne, Herbert, Carew, and Milton that mutual happiness is often much harder to achieve than one might wish, and that, even if achieved, it may veer from the straightforward path that official religion, social convention, and the conscious intent of poet or lover would wish it to take, into byways that are sometimes darker, often more precarious, usually more mysterious and occult, and always more internally conflicted and complicated. We begin with the case of John Donne.

The conditions under which Donne wrote the love poems of the *Elegies* and the *Songs and Sonets* exerted strong pressures toward courtly and social modes of thinking about love. In the love lyrics of Wyatt and Surrey, and even of Sidney, the two lovers may sometimes be alone, but the poet addresses a courtly audience, is sensible of his place in the social system, and – although he may observe the conventions of "secrecy" – never really forgets his or his beloved's rank, position, family, relative eligibility, social connections, duties, relation to the court, or similar considerations. As Arthur Marotti has argued, Donne wrote his poetry under like conditions, which dictated that love was far more a social than a private matter.[5] Yet, although Marotti has well described the pressing constraints under which Donne labored, he has not given him sufficient credit for transcending and, eventually, transforming them. Donne was a chief actor and influence in what may be called the "reinvention of love," from something essentially social and feudal to something essentially private and modern. As I shall argue, he accomplished this reinvention partly through his interest in New-Scientific method, but chiefly by means of a brilliant and unexpected redirection of the communal.

Constructing a history of Donne's changing attitudes toward love is notoriously difficult because of the well-known problems of dating the poems and deciding how a particular poem might relate to his biography and historical situation. The easiest way to curb unscholarly speculation, a method popularized by the New Critics, is to cut the knot of biographical indeterminacy simply by cutting the connections between Donne and the speaker or speakers in his poems. Thus arose that critical figure variously called the "poet," "speaker," "satirist," "lover," "protagonist," or, more broadly, "persona." Although most of us would now resist the unthinking use of such terminology, still from time to time it proves convenient or even indispensable. Employed as a preliminary exercise as well as a final checkrein, New-Critical methods are invaluable: what better way to begin interpretation or test one's theories than to ask a poem what it has to say for itself? Yet a permanent divorce between poem and author, or poem and world, is untenable.

In reaction against New-Critical extremes, recent critics have largely replaced the old-fashioned persona with the new-fangled self-presenter or self-fashioner: an alternative critical terminology that is equally useful yet also limited. Most of Donne's poems, after all, fall somewhere between harmless fiction, brilliant invention, and outright self-presentation or self-aggrandizement. We may deduce that he wanted to please and amuse as well as sometimes take advantage of his friends, mistresses, and patrons; yet in the end he could not help being a good poet even at risk of damaging his prospects. So – to conclude these preliminary observations – the best critical method is an open-minded eclecticism. Invading theories, like invading barbarians, are assimilated as the turmoil subsides; thus they add new vigor to old assumptions.

Because Donne's love poems arise from a social matrix, it is useful to begin with a brief discussion of the satires, which treat the place of the individual in society. Donne's earliest satires reveal a young writer torn between conflicting desires. In "Satire I" he pits a parody of the life of the mind against a parody of worldly ambition. Love is reduced to the margins, as a vent for desire but an impediment to advancement. In Donne's words, little more can be expected in the society he portrays than "ranke itchie lust" for a "plumpe muddy whore" or "prostitute boy" (lines 38–40).[6] More suggestively, as several critics have noted, the compact between the studious speaker and his giddy tempter is described as if it were a marriage vow, a contract first sworn to, then betrayed.[7] Donne mocks and satirizes this relationship yet makes it central to the poem. In the patronage system of his time, ambitious young men needed lateral connections or "friends," on whom they might rely for mutual support in the constant struggle for preferment. Although the two personae have almost opposite characters and methods of proceeding in society, they have certain important characteristics in common: both apparently are young and just embarking on careers and eager for advancement, whether by arduous study or by keen attention to fashions, personalities, and the whims of potential patrons. Thus one subject of the poem – and its central assumption – is the importance and difficulty of what has been called "male bonding" or the building up of a support system among young male equals.

Women have small place in the world of this first satire, except as degraded and degrading impediments. "Cheape whore[s]" (line 53) recurrently trouble the speaker's thoughts. True, he mentions the so-called "Infant[a] of London," a rich heiress, but he need not belabor the point that she is a commodity, not a person to love, and that she is impossibly beyond his reach. No one can guess even who will "beare away" this "Heire to'an India." Such information, of course, would be invaluable. If an ambitious young man could not hope to marry an heiress, his next best move would be to attach himself to the lucky man who did – *before* he did so and thus grew out of reach. The bare news of such a match is a valuable commodity in the patronage marketplace. Far more important than women is the relationship between the two main characters. Such is the nature of Donne's youthful world, which, as satirist, he scorns yet knows well and cannot bring himself to repudiate.

In the second satire Donne pits poetry against law. These two professions represent kinds of writing and ways of advancing in life and love. Donne tells us that poetry has fallen on hard times in the new world of Queen Elizabeth: those who govern consider it dishonorable and dangerous – which, to judge from Spenser's remarks in *The Faerie Queene* and elsewhere, may have been the reaction of Burghley and his circle at least. Donne, however, maintains that it should be pitied: its present state is "poore, disarm'd, like Papists, not worth hate" (line 10). As Thomas Hester has shown, Donne's Catholic upbringing and beliefs play an important part in the satires – a matter to which we shall return later.[8]

Poetry has been reduced, Donne continues, to mere writing for hire, writing for fashion, or plain theft. None of these disorders is simply literary; instead they illustrate how society determines, and in bad times deforms, the writing of poetry. About the second failing, writing for fashion, Donne is relatively mild. As a weakness of the financially secure, it more amuses than concerns him directly. About the first, writing for money, he is harsher. He was too near being forced into that humiliating position himself: "And they who write to Lords, rewards to get, / Are they not like singers at doores for meat?" (lines 21–22). He is harshest on the third failing, theft, because it involves competition among men vying for place and therefore strikes nearest to home:

> But hee is worst, who (beggarly) doth chaw
> Others wits fruits, and in his ravenous maw
> Rankly digested, doth those things out-spue,
> As his owne things; and they are his owne, 'tis true,
> For if one eate my meate, though it be knowne
> The meate was mine, th'excrement is his owne. (lines 25–30)

The anxiety revealed here is that of a man whose wit, his only negotiable asset in the struggle for patronage, may be appropriated by others as hungry as himself. But the crisis is more than personal. The old poetic community, in which the practice of *imitatio* and the communal sharing of tradition depended on common cultural assumptions – which, the imagery implies, were in turn cradled in the certainties of the old religion – has died. Imitation, which should be constructive and communal (in the ancient topos, like bees gathering nectar and converting it into honey) has become a savage war of individuals, who steal food from one another and turn it into excrement.[9]

The new world brings with it more direct and selfish forms of writing and courtship. Coscus, the representative of new man – once a poet, now a lawyer – makes love in legal language. Why not, if the only aim of writing is to serve self-interest?

> [He] wooes in language of the Pleas, and Bench:
> A motion, Lady; Speake Coscus; I have beene
> In love, ever since *tricesimo* of the Queene,
> Continuall claimes I have made, injunctions got
> To stay my rivals suit, that hee should not
> Proceed; spare mee; In Hillary terme I went,
> You said, If I return'd next size in Lent,
> I should be in remitter of your grace;

> In th'interim my letters should take place
> Of affidavits: words, words, which would teare
> The tender labyrinth of a soft maids eare,
> More, more, then ten Sclavonians scolding, more
> Then when winds in our ruin'd Abbeyes rore. (lines 48–60)

Given Donne's earlier reference to disarmed Papists, this last metaphor is especially potent. One may hope that we have got past thinking that the meaning of a conceit can be strictly limited to its logical connections. The natural ambiguities of interpretation might get the line past spies or censors,[10] but the clear implication of Donne's image is that the social fabric, the religious and cultural architecture, within which love poetry once subsisted, has been ruthlessly dismantled by its enemies, leaving Donne and his contemporaries to inhabit the bare ruins.

In Donne's eyes the new society no longer has room for traditional poetic forms and themes. Although he holds Coscus up before his audience as a fool at his wooing and a rogue at the law, unhappily he is a successful fool, who engrosses women as well as land. Donne plays on the familiar similarities between the various forms of "courting," whether in love, in law, or in politics.[11] Just as Coscus treats his mistress like a judge or client, so, bringing the analogy into politics, he "lye[s]" to each legal suitor "in every thing, / Like a Kings favourite, yea like a King" (lines 69–70). These words, which still have power to shock, not only risk "the vast reach of th'huge statute lawes," the dark threat with which Donne concludes, but also anticipate, remarkably, certain prominent images in his own love poems. "Like a Kings favourite"; "like a King": similes which, a few years later, he will appropriate and reverse. In the early satires, however, sexual love is reduced to a subordinate but fully congruent place in a universally grim, treacherous, self-seeking society, a society that lacks true community in its legal and political relationships as in its writings, since the chief concern of its members is personal gain. The social bonds break down, feudalism gives place to a proto-Darwinian market economy, and love, like other social relationships, is commodified.

The elegies are generally harder to date than the satires. In

most of them, Donne views love and sexuality as matters for
Ovidian game-playing. In them Donne turned, for social and
cultural as well as formally "literary" reasons, to Ovid,
Catullus, and Propertius for his models. Love, if that is the right
term for the mostly cynical relationships he portrays, shares in
the general corruption of society. It involves secrecy, adultery,
and betrayal in all directions. At best, it gives the lover brief
pleasure and a sense of superior cleverness for having overcome
obstacles, "out-Machiaveled" other schemers, and bested
rivals; at worst and more predictably, his schemes collapse and
his pleasures turn to self-loathing and disgust.

The parallels with the Elizabethan career system are again
evident. The older generation of men in power must be
hoodwinked or otherwise displaced. By hook or by crook, a
young lover must make room for himself. Those who stand in
the way – a jealous husband, suspicious parents – are often violently wished to death. The most intense relationship in "The
Perfume," for example, is not between the lovers but between
the young lover and his mistress's father. It is not hard to detect
elements of Oedipal conflict in "The Perfume," as also in such
poems as "Jealosie," and "Natures lay Ideot," in all of which
rising young lovers displace and symbolically destroy older
authority figures and then are punished for their transgressions.
It is notable, however, that this psychological pattern also fits
the underlying social pattern. If, as may or may not be the case,
Oedipus is always with us, and some basics of human nature do
not change, still there are times when economic, social, and
political conditions reinforce perennial psychic patterns and
bring them closer to the surface. Anthony Esler and Lawrence
Stone have documented the prominence of generational conflict
in the 1590s, due to the crowding of many more young
gentlemen into London and Westminster than there were jobs
to support or heiresses to marry.[12] The Queen and her chief
advisors are "elders" who exclude the young. More recently,
Richard Helgerson has demonstrated the importance of generational struggle to the writing of poetry.[13]

In the notorious images at the heart of "Going to Bed" one
may read a more complex message, at once idealistic and

cynical: both a groping toward equality and, more obviously, an expression of male dominance:

> License my roaving hands, and let them go,
> Before, behind, between, above, below.
> O my America! my new-found-land,
> My kingdome, safliest when with one man man'd,
> My Myne of precious stones, My Emperie,
> How blest am I in this discovering thee! (lines 25–30)

Most obvious is the attitude of male dominance and the reduction of the mistress to an object or series of objects: he is the king, she the kingdom; he is the explorer, she the land explored. We may recognize imperialistic tendencies that are both literal and sexist. At the same time, vestiges of courtly convention remain: she must be, implicitly, the queen, since she retains the right to "license" his ventures; and, throughout the passage, his eagerness to dominate and his apparent confidence in his power to do so is counterbalanced by a syntax that shows he must ask permission before proceeding. If, as John Carey in his Oxford dissertation and Marotti in his recent book have argued, the lover is a poor but aspiring Inns-of-Court student and the lady a rich wife of the merchant class, then her much-desired stripping represents not only titillation of the reader but the divestiture of social barriers as well as clothes: down to a naked and almost equal meeting.[14] And if the eager, imperialistic politics of this poem are neither exclusively scientific nor middle-class, nevertheless Donne's language and procedure may be thought, in general terms, not only timelessly libidinous but also characteristically modern and scientific. They employ a method and a metaphor that are as nearly Baconian as Ovidian, in that they reduce the woman to an object – an exciting object, to be sure – and then seek to explore, lay bare, and fully possess that object.[15] Having done that, however, and in this way having deposed the mistress from her accustomed Petrarchan throne, "Going to Bed" proceeds to employ other metaphors that are more nearly personal and mutual. Thus it is possible, by leaving out one part of the elegy or another, to argue either that Donne is a sexist or a pioneer of mutual loving. He is both.

In much the same way, several of Donne's daring reversals of traditionally authorized procedures in other elegies may owe as much to pragmatism and to science's willingness to see old things in new ways as to Ovidian cynicism. For example, we remember that in "Loves Progress" Donne insists that the blazon, which traditionally starts from the head and works downward, should instead, in good Baconian or Cartesian fashion, give place to the more direct and practical "method" of working upward from the feet. Significantly, Donne not only justifies his procedure on a pragmatic basis but also reveals that its roots lie in the recent growth of a market economy in England – "our new nature (Use)." One should value women, Donne argues, as one values gold, not for beauty, or goodness, or spirit, but for immediately practical reasons:

> I, when I value gold, may think upon
> The ductilness, the application,
> The wholsomeness, the ingenuitie,
> From rust, from soil, from fire ever free:
> But if I love it, 'tis because 'tis made
> By our new nature (Use) the soul of trade. (lines 11–16)

Although the poet scoffs and invites us to laugh, the serious implications of his willingness to look at everything afresh is evident. The revolutionary social implications potential in this willingness to reexamine established conventions between the sexes are clear as well. There are literary precedents for Donne's misogynistic elegies, but those earlier satires and epigrams were customarily directed against prostitutes or other sorts of lower-class women. Since the "new Philosophy" already is beginning to call "all in doubt," however, these precedents may be put to fresh and original uses. As yet, however, these cannot be called hopeful uses.

To be sure, Donne's elegies are varied and complex. "The Autumnall" is still something of a puzzle – although it seems fairly certain that not even Donne would have risked addressing it to Magdalene Herbert. "Going to Bed," as we have seen, is more problematic than first appears. Perhaps, however, only "On his Mistris" reveals more than faint stirrings of a different and more tender attitude toward love, which later will become more fully realized in the *Songs and Sonets*, though it still is weighed down by an abundance of desperate cynicism. Although these exceptions may add grace notes and counterpoint to the pattern we have sketched so far, they do not dispel it.

Donne continued to make innovative use of scientific metaphor in the *Songs and Sonets*. In several poems, he gives the lovers' traditional exchange of hearts a mock-scientific literalness by referring to medical theories that each act of intercourse shortens one's life by a day, and each deeply felt sigh consumes a precious drop of heart's blood. To understand Donne's meaning requires of his reader not only the usual familiarity with poetic love conventions but also some knowledge of current medical lore: "Since thou and I sigh one anothers breath, / Who e'r sighes most, is cruellest, and hasts the others death" ("A Valediction: of weeping"). Dissection and anatomy also pervade Donne's love lyrics, along with humor theory, propagation of spirits from the blood, and preoccupation with the new difficulties raised by what would come to be known as the Cartesian mind-body problem.

Examples abound, and some are almost too obvious to mention; but we may take "The Dampe" as an especially interesting case. Like many of the *Songs and Sonets*, this poem opens somewhere beyond the point where a Petrarchan poem or lyric sequence might end: with the lover's death. As so often, Donne takes particular pleasure in literalizing an especially worn and "artificial" literary convention and then proceeding to examine what might happen next. Since the lover is dead to begin with, it follows that there is no immediate place for the feudalistic assumptions about social relationships that would be implicit in a haughty mistress rejecting an unsuccessful servant-lover. Nor, to move closer to the social conditions of Donne's time, does his stance resemble that of a client lover pursuing the rewards of patronage and generalized desire from a mistress-patroness, the pattern taken by Sidney's *Astrophil and Stella* or Ralegh's "Ocean to Scinthia." Instead of a social or a human problem – how to overcome the insuperable barriers of the mistress's superiority – Donne presents this unhappy love affair as a scientific puzzle or a medical case:

> When I am dead, and Doctors know not why,
>   And my friends curiositie
> Will have me cut up to survay each part,
> When they shall finde your Picture in my heart,
>   You thinke a sodaine dampe of love
>   Will through all their senses move,
> And worke on them as mee, and so preferre
> Your murder, to the name of Massacre.   (lines 1–8)

The person seeking metaphorical advancement here is not, as we might ordinarily have expected, the lover but the mistress, who, the poet pretends, pursues a kind of grisly social preferment by turning her murder of one lover into a massacre of many. Thus metaphors of the lover's ambition and desire are displaced and reversed. By his witty permutation of conventional Petrarchisms – murder of the lover by his mistress, lodgement of her image in his heart, the lover's assumption that to see her is to love her and therefore to be killed by her – Donne has managed to place both the defunct lover and the pathology connected with this sort of loving under the dissecting knife. The lover disclaims personal "interest" or ambition; instead, while transferring such selfish concerns to his mistress, he pretends to the role of disinterested social critic and scientific pursuer of generalized truth, under the useful metaphorical device of the dissection of surface appearances.[16] As for the mistress, her resistance to the lover's importunities is reduced momentarily to a plague-source.

Having thus disarmed the conventionalities, Donne dismisses all precedence and custom depending on remembrance of things past. "[L]ike a Goth and Vandall rize," he instructs his mistress, "Deface Records, and Histories / Of your owne arts and triumphs over men" (lines 13–15). They will destroy civilization and all its conventions in order to begin again in accordance with rules that only they will set. In the balance of the poem Donne portrays the lover and his mistress as two opposing duelists, who, to play fair, must lay aside all advantages given them by convention, sex, and class to meet as plain human equals. Their naked equality is similar to that which Donne evokes in his elegy "Going to Bed" – and it likewise emerges from New Scientific imagery:

> Kill mee as Woman, let mee die
>   As a meere man; doe you but try
> Your passive valor, and you shall finde than,
> In that you'have odds enough of any man.   (lines 21–24)

Although his argument may seem purely impudent in tone and intent, nevertheless its rejection of a courtly ambience and its clear adumbration of a more modern, equal, and "nuclear" relationship between the sexes can hardly be denied. Precisely the mock-scientific reductionism of the first stanza prepares the way for this seminal shift in attitude. As both Bacon and Descartes were to argue – respectively a few years and a few decades later – before a new system can be erected, the old one must first be demolished. But science still is not enough to solve Donne's problems. "The Dampe" offers more in the way of Cartesian-style demolition than it does of reconstruction. It finds no clear way out of Donne's cultural difficulties.

To say that, in his poems, Donne is Baconian or Cartesian is not to say that he necessarily was "influenced" by reading specific published works by these writers, for there is an apparent anachronism.[17] Descartes, who was born in 1596, published his *Discourse on Method* in 1637. Bacon, born earlier, may have been known to Donne by acquaintance or by word of mouth before his seminal scientific ideas appeared in print. Still he cannot be said to have preceded Donne, for Donne wrote the poems we are discussing in this chapter in the 1590s or, at the very latest, in the early 1600s. At that time Descartes was still a child and Bacon a young and unsuccessful politician. Nevertheless, although these "New Philosophers" were yet to assemble and give definitive form to the revolutionary ideas that we associate with their names, those ideas were beginning to appear, partly developed, partly inchoate, in the earlier writings and specu-lations of others; were beginning, in short, to get into the air. Here, as elsewhere, Donne was among the first to develop and

give expression to the innovative ways of thinking that were
beginning to form the cultural opening and the conceptual basis
of the "New Science."[18]

As much in "The Dampe" as in that apparently far more
serious poem, *The First Anniversary*, Donne assumes that the way
to understand a human mystery is to study it not living but
dead, to subject it to a scientific anatomy or autopsy, and this
assumption gives the verse most of its force. One might protest
that Donne only pretends to a scientific attitude; he doesn't
literally mean what he says. Still there is no question that in his
poetry the new imagery of science often vanquishes and
fragments the old imagery of courtly love, and, by that very
fact, proves clearly the stronger of the two. One might protest
with equal justice that probably, in most cases, the Petrarchan
lover only pretends to kneel, servantlike, before a prospective
mistress. Most men in Donne's time heartily assented to St.
Paul's maxim: "the head of woman is the man" (1 Corinthians
11:3). Really, we may think, it was too customary for the man
to dominate the woman, in love relationships as in formal
marriage. Nonetheless, in Petrarchan poetry the imagery of
feudal service dominates. By means of such pretences and role-
playings, together with the fictions that give them expression,
social relationships grow and subsist and take on the particular
qualities that differentiate one culture from another. Perhaps
male dominance was, at least in part, not only concealed and
mystified by courtly love conventions but actually moderated.
Even though lightly or comically expressed, a living social
convention, as opposed to a dead literary one, may, like
Herbert's rope of sand, grow to become good cable in the hands
of a believer's conscience.

The New Science, which introduced a new pragmatism, was
also connected with the urge to explore and exploit nature. The
Songs and Sonets and the *Elegies* are filled with such tendencies,
too: the replacement of aristocratic pastoral by more pragmatic
and useful georgic, for example, which Donne resented yet was
forced to acknowledge as a force in his world;[19] or by analogies
with mining and alchemy, which, his poetry reveals, he equally
resented yet grudgingly employed. Whether the alchemists and

miners discover and bring back all the wealth of the Indies or merely expose themselves as impostors, still Donne refuses to cease his metaphorical digging and exploring. For him, the female body can become an object to be dug into, uncovered, and laid bare, though sometimes the result may prove miraculously wonderful and sometimes bitterly disillusioning. In "The Sunne Rising," Eastern spices and American gold mines represent unimaginable new splendors of richness and beauty, which Donne appropriates to his mistress:

> Looke, and to morrow late, tell mee,
> Whether both the'India's of spice and Myne
> Be where thou leftst them, or lie here with mee.
>
> (lines 16–18)

In "Loves Alchymie," mining and alchemy illustrate a more cynical mood, as exploration, science, and the search for new wealth through technology are seen to be failed enterprises, beginning in hope but ending in disillusionment:

> Some that have deeper digg'd loves Myne then I,
> Say, where his centrique happinesse doth lie:
>   I have lov'd, and got, and told,
> But should I love, get, tell, till I were old,
> I should not find that hidden mysterie;
>   Oh, 'tis imposture all:
> And as no chymique yet th'Elixar got,
>   But glorifies his pregnant pot,
>   If by the way to him befall
> Some odiferous thing, or medicinall,
>   So, lovers dreame a rich and long delight,
>   But get a winter-seeming summers night.   (lines 1–12)

If this poem has a social origin or purpose, it is to be found in the politics of patronage. As in many of the elegies, it is clear from the beginning that Donne is addressing not a mistress but an audience of male peers. His request for information from this audience implicitly requires their sympathy for his difficulties and their cooperation with his quest: "Some that have deeper digg'd loves Myne then I, / Say, where his centrique happinesse doth lie." As with the telling of off-color jokes when men are among themselves, the poet assumes a community of libertine attitudes at the expense of women, whose deprecation cements the bond between the male speaker and his audience. ("Hope not for minde in women; at their best / Sweetnesse and wit, they'are but *Mummy*, possest" [lines 23–24].) Like "Satire I," "Loves Alchymie" directs much of its energy not toward women as audience or goal, but toward establishing a bond between young men who are equally preoccupied by the task of hunting for a place in the social system.

What is particularly fascinating about these opening lines, however, is that they also resemble quite closely a typical request for experimental data between members of the Royal Society. "I am conducting an investigation of women and sex," Donne announces. "Can any of my readers give me further information about this subject from their own varied experiences or experiments?" What this curious resemblance may suggest is that the concept of science and technology as a cooperative enterprise, an ideal for which Bacon was to be largely responsible, and which we would normally associate with a movement toward democratic and altruistic ideals, may in part have grown out of the maneuvering and the desperate competition that were inescapable aspects of the Renaissance patronage system. Indeed, if we are to believe our scientific colleagues, the Renaissance system of power-sharing between patron and clients may still be an appropriate model for modern scientific enterprises, with their senior and junior scientists who typically must cooperate with one another to complete the task yet who also maneuver constantly for career advantage. Certainly Bacon's *New Atlantis* paints a picture of a scientific enterprise as hierarchical as it is cooperative.

New Science may have helped Donne unleash his creative energies, but often he uses scientific metaphor coldly and destructively. Often he presents the difficulties of love more as dead scientific conundrums to be solved dispassionately or dissected than as living social dynamics to be lived through and humanly resolved. Instead of a courtly or would-be courtly lover striving for the unattainable, we get a puzzled scientist-lover sifting through the evidence or dissecting a corpse. In "Twicknam garden," for example, the truth or falsity of love is to be determined not by confronting the living person in question but by analyzing the tears left over, *ex-post-facto*, from the love-crisis. "[T]ry your mistresse Teares at home," Donne advises, "For all are false, that tast not just like mine" (lines 21–22). Similarly, in "A Valediction: of the booke," by an imaginative projection into the future the living lovers are reduced to a dead text from the unreachable past, to which the detective methods of the scientific humanists must be applied, as if Donne and his mistress were ancient Romans or Greeks:

> Study our manuscripts, those Myriades
>   Of letters, which have past twixt thee and mee,
>   Thence write our Annals, and in them will bee...
>   Rule and example found.   (lines 10–14)

Again, in "A nocturnall upon S. Lucies day" the lover becomes yet another such fragment of dead scientific evidence from the past:

> Study me then, you who shall lovers bee
> At the next world, that is, at the next Spring:
>   For I am every dead thing,
>   In whom love wrought new Alchimie.   (lines 10–13)

In all three poems, we are given the impression that ordinary truths and ordinary knowledge, which might be gained by conversation or by confronting the living human situation, must be abandoned, reluctantly yet necessarily, in favor of a more indirect yet more "objective," more "scientific," and therefore more ultimately truthful, kind of knowledge. Donne, whose remarkable capacity for viewing a situation as if it were immediately alive and in process has so often been admired, also has a remarkable capacity for suddenly, in his prophetic imagination, killing, freezing, and preserving it, as if embalmed, for post-mortem dissection by a future generation of curious and anxious scholars. He portrays these future generations as seeking to reconstruct the secret of a lost vitality and spirituality of which they themselves are no longer capable. This loss of living faith and love, these desperate exhumations, dissections, and anatomies of the past are, presumably, projections of Donne's own anxieties onto future time.

Toward the beginning of 1601, about two years before the death of Elizabeth, two dramatic events worked a decisive change in Donne's life and poetry. These were, of course, his clandestine marriage to Ann More and the resultant destruction of his expectations for advancement within the patronage system.[20] That the marriage changed Donne's love poetry and made it more serious, more spiritual, more idealistic, has long been a commonplace. The difficulty is to decide which poems are pre-Ann, which post; or which were written about her and which about any of the presumed crowd of lesser women in his life. Such speculation, which began even before Walton, is always tempting, though the dangers are familiar. Even the redoubtable Helen Gardner could not resist an attempt, which has not been generally well received, to divide the *Songs and Sonets* into two groups: cynical and idealistic, immature and mature.[21]

It is best to avoid the particular grounds of that dispute, which, barring discovery of new evidence, is presumably insoluble. Instead, I want to reconsider the strong probability that these linked events – Donne's getting to know and marrying Ann More, and his losing for many years all hopes of preferment – drove him to a new kind of love poetry that came to dominate English and Western culture. I do not mean that Donne was the sole originator of such a poetry, but that he gave it early and powerful expression in English. In this reinvention of love, it does not really matter whether the lover in a given poem directly represents Donne-in-person, whether the mistress is Ann More, or whether Ann More is the implied or actual audience. What does matter is that somehow Donne discovered a new kind of love poetry, which generations of readers have found fresh, startling, and – even when they have been at odds with it, as Dryden, Johnson and C. S. Lewis have been – still have found it too significant to ignore.

A critical characteristic of Donne's best love poems is that they are private. Some time ago, Earl Miner suggested that they are so because Donne visited the court and shrank away; that he looked at society and was disillusioned.[22] I think Miner is fundamentally correct; I have long found his distinctions among "public," "private," and "social" modes very useful. I would like, however, to amplify his insight. Donne was among the earliest and most powerful proponents of love as a shelter and defense against the world, which is an idea or an assumption about love that, over succeeding centuries, has come to dominate our thinking and behavior. It is a bourgeois assumption, Marxists would agree, which results from the fragmentation of older, characteristically feudal, extended-family ties, and from the alienation produced by large-scale industrialization and a market economy. Such suggestions are helpful in a way; but one may resist the notion that Donne was somehow an early bourgeois, or had covert capitalist tendencies. As we have seen, he resisted what he saw as a commodification of love, just as he resisted professionalism and money-grubbing generally. Rather, he was presumably driven inward, in what may fairly be called something like "internal migration," by a combination of large-scale social forces and intractable personal difficulties.

The satires and elegies reveal that even before his fall from grace Donne was unhappy with the patronage system and with the accompanying fashionable ideas about love, which in general he reduces to prostitution, adulterous game-playing, and cynical struggling for power. Doubtless his Catholic upbringing, a serious impediment to his career, added to his general malaise. Yet, if Carey and Marotti are right, these elegies not only reveal Donne's perhaps involuntary distaste but also – because he wrote them and passed them around in manuscript – his interest in striking a clever pose among a presumed coterie of cynical young favor-seekers at the Inns of Court.[23] Although the behavior of Donne's protagonists may for various reasons repel a modern reader and indicate the poet's own disgust, still we can see how they might appeal to an audience of young would-be social climbers and thus attest in such circles to the superior cleverness of their author. Even at this stage in his life, Donne shows an impulse toward innovation, but his use of New Science in the elegies and in the more cynical of the *Songs and Sonets*, however creative poetically, however remarkably insightful into the cultural situation, can do little more than expresses his dissatisfactions in a novel way.

Together with his marriage, however, Donne's fall from favor put everything into new perspective. Now he was not just driven by ambition against a troubled conscience but simply debarred from exercising ambition, let alone hoping to enjoy its fruits. At about the same time he discovered in Ann More a possible alternative. So, even if we were to grant that a given poem concerned the love of a fictional protagonist for his fictional mistress, we might still conclude, because of the way Donne portrays that love, that a sea-change had taken place in his mind. That new poetry remains attractive to modern (if not to postmodern) readers because they still share many of its underlying assumptions.

Foremost is the assumption of privacy. As is well known, Donne redefines the term "microcosm" in his love poems. It no longer means only an individual human being who incorporates within himself complexities analogous to the universe and the state, which was its primary significance before and some time after he wrote. Instead, more often than not, it refers to a lover, his mistress, and the private world they inhabit together:

> And now good morrow to our waking soules,
> Which watch not one another out of feare;
> For love, all love of other sights controules,
> And makes one little roome, an every where.
>   ...
> Let us possesse one world, each hath one, and is one.
>   ("The good-morrow," lines 8–11, 14)

As Jonathan Goldberg has observed, political language pervades the *Songs and Sonets*.[24] Almost invariably, however, it is used to deny and to exorcise precisely the world from which it is taken:

> She'is all States, and all Princes, I,
>   Nothing else is.
> Princes doe but play us; compar'd to this,
> All honor's mimique; All wealth alchimie.
>   ("The Sunne Rising," lines 21–24)

In the 1950s, when the New Criticism reached its heights, such lines could be taken at face value – as apolitical and anti-ideological. They belonged to the personal world of mind and feelings: to psychology, not to sociology. Now, however, if we choose, we can read the same words as profoundly political. To stress a term already used several times, Donne's poems mark not just the discovery but, in a real sense, the invention of an inner space, a magic circle of subjective immunity from outward political threat and from culturally induced anxiety. It is notable that "The Sunne Rising" begins with an explicit rejection of the social and courtly worlds:

> Busie old foole, unruly Sunne,
>   Why dost thou thus,
> Through windowes, and through curtaines call on us?

> (lines 1–3)

Critics have compared Donne's comically senile sun to Polonius: with peculiar aptness, I think, because it is a spokesman and enforcer of social norms and representative of the public world. As it attempts to pay a formal call on the lovers, it tactlessly ignores their drawn curtains. Donne advises this "caller" not to bother the lovers, but instead to chivvy those who belong to the world of diurnal time, those who constitute hierarchical society from its bottom to its top: "Late schoole boyes" dragging their feet on their way to their first training for careers and preferment; "prentices," presumably "sowre" because they are at the bottom of the professional ladder; ambitious "Court-huntsmen," who must rise early to court the king and seek further advancement. In a scornfully georgic image, Donne reduces all these figures, caught up in public life, work, and careers, to a common level: "Call countrey ants to harvest offices."[25] Only love, ensconced in its private space behind the barrier of windows and curtains, escapes the universal bondage of the outer world to "houres, dayes, moneths, which are the rags of time."

New Science helped Donne revise his view of privacy in "The Sunne Rising." His major metaphor for the shift from the "houres, dayes, moneths" of worldly time to love's eternal timelessness and privacy is not, as it might have been in a more conventional poem, biblical: to make the sun stand still, the miracle, impossible to reproduce in this late age, that Herrick longingly evokes in "*Corinna's* going a Maying" and Marvell in "To his Coy Mistress." Instead, it is scientific: a deliberate reorientation of the sun's orbit in order to effect a pseudo-Copernican transformation of the universe into a system more satisfactory to lovers. Although we do not take this metaphor literally or, in a sense, absolutely seriously, still its implications – and the reverberations throughout the poem of subjectivity, solipsism, and phenomenological relativism for which the metaphor serves as a focus – are very serious indeed. "I could eclipse and cloud them [Thy beames] with a winke" (line 13), the lover tells the sun; and he ends with the mocking yet ringingly authoritative proclamation: "This bed thy center is, these walls, thy spheare" (line 30). Thus, appropriately, Donne borrows an image from the Copernican reordering of the universe to mark what amounts to a Copernican revolution in the perception of love and personal identity. Here science is being used in quite a different way: to create, not only to tear down.

It might be objected that the Copernican theory moved the center of things outward, from earth to sun, while Donne moves them inward, from earth to lovers. In fact, Donne may not have accepted the literal details of Copernican theory, since in "The Progresse of the Soule" (1612) he pictures Elizabeth Drury traveling to heaven through Tycho Brahe's system.[26] But the essential point is that Copernicus and his fellows showed spectacularly that fundamental axioms might be questioned and fundamental viewpoints shifted. Within the social universe contemporary with Donne's poem, the equivalent of the Ptolemaic or traditional system was to say that the king is both sun and center of all things, the source of social and political life, of patronage, of wealth, even of full personal identity. Donne's revolutionary metaphor implicitly exiles the king and his clients to the periphery and shifts the psychosocial center from the court to the lovers' private space.

The privacy this poem insistently defends is so characteristic of many others that they need no citation. Instead, we may move to a further point. Although science provided Donne with a central metaphor, another cultural force gave him an infusion of psychic energy. In addition to privacy in love, we can also detect in this poem, unexpectedly, a hint of another state, which Victor Turner distinguishes from "society" by the term "community."[27] Human beings divide their lives in the company of others into two distinct kinds of activity, "social" and "communal." These activities, or ways of living, may also be distinguished by other paired oppositions: diurnal and eternal, profane and holy, ordinary and liturgical, working and playful. Communal occasions are often called "liminal," because they can only exist if an imagined *limen* or threshold separates their enchanted rituals from ordinary events. Wayne Rebhorn has shown how Castiglione, in *The Courtier*, portrays Urbino as an ideal community, with timelessly communal, as opposed to social, values.[28] On his way toward staking out and enclosing his characteristically private space, Donne makes similar use of important aspects of communal language and experience. In "The Sunne Rising," for example, he contrasts the lovers' timeless world with the timebound world of daily society, and their playful leisure with the universal, antlike industry that permeates society from schoolboys to the king. In other poems he contrasts the sacredness of the lovers' world with surrounding profaneness. Finally, the window and curtains are a liminal threshold through which the sun attempts to intrude. Should the sun succeed in doing so, without itself undergoing a transformation, it would destroy the separateness that sustains Donne's little world.

The Reformation brought contempt for certain forms of communal life into England. The guilds were diminished; the monasteries were abolished. Religious ritual was subjected to constraint and suspicion; as were playfulness and childlike behavior.[29] That Donne shared a few of these prejudices is evidenced by his contemptuous dismissal of the truant school-boys. He perceives them not as participants in a timeless world of play but as miniature adults, confined by their size and surbordination in the family to the bottom of the social heap. In contrast, the private world of the lovers, despite its miniature scale, reaches imaginatively toward the communal at the same time that it resolutely rejects the social. I do not mean that this is a communal poem in the usual sense but that in it communal notions and feelings persist, though Donne has reduced and transformed them.

One of the most extreme forms taken by community is carnival or the feast of fools – common throughout Europe before the Reformation, but in England mostly driven underground during the sixteenth and seventeenth centuries. Still, as always, it appears marginally in many forms: for example, in Ben Jonson's antimasques, in his *Bartholomew Fair*, in the public theaters generally, and notably in student revels at the universities and the Inns of Court. Milton was chosen to be master of ceremony at one such occasion in Christ's College.[30] Surprisingly, the two lovers in Donne's private room enact one of the central rituals of carnival. They assume the personae of the dominant authority figures of their diurnal society and mockingly invert the social order. As in several other poems, the lovers anoint themselves as princes and declare themselves superior to the rulers of the world. Occasions such as this are also liminal because they can only exist apart from ordinary events.

In other lyrics Donne's lovers assume the roles of king and queen, priest and priestess, and of wonder-working saints. To these seemingly private festivities Donne often invites not only his usual eavesdroppers but crowds of admirers and even worshipers. "And by these hymnes, all shall approve / Us *Canoniz'd* for Love." The lovers of "The Canonization," who reject society, work, ambition, and money, are now alone, but in the future whole crowds will "thus invoke us" (lines 35–37). So, too, in "A Valediction: forbidding mourning," though "Dull sublunary lovers" and "the layetie" are distanced and excluded, their existence is as necessary to define the occasion as the crowds of anonymous friends who, in Donne's simile, surround the deathbeds of single virtuous men, witnessing and attesting to the saintliness of their deaths.

In another poem, "The Relique," Donne typically begins in

privacy, as he anticipates the opening of his grave: "Will he not let'us alone," he complains of the grave-digger, "And thinke that there a loving couple lies[?]" (lines 6–7). The rude interruption is a more extreme form of the interruption and potential boundary-breaking caused by the sun's visit to the lovers' room. Even in the grave – which, as Marvell points out, should be a private place – secure shelter from an officious world is uncertain. In his second stanza, Donne fantasizes a future, however, when the lovers will be not merely private but, through the exhumation of their skeletal remains, transformed into festal leaders in a vast communal celebration:

> If this fall in a time, or land,
> Where mis-devotion doth command,
> Then, he that digges us up, will bring
> Us, to the Bishop, and the King,
>   To make us Reliques; then
> Thou shalt be a Mary Magdalen, and I
>   A something else thereby;
> All women shall adore us, and some men;
> And since at such time, miracles are sought,
> I would have that age by this paper taught
> What miracles wee harmelesse lovers wrought.
>
> (lines 12–22)

Donne anticipates and defuses English Protestant objections to his wild scene by an irreverent use of comedy and by some mild Papist-bashing. Still, the atmosphere he evokes is less reminiscent of formal religious and social proceedings, even viewed through suspicious Protestant eyes, than of the role-playing and communal irreverence that characterize carnival on the grandest scale. The scene and atmosphere are such that Donne's playfulness is more than simply a defense against possible critics: rather, it is a playfulness seriously appropriate to the occasion.

As several critics have pointed out, Donne's cryptic phrase describing himself as "something else" is rhythmically equivalent to the name of the person he covertly impersonates: Jesus Christ.[31] Donne and his mistress are to be visualized as standing before the king and the bishops in this future time, when

England's lost Catholicism has been restored and celebration is general, in the extraordinary guise of Christ and Mary Magdelene – as the king and queen of this feast of fools. Recreated from their bones by a future audience instructed by the text Donne sends them – "this paper" – the mortal lovers are deliriously welcomed, admired, and imitated by all levels of a society transformed into festive community by their exemplary presence.

The more one tries to picture the scene, the stranger it is. How are we to interpret this unprecedented and apparently blasphemous impersonation? In the Middle Ages, clownish actors might dress as bishops with donkey's ears, or the excited crowd might accidentally set fire to the sanctuary, yet few (before *The Last Temptation of Christ*) ever went so far as Donne does in deliberate irreverence.[32] Unlike "The Funerall," which begins solemnly and ends with a joke, "The Relique" grows more serious as it progresses, a movement partly evidenced in the stanza just quoted. The poem is exhilarating yet troubling. Still, it brilliantly exemplifies Donne's use of communal religious elements in a constant effort to define and enclose a safe space for lovers to occupy. As in "The Sunne Rising," Donne does not picture an ordinary community. His saturnalia is at several removes: first it requires the death of the lovers, then their projection into an imagined future as bony relics, finally their reconstruction, by the imaginations of imagined admirers, as living role models and festival leaders. The poem itself will teach these future readers how to accomplish this miracle of imaginative resurrection. The whole process is conditional, hypothetical, and obviously fragile: Donne's poem and its private world represent not natural or traditional versions of reality, but a poet's artifice, a lover's makeshift, a subject's attempt to refashion unsatisfactory objects.

One reason for Donne's indirection and the fragility of his invention is, presumably, that he is engaged in the difficult – some would say impossible – task of transcending and transforming the basic social assumptions of his time. In a perceptive remark directed toward "A Lecture upon the Shadow" but applicable to many of Donne's other love lyrics, Marotti argues that "Donne transformed a problem having to do with the social circumstances of a love relationship into the more manageable one having to do with the personal attitudes of his lovers. The speaker of this lyric thus pretends that if he and his beloved maintain their full reciprocity of commitment and refrain from deceiving one another, their problems will be solved."[33] The operative word here is "pretends." Realizing that Donne is working against the social conventions and assumptions of his time, Marotti argues that Donne can only succeed in fooling himself by converting a social into a private problem. He cannot transcend his situation, but only mystify it. Yet it might equally well be argued that indirectly and tentatively (since the social pressures against which he was working were so great) Donne was not just fooling himself but inventing new ways of thinking about love.

In response to similar social pressures Ben Jonson created the communal worlds of "Penshurst" and "Inviting a Friend to Supper." The Cavalier poets, driven into exile by civil war and expelled from participation in society, created in response communal worlds of friendship.[34] In his verse letters to Sir Henry Goodyere and others Donne occupies himself similarly; but in his love poems – and probably only for a certain period in his life – he takes the ideals and rewards of community and forces them into the love relationship, where they provide much of the positive tone of emotional satisfaction. Yet they lie there oddly and somewhat uneasily.

Social as well as psychological pressures are at the root of these inventions. In psychosocial suffering human beings invent the future. The individual seeks elsewhere satisfactions society denies. For Donne, the disappearance of Catholic community, to which he alludes in the satires, took place in several stages. It had begun before his birth, with the Elizabethan settlement; it came closer to home with the persecution of his family and his brother's death in prison; and it culminated in his loss of faith and apostasy. Presumably, Catholic community originally had for him strong resonances of childhood, home, and family, set against a violent and treacherous outer world to which he later resolved to accommodate himself. After he lost or relinquished his early spiritual home, he needed a new one. During his middle years ambition failed him. As the imagery of the love lyrics suggest, love replaced religion as a reason for living. Of course love poetry often borrows religious imagery, but with Donne this imagery assumes unprecedented importance.

Still another instance of the influence of community and festivity on Donne's invention of a private and sacred love may be found in "A nocturnall upon S. Lucies day," probably a late lyric, which mourns the dissolution of the lovers' special unity through the death of his beloved. Having built his identity not on his position in society but on an intense, private bond with his beloved, the speaker's psyche is consequently annihilated and dissolved, "ruin'd" by her loss, and then reconstituted "Of absence, darknesse, death; things which are not" (lines 17–18). "Love's limbecke," which formerly made the lovers into a "whole world, us two," has also the power to turn them into "two Chaosses" or "carcasses" when absent from each other (lines 21–27). Yet even amidst loss, the distinction between society and community obtains, for festive community offers the lover his only possible hope:

> You lovers, for whose sake, the lesser Sunne
> At this time to the Goat is runne
> To fetch new lust, and give it you,
>   Enjoy your summer all;
> Since she enjoyes her long nights festivall,
> Let mee prepare towards her, and let mee call
> This houre her Vigill, and her Eve, since this
> Both the yeares, and the dayes deep midnight is.
>
> (lines 38–45)

The sun will not renew for the lover, not only because his beloved (like Catullus' lovers)[35] cannot rise again in this world, but because he remains outside the world of diurnal time, within which ordinary, lustful lovers are mired. They live in the world, he even now in a "long nights festivall" of sacred and celebratory timelessness. If she cannot be reborn to him, he can be reborn to her, because this is "her Vigill, and her Eve," a transitional time of penance leading into festivity, and of darkness leading into light. Condemned by the more extreme

Protestants of Donne's time, the old religious festival, with its roots in a Catholic past, offers him a hope for renewal of love and union in another world. Strictly speaking this is not a religious hope or a prayer, but rather the conversion of religion into something that is still spiritual yet essentially de-Christianized. The lover does not, after all, ask St. Lucy to intercede for him or to help reunite him with his beloved; rather he converts his beloved into St. Lucy in the alembic of his poetic imagination, and thus empowers her to draw her worshiper (since she is the ultimate goal, no other word seems so apt) into the intensely desired, timeless, and magically transformative world of her "long nights festivall."

We spoke earlier of Donne's poems as a subject's attempt to reform objectivity, and the same tendency is evident in "A nocturnall." A poem is not only a well-wrought urn but also an action, in Kenneth Burke's terms a symbolic gesture, one of whose central purposes is to solve problems and establish alternative, more satisfactory ways of living.[36] Does Sir Robert Sidney lack funds to tear down Penshurst and build a showplace appropriate to his station and ambitions, as his father intended?[37] Then let Ben Jonson, by the power of poetry, establish a whole different perspective on the matter, and in doing so, invent an ideal life-style not only for Sir Robert but for his whole society.[38] Some transformations are more successful than others. Donne's transformation, I would say, is to loving roughly what Descartes' is to philosophy: enormously influential and long-lasting, yet containing the seeds of its own contradiction.

Donne's similarity to Descartes rests largely on his movement toward a subject-centered viewpoint. At least two important lines of descent may be traced back to Descartes, scientific and Romantic. But these two lines are not so diametrically opposed as they may first appear. Like the two sides of a single coin, both are connected with the growth of subjectivity.[39] The connection is already adumbrated in Donne, since, as we have observed in "Going to Bed," "The Sunne Rising," and other poems, important shifts in his perception are clearly related to his interest in the New Science. In the broadest sense, the methodology of science provides Donne with his metaphors in these poems, with a language and a way of thought that allow him to write as he does. Not only the details of new scientific discoveries – new stars, comets beyond the moon, spots on the sun – energize his poetry.[40] At a deeper level Donne learned from science possibilities for new ways of seeing and new ways of thinking, which had the potential not only to turn the physical world upside down, but love, society, and individual consciousness as well. But science could not achieve these transformations alone; it had to be energized by its obverse, the movement of the individual and his culture toward private subjectivity.

Perhaps the most basic thing that Donne's love poems have in common with Baconian Science and the *Discourse on Method*, as well as with the later flood of Romantic love poetry, is that they all reject tradition, authority, and other forms of discussion based on natural or social values, and instead begin with the absolute subject. I think, therefore I am; or, to paraphrase, I love, therefore I am. Wyatt, Surrey, and Sidney were all to an extent rebels against society. Two were exiled several times from court, and the third was beheaded. Yet none of them – and this has nothing to do with relative merit – could more than struggle against, and incrementally modify, the rules of love encoded in cultural conventions. For them, it was not just a matter of social consensus but of natural law: therefore, ultimately of divine law. For the latest of their poetic lovers, Astrophil, personal will or desire is irresistible, yet finally destructive of the self who wills. For Donne, in the years of which we are speaking, personal will is a determining creative force that seems to alter the world.[41]

We have long been accustomed to say that Donne writes about physical and spiritual love. Some poems, like "Loves Alchymie," deny that love transcends the physical; others, like "The undertaking," celebrate a love that is purely spiritual. As we know, in some of the most finished poems love is both physical and spiritual. But what do we mean by "spiritual"? A. J. Smith and others have established that Donne draws on certain Neoplatonic and Ficinian traditions, yet to know Donne's sources does not altogether solve the mystery.[42]

> This Extasie doth unperplex
> (We said) and tell us what we love,
> We see by this, it was not sexe,
> Wee see, we saw not what did move.
>
> ("The Extasie," lines 29–32)

Like others before and after him, Ficino made a considerable effort to reconcile Neoplatonism with Christianity. Spenser, in the *Fowre Hymnes*, may properly be called a Christian Neoplatonist poet. But in many if not all the *Songs and Sonets*, Donne noticeably is not. This is not to say that he is not Christian but that in these poems two forms of spirituality war with each other. We have already noticed the symptoms of such a conflict in "A nocturnall upon S. Lucies day." There is a minor sign of the same conflict in "The Relique." The "bracelet of bright haire about the bone," the lover explains, is a device "To make their soules, at the last busie day, / Meet at this grave, and make a little stay" (lines 5, 10–11). Here is a lover who credits the reality of the Resurrection but who wants to put it off a little while he attends to his love interests. For us post-Romantics, his sentiment is appealing. Yet it assumes an un-Christian contradiction between divine and human love. In the *Songs and Sonets* we never find anything like the concluding lines of Spenser's Easter sonnet: "So let us love, deare love, lyke as we ought, / love is the lesson which the Lord us taught." Milton hopes to enjoy full sight of his dead saint in heaven; Donne fears that in heaven his love may be lost, or at least impeded. Better enjoy it before the Last Judgment.

This reading may put too much weight on an affectionate joke. Yet what Donne constantly does – substituting love for religion, producing by sheer assertion of his will a magical space in which to love, inventing a world to set against and exclude the social, material, and even religious worlds he rejects, substituting experience or experiment for convention, authority, and tradition, which derive from the social order – is epitomized in this small joke. In short, may we not see Donne as anticipating the whole Romantic complex of individualism, self-assertion, and "natural supernaturalism"? Much recent critical analysis has emphasized the difficulties inherent in natural supernaturalism or has attempted to "demystify" it. This "Romantic" way of thinking was born, so far as a moment is identifiable, at just about the time we are considering, and it has persisted with remarkable vitality ever since.

To pull together the threads of the argument, let us consider a poem not mentioned so far, "The Anniversarie":

> All Kings, and all their favorites,
>   All glory of honors, beauties, wits,
> The Sun it selfe, which makes times, as they passe,
> Is elder by a yeare, now, then it was
> When thou and I first one another saw:
> All other things to their destruction draw,
>   Only our love hath no decay;
> This, no to morrow hath, nor yesterday,
> Running it never runs from us away,
> But truly keepes his first, last, everlasting day.   (lines 1–10)

Once again, Donne establishes a special region, distinguished from the social world of king and court, and by an act of will sets it apart from the destructive powers of time. Within their invisible barrier, the lovers may love one another eternally, without fear of time or death. Then comes the immediate shock of contradiction:

> Two graves must hide thine and my coarse,
>   If one might, death were no divorce.
> Alas, as well as other Princes, wee,
> (Who Prince enough in one another bee,)
> Must leave at last in death, these eyes, and eares,
> Oft fed with true oathes, and with sweet salt teares;
>   But soules where nothing dwells but love
> (All other thoughts being inmates) then shall prove
> This, or a love increased there above,
> When bodies to their graves, soules from their graves remove.
>   (lines 11–20)

Having just been told in the most ringing terms that the lovers will transcend time and humanity and live forever, the reader is jarred by this abrupt turn. Yet if a special immortality for lovers is not to be expected, Donne seems to say, they can still look forward to Christian immortality, which is a guaranteed immortality, so long as nothing but love dwells in their souls. Having already been made suspicious, the reader may also hesitate at this assertion. To what kind of love does Donne refer? Christian love, as the context requires, or romantic love, about which he spoke earlier? Perhaps the third stanza will resolve the doubt.

> And then wee shall be throughly blest,
>   But wee no more, then all the rest;
> Here upon earth, we'are Kings, and none but wee
> Can be such Kings, nor of such subjects bee.
> Who is so safe as wee? where none can doe
> Treason to us, except one of us two.
>   True and false feares let us refraine,
> Let us love nobly, and live, and adde againe
> Yeares and yeares unto yeares, till we attaine
> To write threescore: this is the second of our raigne.
>
> (lines 21–30)

The solution Donne proposes to the threats of time, death, and political treason are not resurrection and eternal life in heaven but, once more, the little kingdom of love, whose safe boundaries the lovers can pull around themselves to keep the world and society at bay. Death and God are put off as long as possible – for sixty years, anyway. Then the lovers can think again.

The attractions of Donne's position for post-Romantic readers are obvious, and so are the difficulties. I am not concerned here with Donne's later work, after he moved back into society and began courting patronesses in verse epistles. But we may suspect that when he emerged from Mitcham his esthetic began to change; and we know that in his later sermon on marriage he takes such a different position that his admirers have been distressed. What Donne proposes in his most idealized love-lyrics is a union between lovers that is essentially communal, sacred, and religious in a certain sense, but neither Christian nor social. But in Donne's day marriage was defined chiefly in Christian and social terms. Among its accepted purposes were to regulate sexuality, produce children, and bring them into society. It was a social, not a private or communal, contract. Spenser illustrates the difference. In the *Epithalamion*, he celebrates his marriage publicly and also celebrates its purpose of producing children, to grow in virtue and follow their parents into heaven.

Although few have doubted Ann More's influence on the later *Songs and Sonets*, Donne says nothing in them about marriage or its traditional functions. In short, he effectively anticipates Romantic and modern views of marriage as a retreat from, rather than an integrated aspect of, the daily interactions of people in society. Such a view best fits a society that has broken down or that separates the workplace and the public realm from the family – unusual in Donne's time and circumstances, but later, with the rise of industrialism, increasingly common. Still the roots of later changes may be found in the conviction Donne shared with Descartes that somehow the individual can cut himself loose from the conventions of the social order and instead construct, on the basis of private experience, a psychological space, within which he can safely live, love, and discover new truths of feeling.

Paradoxically, history has taught us that individualism seeks company. Through his poems, circulated in manuscript among his friends and posthumously published, Donne sought to share his vision with others. His spokesmen in the *Songs and Sonets* are proselytizing saints of love looking for admirers, converts, and followers. It is an irony of literary history that the middle writings of the poet who was later to proclaim that "No Man is an *Iland*," are the remote ancestors not only of thousands of hopeful Romantic love lyrics but also of as many disullusioned ones: for example of Matthew Arnold's bleak vision of "mortal millions" "in the sea of life enisled," each alienated from his fellows by "The unplumb'd salt, estranging sea," each "*alone*."[43] For, by cutting love loose from society and from religion, Donne put a burden on it heavier than it could well bear, so that, as he himself realized: "his first minute, after noone, is night."

CHAPTER 3

John Donne: "the Holy Ghost is amorous in his Metaphors"

It is a "widely publicized observation that Donne expresses religion through human love," as Winfried Schleiner has remarked.[1] In a sermon preached before the King at Whitehall on 24 February 1625/26, Donne indicates why he found the language of sexual love appropriate in speaking about divine matters:

And would GOD pretend to send thee a *gracious Messadge*, and send thee a *Divorce*? GOD is *Love*, and the *Holy Ghost* is amorous in his *Metaphors*; everie where his *Scriptures* abound with the notions of *Love*, of *Spouse*, and *Husband*, and *Marriadge Songs*, and *Marriadge Supper*, and *Marriadge-Bedde*. But for words of *Separation*, and *Divorce*, of *Spirituall Divorce* for ever, of any soule formerly taken in Marriadge, this very word *Divorce*, is but *twice* read in the *Scriptures*; once in this *Text*; and heere *God* dis-avowes it; For when hee sayes, *Where is the Bill*, hee meanes there is no such *Bill*.[2]

There is ample biblical precedent in speaking about both the love between God and man and the love between God and his Church in sexual and marital terms. In this instance, Donne's sermon speaks of an indissoluble marriage between God and the soul.[3] And, of course, although he invokes the authority of the Bible directly here, there is also an ancient tradition of writings based on these originary biblical metaphors – hermeneutical, theological, devotional, and literary – on which Donne also drew.

Having considered Donne's secular love poetry at length,[4] I would like now to consider how his divine poems are related to his secular love poems and to those of other poets in the tradition. There has been a variety of approaches to Donne's use of human love in his divine poems, ranging from Freudian debunking to respectful admiration, and from emphasis on continuity to emphasis on difference.[5]

An exploration of changing attitudes toward love in the seventeenth century will not be adequate unless one takes sacred love into account, since, although religious concerns do not generally loom as large in our eyes as they did in earlier times, sacred love represents an important aspect of the cultural development and changing attitudes we are examining. In the seventeenth century, nearly everything, personal or political, social or psychological, was filtered through, and colored by, religious experience, which as Helen C. White once so aptly argued, and as many critics have since confirmed, was a central concern of the times.[6]

Critics of seventeenth-century literature have often remarked on the resemblances as well as the tensions between sacred devotional and secular love poetry. We know that sacred and secular loves have often been in conflict, but that in the expression they seem to include many of the same feelings and emotions and to employ many of the same images. Even at the highest level of religious verse, for example in the poems of St. John of the Cross, such connections are often easily visible. We might take our departure from Freud and the twentieth century, and posit that religious love is human love "sublimated" – that is, deflected onto other, ghostlier, finally imaginary objects.[7] Or we might prefer Robert Southwell's earlier argument that religious love is human love raised and redirected toward a higher object:

Passions I allow, and loves I approve, onely I would wishe that men would alter their object and better their intent. For passions being sequels of our nature, and alloted unto us as the handmaides of reason: there can be no doubt, but that as their author is good, and their end godly: so ther use tempered in the meane, implieth no offence.[8]

The chief practical difference between these two views, late sixteenth-century and modern, results from their origins in two different sets of assumptions: that God is real and worthy of love above all other objects, or that he is imaginary, no more than an illusory projection of thwarted or repressed libido. Both views posit some degree of continuity between the secular and the sacred. The drawback of the modern view, when dealing with some early religious verse (Donne's and Crashaw's especially), is that it too often results in prematurely patronizing and reductionist conclusions.

It is not within the scope of a merely critical study to prove or to declare which of these views is finally correct. It is useful to remind ourselves of them, however, in order to be conscious of potential blind spots. I would argue that (as is often the case) the best procedure is to suspend disbelief at least long enough to make a thorough effort to understand and to work through the world-views of the earlier writers under consideration, feeling free to use modern insights to intervene and interpret but not to block out older views. We naturally reserve the right to reassume our private or contemporary opinions at the close of the excursion – or perhaps to decide that the past had a better grip on some matters than we do. In any case, most readers will prefer to make their own decisions.

In what sense might we say that Donne's divine poems are "sacred parodies" of his secular love lyrics? As we have seen, Donne struggles with Petrarchism in the *Songs and Sonets*, and in the course of this struggle he invents new ways of thinking about love. Did his struggles and discoveries carry over significantly into his religious verse? Are his metaphors for divine love in the *Holy Sonnets* based only on biblical models, or do they also parody conventional love poetry? And do they imitate, qualify, or dismiss what Donne had learned from experience with his wife, "she whome I lov'd," or with his other "profane mistresses"?[9] If so, what kind of relationship do we find in the divine poems between Donne's speaker and his God?

Two critical comments offer a useful starting-point in understanding the nature of love in Donne's divine poetry. Mario Praz writes that Donne "uses the elements of the Petrarchan subject matter, but in a bizarre, unorthodox way."[10] And Carol M. Sicherman notes that "Although involved in an inward crisis, [Donne's] speaker always conducts his self-examination in relation to another being, either a woman or God."[11] As Donne himself says, relationships are critical in defining the persons who are related. At Pauls Cross, on the anniversary of the King's accession on 24 March 1616/17, he respectfully preaches to the Lords of the Council that, just as there can be no subjects without a king, so there can be no king without subjects. The principle applies even to the Divine Persons within the Holy Trinity: "God could not be a father without a Son, nor the Holy Ghost *Spiratus sine spirante*. As in Divinity, so in Humanity too, *Relations* constitute one another, King and subject come at once and together into consideration" (*Sermons*, 1:184).

"*Relations* constitute one another." These relations are prior to what we would call the individual identities of the persons involved.

> As he that would vow a fast, till he had found in nature, whether the Egge, or the Hen were the first in the world, might perchance starve himself; so that King, or that subject, which would forbear to do their several duties, till they had found which of them were most necessary to one another, might starve one another; for, King and subjects are Relatives, and cannot be considered in execution of their duties, but together. (*Sermons*, 1:183–84)

True, Donne here emphasizes public and not private relationships ("in execution of their duties"), but he also finds an analogy between social relationships and the "familial" relationships within the Godhead itself. And, however much the law might elaborate on the distinction between the king's two bodies, public and private realms were inextricably connected, as so many literary-historical studies have recently demonstrated. In the ordinary thinking of the time, even in the case of a king, the essential identity of the self and, reciprocally, of the other, depend on that person's relationship with the other. Indeed, as we noted earlier, what we think of as the very "nature" of the phenomenal or "objective" world always depends on our relationship with it, on our cultural bias, on the way – normally largely unconscious – we perceive it.[12] Subject and object define themselves in one another.

Three of the significant ways in which Donne relates to God

in the divine poems are as king, master, and father. These three relationships are so closely interconnected with one another as to be almost wholly inseparable and indistinguishable. "Father, part of his double interest / Unto thy kingdome, thy Sonne gives to mee" (lines 1–2). In this sonnet, God is king, father, and property owner, as well as creator. In "Oh my blacke Soule," God is a great king against whom the soul has committed treason. In "Batter my heart," he is a king who has left a deputy to command his city. In "I am a little world" he is lord of a "house," which the poet wants to join, that is, he is head of a family, tribe, or nation. In "Oh, to vex me" he bears the "rod" or scepter of authority, the sign of his ability to punish his subjects. The anxious speaker assiduously courts him, "In prayers, and flattering speaches." These images reflect some aspects of Donne's complex and often passionate relationship with the Father God. Debora Shuger documents the extent of this relationship throughout the Sermons, uncovering in the process the sometimes almost unbearable intensity of feeling with which Donne confronted his Omnipotent Father.[13]

But, strong as Donne's feelings are toward the figure of the authoritative father, the strongest emotion in his divine poems, especially the *Holy Sonnets*, is probably that between man and woman, husband and wife. Donne himself says, as we might expect, that, other than divine love,

The highest degree of other love, is the love of woman: Which love, when it is rightly placed upon one woman, it is dignified by the Apostle with the highest comparison, *Husbands love your wives*, *as Christ loved his Church*: And God himself forbad not that this love should be great enough to change natural affection, *Relinquet patrem*, (for this, a man shall leave his Father) yea, to change nature it self, *caro una*, two shall be one.[14]   (*Sermons*, 1 : 199)

Thus, on the authority of Genesis, Donne explicitly ranks the love of a husband for his wife above a son's love for his father, indeed above any other kind of human love. As we shall see, however, Donne does not succeed in bringing together the love of woman with the love of God without experiencing agonizing inner conflicts and difficulties, which his poems reflect. These poems are far from being pious exercises in the established conventions about love. The focus of Donne's inner psychological or spiritual tensions is on the speaker's sexual identity – on his confusion between what amount to conflicting roles. In the divine poems, Donne is both an insistently masculine seeker after mistresses or truths, and the necessarily feminine and passive recipient of God's love.

"A Hymne to Christ, at the Authors last going into Germany" is among the most powerful of Donne's divine love poems. It begins with a typological metaphor, in which he compares his voyage across the Channel to Noah's preservation from the flood, which was traditionally understood to typify the passage of the Church and its members through the perils of a threatening world, as well as to typify any individual's particular experience in perilous times.[15]

In what torne ship soever I embarke,
That ship shall be my embleme of thy Arke;
What sea soever swallow mee, that flood
Shall be to mee an embleme of thy blood;
Though thou with clouds of anger do disguise
Thy face; yet through that maske I know those eyes,
Which, though they turne away sometimes, they never will despise.
                                                (lines 1–7)

The universal typology of Noah's ark, which Donne understands to be an emblem of salvation linking the two covenants, he also applies specifically to his own threatened situation. Amid ominous threats of outward danger and of inward guilt, there flashes forth in his imagination a strong suggestion of recuperative love, in the powerful phrase: "I know those eyes." As yet, this is a love unspecified, although there are unavoidable suggestions both of a lord's or a father's anger toward his servant or child and of coquetry with a masked lover of indeterminate sex. Although the masking presumably derives from the biblical metaphor of God's turning away his face, to which Donne later alludes (line 7), it more immediately provokes thoughts of casual courtship or flirtation, which in turn are belied by the seriousness of the speaker's response: I know those eyes.

In the second stanza, Donne offers to give up all of his other loves and allegiances for the sole love of Christ:

I sacrifice this Iland unto thee,
And all whom I lov'd there, and who lov'd mee;
When I have put our seas twixt them and mee,
Put thou thy sea betwixt my sinnes and thee.
As the trees sap doth seeke the root below
In winter, in my winter now I goe,
Where none but thee, th'Eternall root of true love I may know.

(lines 8–14)

There is some echo here of the First Commandment: "Thou shalt have no other gods before me" (Exodus 20:3). There is a closer echo of God's pronouncement on marriage in Genesis. And there is an even closer echo of Matthew, where Jesus, who first quotes the Genesis text (19:5), a little later bases a new saying on it: "And every one that hath forsaken houses, or brethren, or sisters, or father, or mother, or wife, or children, or lands, for my name's sake, shall receive an hundredfold, and shall inherit everlasting life" (19:29). Precisely as in this invitation, Donne's pledge to love Christ above all other loves derives from the marriage vow. To love Christ is the new ultimate: he is "th'Eternall root of true love."

The third stanza, like the second, echoes the Commandments: "for I the Lord thy God am a Jealous God" (Exodus 20:5). But this jealousy sounds a note distinctly marital and sexual. It builds on the disparate biblical texts to the point where Gardner, who certainly knew these texts, is nonetheless moved to call it "Donne's own" conceit (p. 107):

Nor thou nor thy religion dost controule,
The amorousnesse of an harmonious Soule,
But thou would'st have that love thy selfe: As thou
Art jealous, Lord, so I am jealous now,
Thou lov'st not, till from loving more, thou free
My soule: Who ever gives, takes libertie:
O, if thou car'st not whom I love, alas, thou lov'st not mee.

Seale then this bill of my Divorce to All,
On whom those fainter beames of love did fall;
Marry those loves, which in youth scatter'd bee

On Fame, Wit, Hopes (false mistresses) to thee.
Churches are best for Prayer, that have least light:
To see God only, I goe out of sight:
And to scape stormy dayes, I chuse an Everlasting night.

(lines 15–28)

The last stanza amounts to a pledge of marriage. Donne will divorce the world and all lesser loves to unite himself indissolubly with God. The biblical tradition is that God is the bridegroom and the soul is the bride. Donne recognizes this polarity of the metaphorical sexes when he plays, in part, the conventional woman's role. He teases and provokes through jealousy; he pleads to be loved; he admits that God must be the one to act, to "free" his soul, to remove him from his attachments to the world, to "Seale" the bill of divorce which Donne himself is powerless to effect. Yet even in this moment of "feminine" passivity and surrender, Donne evokes the reverse polarity of the sexual metaphor. He remains a man, married to "false mistresses."

These mistresses compete with God for Donne's love. By the logic of the metaphor, then, God momentarily becomes a woman, the true bride as opposed to the false mistresses. The implications are disturbing: not just because God is thus seen under a female metaphor – after all, orthodox Medieval and Renaissance writers often picture him under the metaphor of a nursing mother[16] – but because in terms of the hierarchical thought of Donne's age God as bride would be viewed as hierarchically inferior to the speaker. The metaphor thus makes God greater than various created "goods" but still apparently less than Donne himself. These sexual confusions are not especially prominent in the "Hymne to Christ," and might easily be overlooked. But they account for some of the underlying tension and uneasiness (which many readers have found even in the three hymns) and for Donne's inability quite to resign himself in this poem to an appropriately passive role. He admits that he must seek aid and permission before he can possibly be divorced and remarried. Yet even to the last we find him boldly plunging into action and taking control of the situation: "To see God only, I goe out of sight: / And to scape stormy dayes, I chuse an Everlasting night." Donne's flamboyant closing gesture underlines and sets its seal to the hymn's magnificent poetry; but this same gesture undermines the hymn's effectiveness as a work of exemplary devotion.

Of course, there is inevitably some degree of ambiguity or paradox when a male speaker assumes a female role. The more patriarchal the society, the greater the inversion demanded. Yet many other male writers – Crashaw, for example, or St. Francis de Sales – settle into the role with no apparent uneasiness. Christianity is fundamentally posited on the basis of such humbling reversals and willing self-immolations. The case is different with Donne, whose insistent masculinity has so often been noticed by critics of the *Songs and Sonets*. As early as 1633, in "An Elegie upon the death of the Deane of Pauls," Thomas Carew admires Donne for committing "holy Rapes upon our Will," for opening "a Mine / Of rich and pregnant phansie," and most famously for founding "a line / Of masculine expression" (lines 17, 37–39). Many other religious writers of the time, from Catholics to Puritans, easily resign themselves to God's love and play the female part when they invoke the marriage trope,[17] but not even with the all-desirable prospect of union with God in mind can Donne surrender easily to the imperatives of this metaphorical role-reversal. For him the relinquishment of his usually dominant and aggressively masculine stance is never anything but uncomfortable. In the greatest of his *Songs and Sonets*, his will to dominate dissolves into timeless moments of equal sharing and of intimate mutuality, but never into passivity, still less into a posture of admitted inferiority.

Although, however, there is room in sacred love for some degree of mutuality or reciprocity, equality is clearly no more workable than superiority as a suitable stance for loving God. As we have seen, many of the *Songs and Sonets* offer moments of intense, timeless transcendence – but not transcendence of a religious, or at least of a specifically Christian, description. Indeed, as we have also seen, in such poems as "The Anniversarie," "A nocturnall upon S. *Lucies* day," and "The Relique," Donne treats the love of God and human love as mutually exclusive and fundamentally incompatible. In these poems God's eternity must wait on the private eternity of the two lovers. From them society and children are excluded. The sacrament of marriage goes unmentioned. Other poems, such as "The good-morrow" and "The Canonization," borrow from religion but turn inward to exalt the lovers' "little roome." As idealistic and "spiritual" as Donne's love may be in the *Songs and Sonets*, it never claims to represent part of a continuous Neoplatonic ladder leading upward to the pure love of the Christian God. So the road from the *Songs and Sonets* to the *Holy Sonnets* is much more difficult and discontinuous than might first appear. Although Donne's ideal secular love incorporates many of the qualities, feelings, and attitudes of religion, it represents an early forerunner of "natural supernaturalism," which cannot lead spontaneously to sacred Christian love.

Donne directly confronts the difficulties of moving from human to divine love in the first of the three late *Holy Sonnets* from the Westmoreland manuscript. He tries to postulate an easy transference, but the inward tensions soon grow evident:

> Since she whome I lov'd, hath payd her last debt
> To Nature, and to hers, and my good is dead,
> And her soule early'into heaven ravished,
> Wholy in heavenly things my mind is sett.
> Here the admyring her my mind did whett
> To seeke thee God; so streames do shew the head,
> But though I'have found thee,'and thou my thirst hast fed,
> A holy thirsty dropsy melts mee yett.   (lines 1–8)

The first quatrain is ambiguous about Donne's love for God. It implies at least the possibility that there was no room in him for divine love until his wife died. But it also suggests that her ravishment into heaven has directed his mind upward, and thus that love for her has led him to love for God. This suggestion is strongly confirmed in the second quatrain, in which the speaker argues that human love has "whett" his love for God and that she belongs to the same stream of love that leads back to its source in the Godhead. But these positive affirmations are somewhat blunted by the admission that he still thirsts, under a kind of love that rather increases his desire than satisfies it. Thus

Donne implies the absence, not the presence, of the divine object of his love. As yet, the metaphor of thirst may be read simply as a measure of the infinite gulf between man and God. It represents, nonetheless, a retreat from or a severe qualification of his argument for simple continuity.

As yet there is nothing in the imagery to indicate a polarity of sexes between the speaker and his God, except that God takes the place formerly occupied by his wife. The sestet formally introduces the traditional marriage trope, with God as suitor and lover, only to proceed immediately to qualify and confuse it:

> But why should I begg more love, when as thou
> Doest wooe my soule, for hers offring all thine:
> And dost not only feare least I allow
> My love to saints and Angels, things divine,
> But in thy tender jealosy dost doubt
> Least the World, fleshe, yea Devill putt thee out.
>
> (lines 9–14)

God as lover actively "wooe[s]" Donne's feminine soul. Then he immediately seems to switch roles, playing the conventional woman's part and passively "offring" himself in place of Donne's wife. In the rest of the sestet the sexual roles become entirely uncertain. God is said to fear that Donne may "allow" his love to saints and angels, whether as lover or object of love is uncertain, although the Anglican prohibition against praying to the saints on which Donne plays would suggest that the forbidden role must be the former and not the latter. In the same way love for the world, the flesh, and the devil implies Donne's love for them, but that they should "putt" God "out" seems in turn to render him their passive object. What is clear enough, at any rate, is that nothing is clear or easy for Donne in this new love relationship. The marriage trope fragments and breaks into confusing pieces. Donne simply cannot effect the kind of direct, simple transference of love from his wife to his God that he momentarily promised with such assurance, nor can he borrow and build upon the trope without running, as in the "Hymne to Christ," into severe difficulty in accepting the indicated passive female role. Perhaps the speaker's most convincing statement is that "A holy thirst dropsy melts mee yett." That is, he is consumed with unsatisfied desire. He is engaged in an endless and possibly hopeless quest. In this regard, he much more closely resembles the disappointed lover of the Petrarchan tradition – which Donne himself had earlier helped to overthrow – than the happy, mutual lover of the *Songs and Sonets*.

The second of the Westmoreland sonnets is considerably more conflicted and disturbing than the first:

> Show me deare Christ, thy spouse, so bright and cleare.
> What, is it she, which on the other shore
> Goes richly painted? or which rob'd and tore
> Laments and mournes in Germany and here?
> Sleepes she a thousand, then peepes up one yeare?
> Is she selfe truth and errs? now new, now'outwore?
> Doth shee,'and did she, and shall she evermore
> On one, on seaven, or on no hill appeare?
> Dwells she with us, or like adventuring knights
> First travaile we to seeke and then make love?
> Betray kind husband thy spouse to our sights,
> And let myne amorous soule court thy mild Dove,
> Who is most trew, and pleasing to thee, then
> When she'is embrac'd and open to most men.

There is no need to point out how anxious and disturbed Donne is about the life-and-death question of identifying the true Church, the Bride of Christ, and of discriminating it from false, harlot Churches, whether Catholic or Puritan. As many critics have pointed out, it is far from certain whether Donne thinks that a true Church exists in this world to be found, or whether the Anglican Church to which he now belonged escapes his general censure. Most of all, the shocking image of God as a complacent husband, prostituting his wife to as many men as possible, has proven difficult for many critics, who have tried to bring it back within the bounds of acceptable, traditional metaphorical discourse. The underlying source of the indecorum, however, has not yet been noticed.

The fundamental difficulty and source of unease in "Show me deare Christ" is that Donne has crossed the wires between the two traditional versions of the biblical marriage trope: the marriage between Christ and his Church, and the marriage between God and the soul. On its surface, from its opening words, the sonnet seems to be based only on the marriage of Christ and his Church. The problem is simply to discriminate between the true Bride of Christ and the false harlots who may seduce the unwary. But the sestet unexpectedly introduces a version of the individual marriage trope: "Dwells she with us, or like adventuring knights / First travaile we to seeke and then make love?" Donne substitutes the Church for God as an intermediary in the usual trope, however, and incorporates additional imagery from the courtly, romance love tradition.

The soul is a questing, masculine knight; the object of its love is a maiden, who must first be actively sought and courted before she can be loved. The result of Donne's having introduced this strange variant of the biblical metaphors into the poem is that we soon find that we have on our hands a *ménage à trois*, if not worse. Christ and the speaker have essentially been transformed into rivals for the lady's affections. Donne has, in fact, presumptuously inserted himself (and us as readers and presumed fellow-members of the Anglican Church) into the ancient marriage trope, as an additional husband. In spite of all the sexual and marital imagery, love between the speaker and Christ finds no logical place in the poem. Instead, the Church is their common wife. Donne has promoted himself from the normal position of sonship in a mother Church to the position of cohusband with God. Of course, we presume this not to have been his intention. But once more great difficulties arise because Donne simply cannot allow himself to relinquish his habitually masculine role. "First travaile we to seeke and then make love." "[L]et myne amorous soule court thy mild Dove." At most, Donne concedes that he must seek God's permission to go on playing the lover's part. If this were not Donne – and at the top of his form – we might think it almost naive for an aspirant lover to attempt to negotiate the distance between human and divine love by a way so bound up in paradox.

The individual marriage trope plays a part in several of the twelve sonnets printed in 1633 and in the four added in 1635. In

"As due by many titles" it is implied by the rivalry between God and the devil, who has usurped, stolen, "nay ravish[ed]" what belongs to God – although marriage is not cited among the eight or more "titles" God has in him. The trope is characteristically reversed in "What if this present were the worlds last night?" in which the bloody face of the crucified Christ becomes a potential rival of "all my profane mistresses" (line 10) and remains, implicitly, the feminine object of Donne's still masculine (and touchingly Petrarchan) love: "This beauteous forme assures a pitious minde" (line 14). The trope appears very tenuously in "I am a little world made cunningly," in which he asks that God burn the fires of lust and envy out of his soul "with a fiery zeale / Of thee'and thy house, which doth in eating heale" (line 14). This is almost an instance of Donne playing the passive role of love object to the end. Perhaps he can do so precisely because the sexual or marital implications are so tenuous. For Donne speaks of "zeale," not love, and makes envy equal to lust among his prior sins. Moreover, zeal implies an active response to the divine fires.

In one of the four sonnets first published in 1635, intertwined sacred and secular love imagery permeates the entire poem. These two loves are in one sense treated as opposites, for one is idolatrous, the other true. At the same time they are treated as precisely alike. Unexpectedly, in this sonnet, which is probably among the last that he wrote among the first sixteen, Donne presents the two loves, sacred and profane, as essentially Petrarchan, and, at least until the present time, as equally unrequited:

> O might those sighes and teares returne againe
> Into my breast and eyes, which I have spent,
> That I might in this holy discontent
> Mourne with some fruit, as I have mourn'd in vaine;
> In my Idolatry what showres of raine
> Mine eyes did waste? what griefs my heart did rent?
> That sufferance was my sinne, now I repent;
> Because I did suffer'I must suffer paine.
> Th'hydroptique drunkard, and night-scouting thiefe,
> The itchy Lecher, and selfe tickling proud

> Have the remembrance of past joyes, for reliefe
> Of comming ills. To (poore) me is allow'd
> No ease; for, long, yet vehement griefe hath beene
> Th'effect and cause, the punishment and sinne.

Here surprisingly Donne does not accuse himself of lust for mistresses or the world. He is neither drunkard, nor thief, nor lecher, nor proud man, for they at least can comfort themselves with having gained something, with "remembrance of past joyes" to repay them in part for the suffering of repentance. To the contrary, the speaker in this poem has sinned as a Petrarchan lover. He has mourned in vain, he has wasted his sighs and tears without return, he has suffered from a "vehement griefe" that is both cause and effect, "punishment and sinne." His was a fruitless and empty love, lacking even the rewards of lust. Now Donne hopes that he may, in "this holy discontent / Mourne with some fruit, as I have mourn'd in vaine." But no such fruit, no such return of love, is yet evident anywhere in the poem. There is nothing to differentiate Donne's "holy discontent" from his former "Idolatry," except for his prayerful plea for a change of objects, which is less a prayer than a lover's vain complaint to an absent God who seems as distant and unobtainable as any Petrarchan mistress.

The only divine poem in which Donne assumes the female part unequivocally to the end is "Batter my heart." Critics have often commented on this poem as among the most powerful and brilliant as well as among the most disturbing of the *Holy Sonnets*. It is powerful in part precisely because it is so disturbing. Once more Donne characteristically makes great poetry from a devotional stance that is troubled and internally conflicted:

> Batter my heart, three person'd God; for, you
> As yet but knocke, breathe, shine, and seeke to mend;
> That I may rise, and stand, o'erthrow mee,'and bend
> Your force, to breake, blowe, burn and make me new.
> I, like an usurpt towne, to'another due,
> Labour to'admit you, but Oh, to no end,
> Reason your viceroy in mee, mee should defend,
> But is captiv'd, and proves weake or untrue,
> Yet dearely'I love you, and would be lov'd faine,

> But am betroth'd unto your enemie,
> Divorce mee,'untie, or breake that knot againe,
> Take mee to you, imprison mee, for I
> Except you'enthrall mee, never shall be free,
> Nor ever chast, except you ravish mee.

As many explications have argued, there is a three-part development of the imagery in this sonnet: the prayer for destruction and remaking, the prayer for relief of the besieged town usurped by Satan, and the prayer for a forcible divorce from Satan and a divine ravishment. But as other explications have argued, there is also continuity in the imagery. The divine rape that closes the poem casts its influence backward, so that one cannot read the poem a second time without reading sexual implications from the beginning. The summary meaning of the poem is that Donne cannot surrender himself to God. He must be forced, broken, burned, entirely remade, taken by storm, broken away from his marriage to Satan, the knot cut, imprisoned, enthralled, and raped. The poem's power depends on the poet's utter resistance to a role he knows he must but cannot play: that of spouse to God. He must be beaten into submission, because in no other way can he find it within himself to submit to the woman's role.[18]

This is imagery likely to trouble nearly any reader, from a traditional Christian to, say, a feminist-materialist. That Donne wishes to turn the violence against himself does not make such wife-beating imagery much prettier. If this is Christian devotion, it is surely devotion at the extreme verge of the permissible. Some critics have explained the speaker's inability to act or to exert his will in any way, even with God's loving help, as an instance of the Calvinist strain in Donne's thinking. The logic of the imagery, however, argues against that as the whole explanation. If we restate what Donne asks of God in Calvinist terminology, it seems to be that God should violently tear him from a state of hopeless reprobation to election – which no Calvinist of his time would have thought possible. As we shall see, such theological speculations cannot be entirely excluded. Yet they do not in themselves entirely explain why Donne had so much more trouble than any of his contemporaries – many of whom embraced Calvinism far more openly and completely than he ever did – in surrendering himself, here and elsewhere, to the terms of the biblical marriage trope. The simpler explanation is that, unless forced – even when putting himself under extreme psychological pressure – Donne simply cannot submit to the woman's passive role.

Donne does assume a woman's role in two of the secular love poems. But two distinctions may be made. First, it is one thing to take the woman's part playfully – or as we would say, fictively – and quite another to assume it in all seriousness in devotional practice, where (Donne would have believed) it was a matter of spiritual life or death. Second, in neither of these two secular love poems is it clear that Donne can view love from the other side, so to speak, without distaste. In "Breake of day," which depicts the aftermath of love, the speaker does not feel sorrow at parting, as the male speakers in Donne's valedictions usually do, but rather a sense of desertion and of having been used. "Must businesse thee from hence remove? / Oh, that's the worst disease of love" (lines 13–14). Donne captures the woman's sense of her unalterably inferior position well. It is, however, disputable whether he sympathizes, or whether he does not still identify with "the busied man" (line 16), whose role he will, after all, reassume when the poem is done.

His distaste for the woman's part in heterosexual love is unquestionable in "*Sapho* to *Philaenis.*" In this heroical epistle from one woman to another, it seems to me that Donne depicts lesbian desire as infinitely pleasurable but narcissistic: as a love of likeness that becomes a love of self. There may also be some element of the male voyeur's pleasure in imagining two women in love. Whether or not I am right in thus finding on Donne's part fascination yoked with implicit moral disapproval for Lesbian eroticism,[19] there is no doubt that he affects to find, through his persona as Sappho, the prospect of Philaenis's receiving a male lover to be appalling:

> Thy body is a naturall *Paradise*,
>   In whose selfe, unmanur'd, all pleasure lies,
> Nor needs *perfection*; why shoudst thou than
>   Admit the tillage of a harsh rough man? (lines 35–38)

The emotion Donne feels here through "Sapho" is not jealousy but a shuddering revulsion at being forced to *identify* with the woman's part, the heterosexual part that (Sappho imagines) Philaenis may play with a man. Yet Donne seeks this revulsion by the very act of writing this poem – just as he repeatedly seeks it when he invokes the marriage trope in the divine poems. Together, these two secular love poems indicate that Donne was capable of unusual empathy in understanding the woman's point of view and her feelings, but that he does not enjoy performing her role *vis-à-vis* himself as a man. Perhaps he may understand it too well.

In the divine poems, the internal conflict over playing the woman's role may have further religious as well as psychosocial motives. In his middle years at Mitcham, when he wrote the *Holy Sonnets*, Donne was torn between the pull of religion and a life that had been much involved with the world and the flesh – not to mention the devil, God's rival in the sonnets. In the last of the additional sonnets which appear in the Westmoreland manuscript Donne tells how his "devout fitts come and go away / Like a fantastique Ague" (lines 12–13), as he vacillates between worldliness and devotion. But there is another conflict in the *Holy Sonnets*, between Donne's deep youthful roots in Roman Catholicism and his comformity with the Established Church. Later he may have made a successful accommodation, as his sermons suggest. But the sonnets reveal a protagonist still torn between the religion of his youth and the potent strain of Calvinism that invaded the English Church at that time.

Thus Donne is torn not only between the world and God but between two religions. The habitual practice of such youthful devotions as Ignatian meditation and, presumably, the biblical marriage trope conflicted with the growing influence on him of the Calvinist doctrine of grace. The *Holy Sonnets* reveal Donne's constant preoccupation with helplessness, with the conviction that any initiative to resolve his predicament must come first from an inscrutable God. Donne seems not only to have confronted the Calvinism of his adoptive Church, but to have feared that God himself might be a Calvinist. I say "fear," because in these poems Donne obviously fears that he is fixed on the wrong side of the unbridgeable chasm between election and reprobation. The intense pressures between a Catholic past and a Calvinist present, with its God who is not only masculine but all-powerful in relation to Donne's absolute powerlessness, impact, in the context of the marriage trope, on Donne's sexual anxieties and severely exacerbate them.

For the convenience of the argument, I have looked at Donne's divine poems in approximately the reverse of their chronological order. The main body of the *Holy Sonnets* were probably written about 1609, the Westmoreland sonnets, or at least "Since she whome I lov'd," after his wife's death in 1617, and "A Hymne to Christ" in 1619. But the imagery in these various poems reveals no noticeable evolution in Donne's general attitude toward or treatment of the marriage trope. In some poems he escapes the feminine imperative in one way, in others he escapes it in another. In none does he simply and gracefully surrender. Donne was ordained on 23 January 1614/15, so at least two of these poems, and probably also "Show me Deare Christ," were written after he joined the Anglican ministry. The only other poem certainly written after Donne's ordination that makes significant religious use of sexual imagery is "To Mr. Tilman after he had taken orders." Donne does not employ the marriage trope, but he does use several related metaphors that cast some light on his feelings about sexual role reversal.

Donne sympathizes with Tilman on his joining the profession to which Donne also belongs. (Donne's tone is very much that implied by today's colloquial saying: "Welcome to the club.") He makes much of the "Lay-scornings" (line 3) and worldly "disrespect" (line 35) that render a minister's office shameful. Donne's underlying argument is that a Christian should accept this worldly shame and glory in it.[20] Therefore it may be inferred that many of the images he introduces in the course of his argument carry a paradoxical burden combining feelings of worldly shame and compensatory heavenly glory:

> Let then the world thy calling disrespect,
> But goe thou on, and pitty their neglect.
> What function is so noble, as to bee
> Embassadour to God and destinie?   (lines 35–38)

Donne then illustrates his point in a striking trope that compares the office of minister to the Virgin Mary:

> *Maries* prerogative was to beare Christ, so
> 'Tis preachers to convey him, for they doe
> As Angels out of clouds, from Pulpits speake;
> And blesse the poore beneath, the lame, the weake.
>
> (lines 41–44)

The further comparison of the preacher to angels in clouds attenuates the impact of the first simile. Still we are left with the thought that preaching a sermon is like, or is a furthering of, Mary's giving birth to the Savior. Implicit in the comparison is the common view that ordinary childbirth, which falls under the curse, is shameful – yet Mary's acceptance of humiliation brings salvation. Hers is a glorious "prerogative."

If Donne safely skirts the implications of this metaphor, which has the preacher giving a kind of birth to his God,[21] the same cannot be said of the trope with which the poem ends:

> These are thy titles and preheminences,
> In whom must meet Gods graces, mens offences,
> And so the heavens which beget all things here,
> And th'earth our mother, which these things doth beare,
> Both these in thee, are in thy Calling knit,
> And make thee now a blest Hermaphrodite.   (lines 49–54)

Here the priest, as mediator between heaven and earth, is God's hermaphrodite, male and female, shameful and "blest," doubly a parent of his flock. Although, as Helen Gardner notes (p. 102), "hermaphrodite" is "used figuratively at this period for any striking conjunction of opposites," the "wit of this climax" lies in Donne's near literalization of the sexual metaphor in its unexpected context. The metaphor shows, with those we have discussed before, that Donne did not hesitate to use almost any variation of sexual imagery in his religious poems. He hesitated, rather, to play a passive part, to surrender himself to the divine lover.

In his sermon of 1626, cited near the beginning of this chapter, Donne recognizes the central significance of the marriage trope in describing the individual's relation to God, as sanctioned by many passages in the Bible. Yet to offer up his soul as the willing bride of God is a trope representing a devotional practice from which – although he often touches on it or narrowly skirts it – he nearly always turns away as soon as it comes to the point of personal surrender. Donne's experience with human love enabled him to write some of the best and most innovative love lyrics in the language. But that experience did not carry over successfully into the divine poems. He could surrender himself to an unspecified, Romantic feeling of transcendence and of participation in something larger than himself – to what in more recent times has sometimes been called the "oceanic feeling," but he could not surrender himself to a specific, personal, masculine Christian God.

Instead, we find Donne in some poems reverting to sterile Petrarchism and in others wrestling with biblical passages he could confidently recommend to others but not bear to apply to himself. As I have several times suggested in the course of the discussion, the result is that love in his religious poems is powerful, moving, shocking, memorable, but (to borrow a phrase of his time) seldom worthy of imitation. Donne's inner struggles remain unresolved. His inability to break through the barrier between himself and a state of peaceful and loving receptivity to God is clearly revealed in the mounting tensions and the outrageous conclusions of such poems as "Batter my heart" and "Show me deare Christ." His efforts to resolve his psychological conflicts, to accommodate his aggressive personality to a passive devotional stance based on an ancient system of religious metaphor, repeatedly fail. But the issue of his struggle is strong, admirable poetry.

The repeated failure of love in Donne's divine poems meant that, in spite of his generally high contemporary reputation as Dean of St. Paul's and as a poet, he had far less direct influence on the devotional poets who followed him than George Herbert. His contemporaries and major successors admired his divine poems but did not closely imitate them. The preferred pattern among devotional poets of the century is doubt followed by faith and questions followed by answers – not struggle followed by failure or prayer followed by silence. But Donne could speak strongly to the troubled and disillusioned religious sensibilities of later ages: to Gerard Manley Hopkins in the "terrible" sonnets, to T. S. Eliot before his public conversion, to the many modern composers who have set his *Holy Sonnets* to music, and to many others of our century who have found God harder to reach than Donne's contemporaries did. Still more, perhaps, he speaks to those who live in the absence of God and find all talk of "relation" inconceivable in such a context.

CHAPTER 4

George Herbert: "the best love"

As we have seen, John Donne recognized the marriage trope, which he inherited from the tradition, to be the dominant biblical metaphor for divine love. Yet his naturally aggressive, masculine personality made it hard for him to accept the feminine role the trope demanded in loving God. His difficulty may have stemmed, as well, from a habit of mind in the English Protestant Church. As a result of various historical and religious developments, the Anglican Church was so constituted as to accustom its members to patriarchal governance and to incline them toward greater militancy and "masculinity" than was the case with its Roman-Catholic counterpart.[1] These habits of mind stemmed not so much from religious principles or from theological doctrines as from broad cultural practices.

On the lay level, within the institution of marriage, and increasingly in the various separatist and congregationally organized sects, women may have gained something in their relations with men.[2] Scholars have disagreed, however, as to whether women were generally better off in the Renaissance and Reformation than they had been in the Catholic Middle Ages.[3] In England, the abolition of women's (as well as of men's) religious orders and the ejection of the Virgin Mary and of female (as well as of male) intercessory saints from devotional and liturgical practices left the Anglican State Church, which was also now subordinate to the King, to the two Houses of Parliament, and to lay authority,[4] almost entirely masculine, both administratively and in its spirit.[5] The place of women in the Church, which was subordinate to men in the Catholic Church on the Continent, was far more subordinate in England.

87

The impact of these religio-cultural forces on Donne, who was brought up a Roman Catholic but subsequently became (as far as we can tell) a committed Anglican, must have been considerable. Already predisposed by his character to attitudes of masculine aggressiveness, he found nothing in the milieu of the Anglican Church in which he was eventually ordained to moderate his natural tendencies. In principle, he accepted the biblical marriage trope and the traditional theological and spiritual principles it embodied. Situated and constituted as he was, however, this belief was not enough to permit him to break through the restraints of personal inclination and of cultural inhibition to assume, at least in the devotional practices that form the basis of his poetry, the feminine role that the trope required.

Herbert, too, found some difficulty in accepting the full implications of the traditional biblical tropes of love and marriage. He often employs the language of sexual love in his poetry but, as we shall see, he always uses it to figure forth what we may call the "courtship" stage of the divine-human love affair, never the consummation or the marriage stage.[6] Herbert reveals none of Donne's particular nervousness or his inner conflict upon assuming the female role. Rather, he avoids continuing in that role to the point of consummation or of marriage. As we shall find, before that point – and sometimes during the course of a single poem – he substitutes for the male-female model of love an entirely different model. So, while Donne revels in the imagery of human sexuality, of marriage, of consummation, even of rape – yet always squirms at assuming the obligatory feminine role – Herbert easily accepts that role – until the moment of consummation. Then he drops it. In its place, as I shall argue, he introduces another, apparently incompatible, love relationship, which is embodied in another traditional biblical trope – the trope of father and son. Donne too uses both marital and parental imagery; but he does not, as Herbert does, substitute the one for the other just at the point where courtship gives place to consummation and marriage. Herbert uses the marital trope for longing love, the parental trope for satisfied love.

What we know about Herbert's basic attitudes concerning human love in its various forms, and especially concerning the love of man for woman, is mainly based on his two well-known sonnets rejecting secular love as a subject for his poetry. According to Izaak Walton, he wrote and enclosed them in a letter to his mother Magdalene Herbert as a "New-years gift" during his first year at Cambridge.[7] A few small clues from Herbert's other writings may usefully be touched on, however, before we consider these sonnets. In his collection of *Outlandish Proverbs* (London, 1640), some of which he may have thought wise, others merely telling or amusing, there are a number of scattered sentences on the subjects of love, women, and marriage.[8] It is useful to cite them all, in order of appearance, to get some idea of the total picture. First those on love: "Hee begins to die, that quits his desires" (2). "Love and a Cough cannot be hid" (49). "No love to a Fathers" (121). "He that hath love in his brest, hath spurres in his sides" (426). "To bee beloved is above all bargaines" (631). "Love makes one fitt for any work" (646). "The best smell is bread, the best savour, salt, the best love that of children" (741). And there is a cluster of five sentences on love: "Love is the true price of love." "Love rules his kingdome without a sword." "Love makes all hard hearts gentle." "Love makes a good eye squint." "Love askes faith, and faith firmnesse" (540–44). Of all these sayings, only one is predominantly cynical: "Love makes a good eye squint." The others acknowledge love's power, its ability to spur worthy ambition and to gentle the hard of heart, its irrepressibility, its inseparability from simply being human and alive. We cannot know whether Herbert thoroughly approved of all of these sentiments, or some of them, or whether he simply recognized the importance of understanding love's force in the world. Unsurprisingly, the sum of these proverbs is – proverbial. That is, they represent the wisdom of the world and of the times, the kind of knowledge we are well advised to turn over in our minds and try to understand, whether or not we always agree.

On the subjects of women and marriage Herbert's proverbs are, as we might expect, also at one with his times, which is to say that they are usually more diminishing and cynical than those on love. "A faire wife and a frontire Castle breede quarrels" (103). "The wrongs of a Husband or Master are not reproached" (139). "Shee spins well that breedes her children" (144). "Dally not with mony or women" (150). "Advise none to marry or to goe to warre" (236). "A woman and a glasse are ever in danger" (244). "The more women looke in their glasse, the lesse they looke to their house" (250). "A married man turns his staffe into a stake" (366). "Mills and wives ever want" (388). "Hee that hath a Fox for his mate, hath neede of a net at his girdle" (428). "Who letts his wife goe to every feast, and his horse drinke at every water, shall neither have good wife nor good horse" (434). "A house and a woman sute excellently" (468). "A poore beauty finds more lovers then husbands" (481). "Discreet women have neither eyes nor eares" (482). "Prettinesse dies first" (484). "In chusing a wife, and buying a sword, we ought not to trust another" (490). "He that hath hornes in his bosom, let him not put them on his head" (567). "Gaming, women, and wine, while they laugh they make men pine" (604).

Even when a proverb is less cynical than most of these are, it is unlikely to reassure a modern sensibility: "In the husband wisedome, in the wife gentlenesse" (658). And even such limited compliments to women are few. "Hee that hath a wife and children wants not businesse" (778). "A shippe and a woman are ever repairing" (780). "Words are women, deedes are men" (843). "He that marries late, marries ill" (863). "A morning sunne, and a wine-bred child, and a latin-bred woman, seldome end well" (866). "Chuse a horse made, and a wife to make" (871). "The wife is the key of the house" (904). "Hee that tells his wife newes is but newly married" (987). The gist of these sayings is that marriage is a burden and a trap, that virtue and meekness are better in a wife than beauty, and that women are best kept firmly in their place. Do these sentences tell us that Herbert was more patriarchal and oppressive than the norm of his times, as the collective wisdom of our time is likely to conclude? Or do they simply confirm that the stream of folk wisdom on which he drew was usually antifeminist? It is notable that Herbert's selection of proverbs shows no tendency to quarrel with a general pattern characteristic of his and of earlier periods: a tendency to see love or being in love as something positive but the ordinary objects and ends of love – women, women's aspirations, and marriage – as dangerous, burdensome and disillusioning.

Altogether, Herbert's *Outlandish Proverbs* are congruent with the typical world-view of a courtly lover, largely disillusioned, who prefers to dwell on unrequited love, to treat woman as an unattainable ideal or as an inspiration to other, implicitly worthier activities. (Even though theory claims that the woman's worth inspires worthiness.) When a man's love is accepted or returned, and the ideal comes down to earth to be embodied in a real-life partner or wife – another person who must be dealt with – the picture immediately darkens. But since it is so difficult to know, without cross-bearings, what Herbert thought about these sometimes conflicting pieces of folk-wisdom, let us take them under advisement for the moment and proceed.

When Herbert wrote in *A Priest to the Temple* that "The Country Parson considering that virginity is a higher state then Matrimony ... is rather unmarried, then married" (pp. 236–37), he had probably been married to the former Jane Danvers for two or three years.[9] But in giving virginity the preference he was presumably just echoing St. Paul, not regretting his choice.[10] In the latter part of this chapter, he continues: "If he be marryed, the choyce of his wife was made rather by his eare, then by his eye; his judgement, not his affection found out a fit wife for him, whose humble, and liberall disposition he preferred before beauty, riches, or honour" (p. 238). The sentiment, that a man should prefer inward virtue in a woman to outward beauty or worldly advantage, is not unusual, but the two particular aspects of virtue that Herbert specifies, humility and liberality, are worth dwelling on a little further.

The husband, Herbert argues, is "*the good instrument of God to bring women to heaven.*" Out of his wife's humility he can produce "*any speciall grace of faith, patience, meeknesse, love, obedience, etc. and out of liberality, make her fruitfull in all good works.*" This may certainly appear to us to be marriage as a limited partnership.

We may recall Milton's often-deprecated phrase, "Hee for God only, shee for God in him," words that the narrator uses to describe the prelapsarian relationship between Adam and Eve when they are first introduced in *Paradise Lost* (4.299). Herbert's clerical husband too is the guide and master, and his wife, much more than Eve, may seem to be nearly his servant. Elsewhere Herbert distinguishes between servants and family: "To his Children he [the country parson] shewes more love then terrour, to his servants more terrour then love" (p. 241). A wife normally came above her children in the family hierarchy. Still, Herbert has a firmly subordinationist view of marriage. Whether he was able to put his theories entirely into practice, however, is another question. Walton (though he suggests that Herbert went out and found a wife without much romantic fuss) presents a generally idyllic picture of his marriage. But Aubrey's brief comments raise a discordant note: "His mariage, I suppose, hastened his death. My kinswoman was a handsome *bona roba* and ingeniose" – which seems to imply that he found her dangerously beautiful and willfully clever.[11] Not only was Aubrey related to Jane Danvers Herbert, but he indicates that he had a knowledgeable informant in "H. Allen, of Dantsey," who was "well acquainted with" Herbert during the first year of his marriage.

In her favor, we know that Jane Herbert agreed to take on a large household, which included Herbert's three orphaned nieces. Walton also credits her with cheerfully putting into practice that part of Herbert's plan that involved converting his wife's natural "liberality" into Christian charity: "he was most happy in his Wifes unforc'd compliance with his acts of Charity, whom he made his *Almoner*, and paid constantly into her hand, *a tenth penny* of what money he receiv'd for Tythe, and gave her power to dispose that to the poor of his Parish ... which trust she did most faithfully perform ... for she rejoyc'd in the employment."[12] We may guess from these mixed testimonies that Herbert put his plans for an ideal marriage into effect as well as he could, but that he found that a husband, not unlike that God in whose place he deemed himself to stand, must sometimes work with a refractory subject, with a person having a will of her own.

Now we may return to the two sonnets from Walton's *Lives*. They delineate a love that falls entirely within the Petrarchan, courtly love tradition.

> My God, where is that ancient heat towards thee,
>> Wherewith whole showls of *Martyrs* once did burn,
>> Besides their other flames? Doth Poetry
> Wear *Venus* Livery? only serve her turn?
> Why are not *Sonnets* made of thee? and layes
>> Upon thine Altar burnt? Cannot thy love
>> Heighten a spirit to sound out thy praise
> As well as any she? Cannot thy *Dove*
> Out-strip their *Cupid* easily in flight?
>> Or, since thy wayes are deep, and still the same,
>> Will not a verse run smooth that bears thy name?
> Why doth that fire, which by thy power and might
>> Each breast does feel, no braver fuel choose
>> Than that, which one day Worms may chance refuse?

Even in repudiation, none but conventional courtly or Petrarchan love themes and images are embodied in this first poem. Here we find Venus and Cupid, hot flames of passion, elevation of the lover's spirit by love of his mistress, and conversion of love into the production of smooth verses, offered up in sacrifice to a deified mistress on a pagan, venerian altar. The rejected lover's stance, too, as exemplified by his language, is entirely courtly. His poetry wears "*Venus* Livery" like a feudal servant, and it elevates his mistress into the heavens while it offers itself up to be burnt. Ironically, Herbert turns this worship of the mistress, which originally derived its terminology from the parody of religion, back toward its original object, as the sonnet becomes a parody of a parody.[13] Of course, Herbert evokes the old Petrarchan formulas only to criticize and reject them. Still, in vowing to turn to God he rejects neither the courtier's manner and stance nor his longing to serve and adore, but only his object.

As Louis Martz has pointed out, the classical English statement on sacred parody of secular love poetry is provided by

Robert Southwell, who argues that the sacred lover may employ
the same passions and affections as the secular lover, provided
that he redirects them upward toward God.[14] Herbert's final
tercet follows Southwell's advice strictly. The fires of love, the
improving pains of passion and longing, are not to be
condemned or expunged, but simply redirected from the
worship of a falsely deified mistress to the living God who
created human passions and is their best and fittest object.

The second Walton sonnet focuses on the proper use of
imagery. As with the passions, the images of secular love poetry
are not to be condemned but converted to better and more
legitimate uses. The right use, in each case, is to praise the
Creator. All of creation mutely praises its maker, and, as
Herbert will make explicit in "Providence," one of the poet's
proper offices is to become their articulate spokesman, the
"Secretarie of [God's] praise" (line 8).

> Each Cloud distills thy praise, and doth forbid
> *Poets* to turn it to another use.
> > *Roses* and *Lillies* speak thee; and to make
> > A pair of Cheeks of them, is thy abuse ...
> Such poor invention burns in their low mind
> > Whose fire is wild, and doth not upward go
> > To praise, and on thee, Lord, some *Ink* bestow.
>
> (lines 4–7, 9–11)

Thus the second sonnet continues along the general lines set by
the first. Poetic images, like passions, should be restored to the
true Creator of the objects from which the poet originally draws
them. God is the author of beauty. The poet's misused faculty of
invention, which finds these images and puts them to false ends,
should be tamed and redirected upward.

The final tercet, however, introduces a shocking turn, which
echoes but far exceeds the troubling but more nearly conventional tercet of the first poem:

> Open the bones, and you shall nothing find
> > In the best *face* but *filth*, when, Lord, in thee
> > The *beauty* lies in the *discovery*.   (lines 12–14)

In part, the sentiment is ancient: flesh dies, but God and the spirit are eternal. Yet the particular imagery and the nature of the poetic gesture are, for Herbert's time, disturbingly modern and scientific. They evoke not only the traditional *momento mori* but also the most disillusioning aims and discoveries of the New Philosophy. They involve the true poet in actively attacking and metaphorically mutilating the false poet's imagined mistress, and not merely in pointing out her eventual mortality or even her sinfulness. They are an anatomy, which murders to dissect. They violently cut open and savagely destroy not only the Petrarchan mistress's lovely face, but the ideal Petrarchan vision itself.[15] They recall the deeply disillusioning yet fascinated unease with which Donne reacted to the New Philosophy, of which the anatomy is so characteristic a manifestation. Donne too uses the literary anatomy as a method to disturb the air of some of his stranger love poems.[16]

Of course, had he not written *The Temple*, no one but a few specialists would now read Herbert or trouble to ask what he thought about love. But love is central to *The Temple*. In a significant article Rosemond Tuve estimates that "all but some twenty of the hundred and seventy-odd poems raise one or more of the many traditional questions which surround the problem of the nature of Christian love."[17] Tuve rightly argues that the form of love that dominates *The Temple* is *agape*, God's perfect love for man. She has much of value to say concerning the major traditional treatments of that love, with which Herbert would certainly have been familiar.[18] Some of the best-known and most important exponents in the main tradition were St. John (the Evangelist), St. Paul, St. Augustine, St. Bonaventura, St. Thomas Aquinas, and St. Bernard.[19] But if divine love comes initially and overwhelmingly down from God, it also poses the problem of how, or whether, or in what way, God's love can be returned by man.[20] Unlike Martz, Tuve is largely concerned to draw a sharp distinction, one might almost say a wall of separation, between human love and divine, which, she thinks, certain unnamed critics have been guilty of blurring and confusing.[21] To a degree, she makes a valid theological point but (I think) does less than justice to Herbert the human being as opposed to Herbert the theologian. Perhaps Herbert strove to find a way of returning *agape* in all its purity to God, if only by admitting the human impossibility of doing so. But in even the purest and most elevated of devotional poets, sacred love takes on the coloration of human emotions, sensibly accommodates itself to human understanding and feelings, and, in putting itself into words and images, models itself on familiar human relationships. As Donne argued in his Paul's Cross sermon of 24 March 1616/17, "*Relations* constitute one another."[22] So the question still arises. What view of human love or human relationship lies behind Herbert's great religious lyrics?

Rosemond Tuve has already argued extensively and persuasively that courtly love is not a model for *The Temple*. The essence of courtly or Petrarchan love is that the mistress should be haughty and unapproachable, but, as Tuve points out, "Here is a love poet who never mentions, or implies, or fears, that his love is unrequited." As she also points out, "The forms and attitudes of secular love pleas are little use as models in a situation where the partner who pleads is also the partner who is unready." Finally, she observes that the "speaker is a most well-beloved one asking help against self-caused suffering, not an unregarded servant in love with submission."[23] In brief, Herbert's devotional poems simply lack the main characteristics of the Petrarchan love relationship. He borrowed much of his style or verse technique from Sidney, as Martz argues, but not his amatory technique.

To Tuve's cogent observations we may add another. There is hardly a suggestion, anywhere in *The Temple*, of fulfilled love between the sexes, whether courtly or of any other kind. Nor does Herbert noticeably represent sacred love by means of sexual or marital metaphors. This relative lack of secular love imagery is especially surprising when we remember the devotional poems of two of Herbert's fellow poets and near-contemporaries, Donne and Crashaw, often thought of as belonging to the same school, one his predecessor and the other his successor. Or we may also remember the ancient and (however troubling to the modern mind) thoroughly orthodox tradition of devotional writings along similar lines stretching all the way back to the Song of Songs.[24] This devotional tradition included, in seventeenth-century England, writers as diverse as the Laudian and Catholic Crashaw and the Calvinist Francis Rous, who produced such observations as: "There is a chamber within us, and a bed of love within that chamber wherein Christ meetes and rests with the soule."[25]

Calling to mind, too, St. John of the Cross's typically lush and passionate imagery, let us consider the last stanza of Herbert's "Even-song," which is about the closest that he comes to the biblical tradition of the divine marriage between God and the soul or God and the Church:

> I muse, which shows more love,
> The day or night: that is the gale, this th' harbour;
> That is the walk, and this the arbour;
> Or that the garden, this the grove.
> My God, thou art all love.
> Not one poore minute scapes thy breast,
> But brings a favour from above;
> And in this love, more then in bed, I rest. (lines 25–32)

The imagery is movingly beautiful, with its walks and arbors, gardens and groves, which insistently recall the Song of Songs, or such poems based on that work as St. John's "En una noche oscura" and (at a later date) Vaughan's "The Night." Characteristically Herbert's language is understated but the feelings he expresses still are powerful. We are persuaded that for Herbert God is, indeed, "all love." Nevertheless, the love in which the poet finally rests, as in a bed, is not the "bed of love" that Rous derives from the Bible. It is a bed not of near-sexual ecstasy but of secure feelings. One might more appropriately imagine the poet not as a bride enjoying her husband's embraces, but as a child, content after a long absence to be home in bed.

Once we have realized that this is so, that Herbert sometimes skirts the sexually suggestive yet avoids fully evoking it, we find that the same is true of other poems in which we might expect him to employ traditional metaphors of sexual passion or of marriage. "Love" 1 and 2, for example, which have often been read as mature versions of the two Walton sonnets – as, in fact,

precisely the kind of love sonnets to God that Herbert had
earlier promised to write, prove to be nothing of the kind.
Although he addresses God in the opening of the first sonnet as
"Immortall Love," and in the opening of the second as
"Immortall Heat," any expectation we might have of finding a
continuous imitation or parody of secular love poetry is aroused
only to be dissipated. "Thou shalt recover all thy goods in
kinde,/Who wert disseized by usurping lust," Herbert promises
his God, toward the close of "Love" 2. But in the very next lines
he discloses a chaste resolution of this promise. His former lust is
replaced not by sanctioned love and marriage but by an
obviously joyous yet sexless obeisance: "All knees shall bow to
thee; all wits shall rise,[26] / And praise him who did make and
mend our eies" (lines 11–14).

Likewise "The Search" seems to begin in the tradition of the
Song of Songs, evoking the love-sick bride overcome with
longing for her absent spouse:

> Whither, O, wither, art thou fled,
>   My Lord, my Love?...
>
> I sent a sigh to seek thee out,
>   Deep drawn in pain,
> Wing'd like an arrow: but my scout
>   Returns in vain.   (lines 1–2, 17–20)

But when at length the poet imagines his God returning to him,
there is no longer any suggestion of a sexual or marital
relationship:

> When thou dost turn, and wilt be neare;
>   What edge so keen,
> What point so piercing can appeare
>   To come between?
>
> For as thy absence doth excell
>   All distance known:
> So doth thy nearnesse bear the bell,
>   Making two one.   (lines 53–60)

The image of two persons who have grown so close that they
become inseparably one reminds us of the secular love tradition – for example, of Shakespeare's "The Phoenix and the

Turtle" or Donne's "The Extasie." Yet once again Herbert excludes from the consummation he has longed for any explicit hint of a sexual metaphor or even the chastest of marital comparisons.

I should add that the few poems I have cited in this connection are exceptional in *The Temple*, not because they refrain from extending the initial suggestion of a sexual metaphor to describe sacred love itself, but because they even begin to allow that such a metaphor may be possible. Most poems in *The Temple* refrain entirely from alluding to even the most refined sort of secular love, and certainly from anything noticeably sexual, except when they describe truancy or sin. "Discipline" is our final example of a poem that introduces a refined metaphor of sexual love, which the reader might expect Herbert to develop to its logical conclusion. Once more, however, he refrains.

> Throw away thy rod,
> Throw away thy wrath:
>   O my God,
> Take the gentle path.
>
>   For my hearts desire
> Unto thine is bent:
>   I aspire
> To a full consent...
>
> Love is swift of foot;
> Love's a man of warre,
>   And can shoot,
> And can hit from farre.
>
> Who can scape his bow?
> That which wrought on thee,
>   Brought thee low,
> Needs must work on me.
>
> Throw away thy rod;
> Though man frailties hath,
>   Thou are God:
> Throw away thy wrath.   (lines 1–8, 21–32)

This, one of Herbert's strongest, simplest, and most affecting lyrics, comes perhaps as close as any of his poems to the language and the characteristic stance of the Song of Songs. But

even here Herbert is, to say the least, reticent. His lines
irresistibly recall the imagery of pagan lyrics and of elegies to
Cupid as well as the Song of Songs. Yet, even though an
undeniable element of sexual longing shows through the poet's
expression of dissatisfaction, no corresponding scene of sexual
fulfillment or of marriage ultimately emerges.

Herbert explicitly dismisses the marriage metaphor for
Christian love in "The Size."

> Content thee, greedie heart.
> Modest and moderate joyes to those, that have
> Title to more hereafter when they part,
>   Are passing brave...
>
> A Christians state and case
> Is not a corpulant, but a thinne and spare,
> Yet active strength: whose long and bonie face
>   Content and care
>   Do seem to equally divide,
> Like a pretender, not a bride.   (lines 1–4, 31–36)

Given the context, a praise of fasting, and the tone, which seems
comical, this cannot be taken as Herbert's definitive rejection of
the bridal metaphor for a Christian's relation with God. But it
certainly falls in with his reluctance to employ it elsewhere, and
it may be read as an implicit criticism of those who presume to
cast themselves in such a role.

As Herbert avoids speaking clearly about the marriage of
God and the soul, he also avoids the long accepted, closely
related image, on which Donne plays so shockingly in "Show
me deare Christ, thy spouse, so bright and clear," of the Church
as the bride of Christ. In Herbert's poems the Church is
regularly the dignified and beloved Mother of its incorporate
members, but, with one minor exception, never the bride of
God. Once in "The Church Militant" Herbert uses the formula
to describe the Church's origins (lines 9–16), but in the balance
of the poem, as the Church descends from its first origins and
grows increasingly corrupted, he drops it. In "The British
Church" he noticeably uses conventional variants of this
traditional image only in speaking about those churches he
considers to be false.[27] The Catholic Church, like the Whore of

Babylon, "wantonly / Allureth" her followers. She has so often kissed her "painted shrines / That ev'n her face by kissing shines" (lines 13–16). The Puritan ideal of the Church, to the contrary, is so "shie / Of dressing" that, in another surprisingly suggestive image, she "nothing wears" (lines 19–24). Only the Anglican Church deserves to be legitimately honored as our "dearest Mother." Yet God shows his love for Herbert's Church more as an architect or as a military commander than as a familiar husband: he can be counted on to "double-moat" her with his grace. Herbert depicts only false religion in sexual terms, while the true Church, apparently, has become the loving mother of its members without ever having been Christ's bride.

Nowhere does Herbert explicitly put forward the view, Neo-gnostic rather than strictly Christian, that sex is simply and intrinsically evil. Yet he was clearly uncomfortable with the use of sexual imagery in certain religious contexts in a way that Donne was not. One might speculate from the mainly negative evidence of *The Temple* that he was naturally inclined to such tendencies. His poems evoke the seductive, the sensual, and the scatalogical only in order to exemplify sin or temptation. Sometimes they embody religious longing in the language of romantic love, but they refrain from even the mildest suggestion that there might be a resemblance between a man's pure love for a woman and Christian *caritas*, or that God's love for souls and for his Church might be like a husband's love for his wife.

Although Herbert's two sonnets to his mother seem to promise that he intends to take Southwell's advice and to rechannel his secular passions into similar but higher sacred passions, and the same promise is at least implied in several of his other poems, Herbert always disappoints us. Or, more accurately, he manages quietly and very unobtrusively to redirect us, since (so far as I know) none of these poems has given its readers the impression that the poet has wavered, or has failed to deliver what he promised.[28] I think this would not be the case if Herbert simply went from concrete, human imagery in describing his repudiation of secular love to vague, merely abstract, imagery in describing his conversion to the sacred. His poems often move

from body to spirit, certainly, but without a corresponding loss
of human warmth. I think that this paradoxical result is possible
because Herbert substitutes for romantic love certain other,
equally human, kinds of love, which help make his poems
emotionally convincing.

One of these kinds of love is a servant's loyalty to his master.
This is, of course, a stance or an attitude very similar to the love
of a Petrarchan poet for his mistress, but as we have seen
Herbert simply avoids making this timeworn connection when
he moves from the secular to the sacred. In "Jordan" 1, he
exchanges the "fictions" and "false hair" (line 1) of the courtly
lover not for a redirected love of God leading to spiritual
betrothal, but for a simple yet loving act of obeisance to an
absolute superior and ruler: "Nor let them punish me with losse
of rime, / Who plainly say, *My God, My King*" (lines 14–15).[29]
In "Jordan" 2, although he closely parodies the first love sonnet
of *Astrophil and Stella*, he replaces Sidney's mistress with a
"friend" (line 15) whom he would honor and serve. In
"Discipline," as we have seen, he does not approach God as a
lover. Rather, here too he is the most abject of subjects, of a
great king, not of a mistress: "Yet I creep / To the throne of
grace" (lines 15–16).

Michael Schoenfeldt has so thoroughly and convincingly
discussed the poetics of patronage in Herbert's poetry that it is
unnecessary for me to argue again how important, pervasive,
and subtle this pattern is.[30] The imagery of God as King or as
feudal superior and of the poet as his servant runs all through
The Temple. In perhaps the greatest of Herbert's poems on
caritas, "Love" 3, a conversation takes place between a host and
a guest, a master and a servant. They contest the nature of love
indirectly by contesting the nature of service. Although the poet
sits down to a meal which represents both the Eucharist and the
heavenly banquet, there is no recollection of the particular
occasion for the banquet in what has seemed to many critics to
be Herbert's chief biblical source, the parable of the guests
invited to a wedding feast.

The poet typically begins "Redemption" by identifying
himself as "Having been tenant long to a rich Lord" – as a

retainer, not a lover. "What pleasures could I want, whose King I served?" he asks in "Affliction" 1 (line 13). "Rise heart; thy Lord is risen," he begins in "Easter" (line 1), with a celebratory emphasis on Christ's title that immediately conveys his own inferior position.[31] The relation between Herbert and his God is that of a subject and his king, a servant and his master, a client and his patron. The subject rejoices in his master's glory. Yet if that were all, and if Herbert's religion were merely a matter of power politics, of dominance and submission, or even of what has come to be called hegemonic mystification, it is unlikely that his poems should be so widely liked and so accessible in an age that so deeply suspects and resents all such political and economic relationships – or for that matter, in any other age. Mere subservience to power would scarcely move most readers.

The answer to this puzzle, as I have suggested earlier, is to be found in still another kind of loving relationship that pervades *The Temple*, that of father and child. Donne had argued, on the evidence of Genesis, that the highest of human loves is that of a man for a woman in marriage. But only two of Herbert's sayings about love in *Outlandish Proverbs* are couched in superlatives. In those two Herbert also speaks with noticeably greater warmth. One of them says that "The best smell is bread, the best savour, salt, the best love that of children." The imagery in this proverb is homely, fundamentally nourishing – and biblical. The other saying is the obverse of the first: "No love to a Fathers." We might rather have expected Herbert to say "No love to a mother's," knowing the story of his life and remembering the sequence of poems he wrote on her death, *Memoriae Matris Sacrum*. They reveal an intense love for his mother, as obsessive and all-consuming in its way as D. H. Lawrence's. Herbert's father died when he was three and a half. Although Herbert seems to have liked and respected his step-father, Sir John Danvers, that later relationship could not have accounted for what, in his poems, appears to be such a deeply felt psychological imprinting.

It is tempting to indulge in amateur psychologizing. We have in Herbert's case an absent father, an overwhelmingly powerful mother, and a child who was the youngest of several dominating brothers.[32] God filled the lacuna. But it is safer simply to turn back to the poems and to note again the pervasive longing for a father's love they so clearly reveal. "H. Baptisme" 2 is typical:

> Thou didst lay hold, and antedate
>   My faith in me.
>
> O let me still
> Write thee great God, and me a childe:
> Let me be soft and supple to thy will,
>   Small to my self, to others milde...
>   Childhood is health.   (lines 4–9, 15)

Herbert draws, with great warmth and seeming intimacy, on the biblical imagery of childhood as a state of receptiveness to grace, in a way that he never does on the imagery of marriage. In *The Temple*, divine courtship and human desire are sometimes the preludes to love, but only in sonship does Herbert find loving contentment.

Rebellion against a mere political tyrant or an economic master would be admirable, but it would be inadmissable if that master were also a loving and beloved father. Even when the familial relationship is not spelled out, the bond between father and son, more than any kind of sexual love, seems to underlie the tone of overtly political relationships. "Nature," which follows "H. Baptisme," is such an instance:

> Full of rebellion, I would die,
> Or fight, or travell, or denie
> That thou hast ought to do with me.
>   O tame my heart.   (lines 1–4)

This, the voice of a subject addressing his lord, could also conceivably be the voice of a bride addressing her husband-to-be, but it sounds far more like a disobedient child penitently addressing his father. In "Affliction" 1, he reveals that obedient service to his lord and master is synonymous with love:

> Well, I will change the service, and go seek
>   Some other master out.
> Ah my deare God! though I am clean forgot,
> Let me not love thee, if I love thee not.   (lines 63–66)

Despite the urgency of his complaints, the speaker never really considers a change of service, I believe. One can no more change such service than one can repudiate a father. As even the arch-individualist Satan ironically realizes in *Paradise Regained*, "relation stands" (4.519). So in "Assurance," the troubled poet proclaims that there is only one answer to those who say that the "league was broke" between him and his God: "But I will to my Father" (lines 11, 19).

We should remember that in the seventeenth century public service, professional employment, personal loyalty, and family relationship often converged in a single bond. The term "family" included not only the nuclear family of parents and children, and the larger blood family of uncles, aunts and cousins, but also the full extended family of inlaws, clients, retainers, and servants. Herbert seems temperamentally to have been inclined to ignore or tacitly to reject the natural parallel which others of his time so often drew between the attraction of exogamous love and service to a patron, but he embraced the other familial model, so often evoked by James I and so many lesser lords and masters, of a loving father and his children. In "The Collar," no more than a word is needed to calm the poet's bitterest doubts and his passionate feelings of resentment against duty and obligation:

> Me thoughts I heard one calling, *Child*!
> And I reply'd, *My Lord*.   (lines 35–36)

That one word "child," of course, is a reminder that the servant is also a beloved son, and that his omnipotent and demanding Lord is also a loving father.

Although "patriarchal" has in recent years become a term of abuse and resentment, in the Renaissance, as Debora Shuger reminds us, the fatherly had broadly positive implications, which people willingly extended to God and to the king.[33] "Power" and "authority" have been subjected to wide-ranging (if sometimes suspiciously obsessive) inquisition at the hands of New Historicists and others, from political deconstructionists to feminists to Marxists. But George Herbert shows us what it is like to think and to feel that ultimate power and authority can

coexist with perfect, selfless love, as in the loving, fatherly figure
of God in *The Temple*. If this observation is credible, one hopes
it will not dissuade readers who love justice from continuing to
read, to like, and to ponder Herbert's poetry.

In what respect might Herbert be said to change or to
"reinvent" received, conventional ideas about sacred love? For
him to say that God is a loving father appears, at first sight, to
represent not much more than the height of conventional
orthodoxy. To say that one should love one's father is to agree
with the Elizabethan Book of Homilies and to reaffirm the social
order. But I know of no other important writer after the English
Reformation and before Vaughan, Milton, and Traherne, who
captures as well as Herbert what it feels like to be the loving and
trusting child of a fatherly God.[34] Although God as a loving
father – as *avinu malkenu*, "our father, our king," in the Hebrew
hymn, as *abba* in Mark 14:36, and as "Our Father" in the
Lord's Prayer – is deeply encoded into the very fabric of both
Judaism and Christianity, the relationship may seem more
natural, affectionate, and comprehensible to some ages than to
others. Our own recent times are a negative case in point.
Herbert may be said to have helped prepare the way for the
benevolent God of the eighteenth-century man of sentiment
and the fatherly God of Victorian piety – now so much out of
fashion and so subject to ignorant caricature as almost to be
unmentionable.

At the same time, and more radically, Herbert nearly excised
from his devotional poetry the ancient idea of God as the spouse
of the Church and of the individual soul. What seemed so
natural to the middle ages and to many of Herbert's contemporaries – to speak of God as a loving husband, or (in another
tradition) as a tender nursing mother – came in the England of
succeeding centuries to seem grotesque and unsuitable.[35] We
have no evidence that Herbert felt anything like this sort of
"wheyfaced" priggishness.[36] Yet we do find him, in such poems
as "Jordan" 1, repudiating the love of mistresses for the service
of a Father God, and in "Even-song" and "Discipline,"
moving from the woman's role in sacred courtship borrowed
from the Song of Songs to the alternative role of a loving and

obedient child. Although the changes that took place in religious attitudes in succeeding centuries obviously cannot be laid entirely at Herbert's door, he was, as we know, extremely influential among later English devotional poets and, over a longer stretch of time, among Anglican and Methodist hymn writers. Herbert may well have been at least partly responsible for furthering the characteristic Anglo-Saxon attitude of reserve in religion. Much of the English-speaking world shrinks or bridles at any suggestion of connecting sexual matters with religion. Alternatively, as if in over-compensation, others can no longer tell them apart.

CHAPTER 5

Richard Crashaw: "love's delicious Fire"

Among the most notable marks of the courtly and Petrarchan love traditions is the centrality of the lover's longing or desire. Ordinarily, a Petrarchan lover can never expect to satisfy his all-powerful desire on this side of the grave. In versions of courtly love in which the lover's desire is requited, and he joins with his mistress as Tristan does with Iseult, fate or the lovers themselves usually manage to produce further obstacles to their happy union. In the Petrarchan tradition of the English Renaissance, frustration and unsatisfied desire are the almost universal story.[1] It has even been suggested, on reasonable grounds, that a haughty mistress is, as we would now say, unconsciously necessary to such a Petrarchan lover, because only her refusal can empower him to indulge his longing to the full. As Denis de Rougement and Mario Praz among others have suggested, these lovers typically seek to be thwarted or otherwise disappointed; they are in love with desire itself, not with fulfillment. Indeed, although a Petrarchan lover, like his Romantic descendants, may say otherwise, often in the depths of his psyche he really seeks frustration, disappointment, destruction of himself and others, and ultimately death.[2]

Richard Crashaw has no reputation as a writer of secular love lyrics. Few of his poems in this vein can stand beside his devotional poetry. Yet all of his love poems and translations share a surprising characteristic: a near absence of raw desire. The concordance to his English poems provides a rough indication of his relative lack of interest in desire.[3] Although in one of his most memorable lines he addresses St. Teresa as "thou undanted daughter of desires!" ("The Flaming Heart," line 93),[4] variants of the word "desire" appear in his English poems a total of only 16 times, while variants of the word "love" appear 324 times.[5] We know that "love" may be made to mean almost anything, depending on the speaker and the context, but the numbers are suggestive. By way of comparison, Sidney uses variants of "desire" 92 times and of "love" 427 times. Thus in Crashaw the ratio of "love" to "desire" is roughly 20 to 1, and in Sidney 4.6 to 1. We might conclude that Sidney, as a result of his personality, his family and political situation, and his greater involvement in the Petrarchan love tradition, was four or five times more wedded to, or obsessed by, desire than Crashaw. Granted, there is more than a little comedy in applying these dry statistics; yet the numbers are suggestive and, as we shall see, supported by Crashaw's poetry itself.

Crashaw seems to have had a natural bent toward religion, a personality that led him as an adult, without notable hesitations or signs of internal conflict (as expressed in his surviving writings) to become a college fellow, an Anglican clergyman, and then a Roman Catholic.[6] We find no evidence of the kind of serious initial doubts or of resistance to entering into an ecclesiastical career that so strongly, if differently, characterize the writings of both Donne and Herbert. Yet surprisingly, and contrary to what we might expect of a man of religion, Crashaw's writings also reveal a strong bent not toward the poetry of desire but the poetry of pleasure, of enjoyment, and of delight. His love poems are much less Platonic or Petrarchan than Anacreontic. They revel in the simple gratification of the senses by what is presently in view, rather than in longing for something perfect, distant, esoteric, and unobtainable.

The best known of his love poems, "Wishes. To his (supposed) Mistresse," is platonic in some ways – if only because she is always confessedly "supposed" and not real flesh – and essentially chaste. Nonetheless, it combines a tale of Platonic origins with considerable enjoyment of an imagined embodiment. We begin with the Platonic:

> Till that Divine
> *Idaea*, take a shrine
> Of Chrystall flesh, through which to shine. (lines 10–12)

But we also have a kind of pleasurable lingering over the fleshly details, so lovely and abundant by nature that no cosmetic artifice is required to supplement them:

> A Cheeke where growes
> More then a Morning Rose:
> Which to no Boxe his being owes.
>
> Lipps, where all Day
> A lovers kisse may play,
> Yet carry nothing thence away. (lines 34–39)

The poet declares all these physical beauties to be innocent, but in doing so, he diminishes none of their pleasurable or sensuous charms:

> Smiles, that can warme
> The blood, yet teach a charme,
> That Chastity shall take no harme.
>
> Blushes that bin
> The burnish of no sin,
> Nor flames of ought too hot within. (lines 61–66)

As Crashaw declares that the physical delights of his mistress are chaste, without depriving them of their pleasurability, so he makes her intellectual virtues seem equally pleasurable by setting them forth in imagery that is insistently, almost physically, sensuous:

> *Sydnaean* showers
> Of sweet discourse, whose powers
> Can Crowne old Winters head with flowers,
>
> Soft silken Houres,
> Open sunnes; shady Bowers,
> Bove all; Nothing within that lowres. (lines 88–93)

Most noticeably, even though Crashaw is writing about an ideal woman who, if "not impossible" (line 2), still scarcely belongs to this world, he does not write with any sense of longing, as if she were – as indeed she is – infinitely desirable but absent. Instead he writes with a clear, untroubled, lingering enjoyment, which he conveys through each loving and appreciative detail of his description. His is a poetry in which the reader's pleasure resides not in the suspenseful building-up of desire and of deprivation to a climactic resolution, still less in the frustration of desire to the end, which is so often the bittersweet fate of the Petrarchan lover, but rather in a leisurely appreciation of and dwelling on each lovely image, word, and stanza for its own sake.

Some further observations may be offered concerning Crashaw's impressive treatment of pleasure in this poem. First, we find in it signs of the same kind of wonderful empathy that characterizes his later sacred poems. That is, we find an identification with, and a feeling through the viewpoint of, his subject. One of the characteristic habits of the Petrarchan poet is to project his own wishes and imaginary ideals onto a real person (in the familiar Jungian terms, called a projection of his *anima*) rather than to see and to acknowledge the presence of an actual person, with a mind and a viewpoint of her own. The terms of Crashaw's poem, as its title indicates, would seem to invite such an act of pure wish-fulfillment and self-gratification. Yet one finds that he respects the identity and integrity even of his purely imagined mistress. "I wish her Beauty" (line 16), he says. He *might* have said, "I wish her *beautiful* (to gratify my own desires)." Instead, his phrasing requests beauty as a free gift to her, for her sake, not his. True, he asks of the mistress a certain passivity: not submissiveness to his desires, however, but receptiveness to a wise and impartial love:

> A well tam'd Heart
> For whose more noble smart,
> Love may bee long chusing a Dart.   (lines 55–57)

He asks of her, in fact, nothing that he will not often ask of himself, openness to a higher power – but not simply submission to his own wishes. Most men of Crashaw's age believed that, as St. Paul advised, women should be firmly subordinated to men, and should do what their fathers and husbands told them to do. The husband, as George Herbert puts it in *A Priest to the Temple*, is "the good instrument of God to bring women to heaven."[7] Likewise, it might be thought that the mistress should submit passively to the poet. Even in this early poem about an imaginary woman, however, Crashaw shows an almost Miltonic recognition that (although men and women alike are not free to choose wrongly without suffering the consequences) a woman possesses her own independent free will and, like a man, must ultimately be allowed to exercise it:[8]

> Her flattery,
> Picture and Poesy,
> Her counsell her owne vertue bee.   (lines 100–02)

If she acts well, it should be according to internal consent to her own wisdom. Pictures of her, and poetry about her, are mere "flattery." They are the outward and inessential equivalents of cosmetic beauty, as her inward virtue is the equivalent of true natural beauty. Paradoxically, the poet expresses no wish to govern or to direct her, even though she is his own creation.

In his closing stanza, Crashaw in effect releases his imagined creature from the bonds of his poetic fancy to her own autonomy:

> Let her full Glory,
> My fancyes, fly before yee,
> Bee ye my fictions; But her story.   (lines 124–26)

Curiously, there is scarcely another love poem of the period in which the mistress – although often based more or less directly on a real woman – has as much ungrudging leave as Crashaw's "supposed" mistress to express her will freely.

As Rosemond Tuve long ago observed, "Wishes. To his (supposed) Mistresse" is largely structured on the blazon, the catalogue of the mistress's beauties.[9] More recently feminist critics have complained, with some justice, that the blazon, although ostensibly a method of praising the mistress, often amounts to no more than a dismemberment, a cutting-up of the whole person into images and poetic pieces, which the poet then manipulates and controls to advance his own aims and to gratify himself.[10] Much the opposite may be said of Crashaw's poem. He uses the blazon not to break down a woman and to gain a kind of indirect control over her, but instead to build up and to set free a woman whose origins are in his imagination. At least he offers to do as much until the real woman should appear to speak for herself:

> Till that ripe Birth
> Of studied fate stand forth,
> And teach her faire steps to our Earth.   (lines 7–9)

Once again, Crashaw's practice is almost the opposite of most of his contemporaries.

Crashaw's consent to the relative autonomy of even an imagined mistress leads to another observation. Although he is a poet of pleasures rather than desires, his pleasures are purified and made licit because he has no desire to possess what he describes, whether a woman or an object – or to stimulate the reader with the desire to possess it. Crashaw's is an impartial pleasure, which delights in the thing itself and not in wanting to own or to control it. He is far from being withdrawn or cool; he is not an impassive witness; he participates in, he feels intensely, and he enjoys what he describes; but he allows it what I have already called its own autonomy. In this regard, Crashaw resembles Thomas Traherne, who values what he calls right seeing, values feeling and appreciating the world's treasures, but treats possessiveness – the desire to own and to control – as if it were effectively the equivalent of original sin.[11]

As far as we know, Crashaw took early to a view of life and religion that served him well when he decided to leave the Anglican for the Roman Catholic communion. That is, he early relinquished the prospect of love and of marriage. As he writes in his short epigram "On Marriage": "I would be married, but I'de have no Wife, / I would be married to a single Life." According to the testimony of Thomas Car in his prefatory poem to *Carmen Deo Nostro*, Crashaw was naturally abstemious in all worldly matters. "No care / Had he of earthly trashe."

His thoughts and his words, Car emphasizes, were virginal, and even his foes styled him "the chaplaine of the virgine myld."[12] Yet a strong element of sensuous pleasure runs through all of Crashaw's poems, secular and sacred.

Crashaw's translation of Moschus, "Out of the Greeke *Cupid's Cryer*," is typical of his early translations of classical and Italian love-poetry as well as of his original love-poetry. The poem is a warning against Cupid spoken by Venus – who is hardly a spokesperson for stern morality. Her tone and personality (which Crashaw captures so appreciatively), and the way she revels in the pleasures against which she pretends to warn us, are suggested by the rewards she offers to anyone who can capture the errant boy, her son:

> The glad descryer shall not misse,
> To tast the *Nectar* of a kisse
> From *Venus* lipps. But as for him
> That brings him to mee, hee shall swim
> In riper joyes: more shall bee his
> (*Venus* assures him) then a kisse.   (lines 11–16)

Crashaw shares and well conveys Moschus' delight in the sensuous pleasures of the moment. Love may burn and consume his innocent victims (line 74), but the poet and the translator alike revel in the fires of this consumption. We see how affably and discerningly Crashaw assumes in his verse, perhaps for the first time, a female persona.

Crashaw's two short translations "Out of the Italian" reveal a similar penchant. The opening lines of one of them epitomize the spirit of the whole: "Love now no fire hath left him, / We two betwixt us have divided it." There is nothing but present delight in the poem, in which the lovers share equally: "And so in mutuall Names / Of Love, burne both together" (lines 1–2, 13–14). The other poem tells how Cupid became "nak't, a Boy, and blind" as a result of listening to the poet's "Mistresse Song." "And so he lost his Clothes, eyes, heart and all" (lines 2, 8). Here again is present pleasure, not pining desire. Desire is present only in its absence or in its satisfaction: to borrow Blake's phrase, in "the lineaments of gratified desire."

In a similar spirit, for his translation "Out of *Catullus*," Crashaw chose the most pleasurable, the least bitter, cynical, or psychologically conflicted, of that poet's sometimes dark lyrics, the one (which Ben Jonson also imitated) on the infinite and mutual pleasures to be found in multiplying kisses:

> Then let amorous kisses dwell
> On our lips, begin and tell
> A Thousand, and a Hundred, score
> An Hundred, and a Thousand more,
> Till another Thousand smother
> That, and that wipe of another.
> Thus at last when we have numbred
> Many a Thousand, many a Hundred;
> Wee'l confound the reckoning quite,
> And lose our selves in wild delight.   (lines 9–18)

To lose oneself in "wild delight," to dwell in the pleasure of the moment, is the central theme of this and of the other love poems Crashaw chose to translate. It is even the theme of his far chaster "Wishes. To his (supposed) Mistresse," a poem in which the reader is nonetheless never frustrated, always gratified, by a poetry that is never yearning, always sensuous. Along with the absence of want or desire in Crashaw's poetry goes an absence of egoistic projection, of ambition, and of possessiveness. These attitudes are replaced by pleasure in recognizing the woman's independent reality, sympathy for her viewpoint, and delight in what Milton's Comus less innocently describes as "mutually partaken bliss."[13]

Crashaw's sacred poems depict a love equally characterized by an absence of empty longing and an emphasis on present, sensuous enjoyment. In this respect he is very different from Donne, whose divine poems are always filled with passionate longing for a love he can never enjoy in this present world. And he is also very different from Herbert, whose God reciprocates his love, but never in a way that can be expressed in sexual, sensual, or marital metaphors. Donne yearns without expecting any answer in this world; Herbert yearns like a lover and is answered lovingly, but as a child by its father or a servant by his king. Crashaw never yearns. Although in life he was often deprived – of his family, of his college living, of his friends and country, and even of the generous patronage he might have expected from Henrietta Maria – in his poetry he seems always to be already satisfied, already emotionally espoused to his mistress or his God, content even at a distance.

Among Crashaw's ripest expressions of sacred love is his Hymn "To the Name … of JESUS." From its beginning the poem invokes emotions of life, warmth, peace, and contentment, not of desire:

> I Sing the NAME which None can say
> But touch't with An interiour RAY:
> The Name of our New PEACE; our Good:
> Our Blisse: and Supernaturall Blood:
> The Name of All our Lives and Loves.   (lines 1–5)

The poet's emotional investment in the object of his praise raises him to the ecstatic heights of "Blisse," but with the calm warmth of someone already securely in possession of his love and without the effort and the violent perturbations that often accompany such strong feelings. Although the affective structure of the poem follows a tripartite pattern, of expectation, presence, and relinquishment, there is no prelude of desire, and there will be no epilogue of loss.

The Hymn begins as an invocation as well as a work of praise. Crashaw appropriately recognizes that he is nothing compared to God, that he is empty unless God fill him. He tells his soul:

> O thou art Poore
> Of noble POWRES, I see,
> And full of nothing else but empty ME,
> Narrow, and low, and infinitely lesse
> Then this GREAT mornings mighty Busynes.
>   One little WORLD or two
>   (Alas) will never doe.
>   We must have store.   (lines 19–26)

Even here, in his confession of emptiness, Crashaw's emotional emphasis glides over what the experience of such a state might feel like. Instead, he passes swiftly on to anticipate the profusion

of God's abundant "store." Forgetting his own emptiness, he
seems already to enjoy abundance on the level of feeling. His
soul goes forth on a quest but passes through no dark night of
suffering; it feels no personal sense of loss or of deprivation:

> Goe, SOUL, out of thy Self, and seek for More.
>   Goe and request
> Great NATURE for the KEY of her huge Chest
> Of Heavns, the self involving Sett of Sphears
> (Which dull mortality more Feeles then heares)
>   Then rouse the nest
> Of nimble ART, and traverse round
> The Aiery Shop of soul-appeasing Sound:
> And beat a summons in the Same
>   All-soveraign Name
> To warn each severall kind
> And shape of sweetnes, Be they such
>   As sigh with supple wind
>   Or answer Artfull Touch,
> That they convene and come away
> To wait at the love-crowned Doores of
>   This Illustrious DAY.   (lines 27–43)

Crashaw has declared his soul to be narrow, low, and empty.
Yet before he has even begun to seek a response from the Name,
a return of love, his soul has been filled with harmony and
sweetness, with crowds of happy images, which seem to bring
him pleasant and responsive company and already to fill and to
satisfy any possible sense of lack he may feel.

As Crashaw turns his address to "every sweet-lipp't Thing"
(line 47) and continues to mobilize the world's forces to help
him invoke and praise the Name, it grows ever more evident
how different his attitude as a sacred lover is from Donne's or
from Herbert's. It is hard to imagine either of those devotional
poets assuming such a confident, joyful, and almost completely
desireless, stance:

> Nor must you think it much
> T'obey my bolder touch;
> I have Authority in LOVE's name to take you
> And to the worke of Love this morning wake you

Wake; In the Name
Of HIM who never sleeps, All Things that Are,
    Or, what's the same,
    Are Musicall;
    Answer my Call
    And come along;
Help me to meditate mine Immortall Song.   (lines 51–61)

Where in Donne and Herbert we would expect to find a strong sense of isolation, personal inadequacy, and longing (though with each poet differently resolved), in Crashaw we find only companionable pleasure and quiet confidence. The difference in their stances as sacred lovers is not attributable only to what their respective Churches, Catholic and Anglican, authorized, or to their possession of what we might loosely call "Catholic" and "Protestant" sensibilities. For we can more easily imagine Milton, from the opposite, Puritan wing of the seventeenth-century Christian spectrum, than either Donne or Herbert, from the Anglican middle-ground, speaking in such warmly confident tones.

Even when Crashaw specifically evokes intense desire in a series of vivid images, he makes desire, too, a matter for present pleasure and subsumes it into the general rejoicing:

    Lo how the thirsty Lands
Gasp for thy Golden Showres! with long stretch't Hands
    Lo how the laboring EARTH
    That hopes to be
    All Heaven by THEE,
    Leapes at thy Birth.   (lines 129–34)

For Crashaw, anticipation becomes another link in a chain of assured delights.[14] Similarly, the painful and expectant process of giving birth, freed of all memory of the original curse pronounced in Genesis, seems to become as happy as the results of that birth. The original source of Crashaw's vivid image is St. Paul's Epistle to the Romans: "For I reckon that the sufferings of this present time are not worthy to be compared with the glory which shall be revealed in us. For the earnest expectation of the creature waiteth for the manifestation of the sons of God

... For we know that the whole creation groaneth and travaileth in pain together until now" (8:18–22).

The whole of Romans, chapter 8, moves between the opposite poles of suffering and joy, death and life, expectation and fulfillment, the old burden of original sin and the new freedom of divine grace. In choosing to emphasize one pole, Crashaw is not necessarily demonstrating his unorthodoxy. At other times and in other poems he meditates movingly on Christ's Passion and acknowledges the continuing reality of sin and suffering. But in the old debate about the comparative efficacy in renewing the world of Christ's First and Second Comings, he puts great weight on the First.[15] Before the climax of the poem, Crashaw finally expresses some sense of real grief and longing:

> O see, so many WORLDS of barren yeares
> Melted and measur'd out in Seas of TEARES.
> O see, The WEARY liddes of wakefull Hope
> (LOVE's Eastern windowes) All wide ope
>   With Curtains drawn,
> To catch The Day-Break of Thy DAWN.   (lines 143–48)

He depicts the grief and longing of the expectant world in heartfelt terms, but he feels them more empathically than personally. This is not so much his own personal longing, except insofar as he sympathizes with others, but his sympathy for the world's longing. Even here his images are so beautiful and so often emotionally positive that a strong counterlogical impulse of joy resists the general sadness and longing expectancy. Against the "WEARY liddes" is balanced "wakefull Hope," against the "seas of TEARES" are balanced "LOVE's Eastern windowes," which are "All wide ope ... To catch The Day-break of Thy DAWN." Even as it waits through long "barren yeares" of suffering expectation, the world's longing is soothed and consoled by the poet's anticipatory joy.

Crashaw's short moment of desire is quickly answered. The Name descends, Love responds, with an overwhelming gratification of the senses:

> Lo, where Aloft it comes! It comes, Among
> The Conduct of Adoring SPIRITS, that throng

> Like diligent Bees, And swarm about it.
>   O they are wise;
> And know what Sweetes are suck't from out it.
>   It is the Hive,
>   By which they thrive,
> Where All their Hoard of Hony lyes.
> Lo where it comes, upon The snowy Dove's
> Soft Back; And brings a Bosom big with Loves.
>
> (lines 151–60)

Crashaw's imagery overloads the senses with intense, pleasurable sweetness, not to exhaust them and to replace them with some better and more spiritual form of devotion, as Louis Martz has suggested, but from sheer, childlike pleasure in the reception of limitless abundance from a nurturing divinity.[16]

The poet revels in the sanctioned pleasures that the Name brings to him and to us with its climactic entrance into the poem. As that climax inevitably recedes, he recognizes that such exalted moments do not eliminate the penalties of living in this world, where we are subject to suffering, deprivation, and death. Still he feels no pangs of withdrawal. Not even the anguish of the martyrs who have helped bring the Name into the world can dampen his joy. The weapons the persecutors wield against them can do no more than "Inlarge thy flaming-brested Lovers" (line 212) to let in more love:

> What did their Weapons but sett wide the Doores
> For Thee: Fair, purple Doores, of love's devising;
> The Ruby windowes which inrich't the East
> Of Thy so oft repeated Rising.
> Each wound of Theirs was Thy new Morning;
> And reinthron'd thee in thy Rosy Nest,
> With blush of thine own Blood thy day adorning,
> It was the witt of love o'reflowd the Bounds
> Of Wrath, and made thee way through All Those Wounds.
>
> (lines 216–24)

The entry of Christ into the world is multiple. He comes at the Incarnation, in the experience of each individual person (martyr, poet, and reader especially), and finally at the Last Judgment. These events, although separate in time, are all interrelated and typologically connected in ways that tradition has explained.[17] Crashaw embodies these various Comings in the emblem of Christ as the Sun (originally from Malachi's *Sol justitiae*), rising in the East and bringing eternal day.[18] Christ comes in the deaths of his followers as well as in his human birth, and he will come again in the last day when the remaining resistance of the persecutors to his demanding love will be broken:

> Next to their own low NOTHING they may ly,
> And couch before the dazeling light of thy dread majesty.
> They that by Love's mild Dictate now
>   Will not adore thee,
> Shall Then with Just Confusion, bow
>   And break before thee.   (lines 234–39)

This is the terrible love that destroys those who reject it.[19]

Thus there are no signs in the Hymn of anything resembling Petrarchan love. There is no fruitlessly longing lover, no unattainable mistress (or God to take her place, or simple reversal of roles), no indulgence in the bittersweet pangs of unsatisfied desire. Yet throughout there are, clearly, an abundance of sensuous and even sexual affects. Martz has rightly cited, in connection with Crashaw, Southwell's famous observations on the legitimacy of the passions in sacred devotion: "Passions I allow, and loves I approve, onely I would wishe that men would alter their object and better their intent. For passions being sequels of our nature, and alloted unto us as the handmaides of reason: there can be no doubt, but that as their author is good, and their end godly: so ther use tempered in the meane, implieth no offence."[20] What are these passions, then, if not those ordinarily expressed in conventional love songs? We find several kinds of secular love reflected in Crashaw. One is mutual and fulfilled sexual love, in which desire no longer has such overwhelming relevance. As we have seen, even in his early love poems Crashaw gravitates naturally to writing about fulfilled love of this kind. His concentration on pleasure rather than on desire carries over into his sacred poems.

It may seem strange that religious poetry should more closely resemble Moschus, Catullus or those writers whom Crashaw's contemporaries regarded as wicked and lascivious Italians than the more "refined" love of the English Petrarchans. But as C. S. Lewis has argued, in the view of Christian moralists, there was no necessary equivalence between unsatisfied love and virtuous love.[21] The best and healthiest human love was thought to be mutual, married, and fruitful. As Milton writes, the state of pining away in unsatisfied desire, about "which the starv'd Lover sings / To his proud fair," is "best quitted with disdain" (*Paradise Lost* 4.769–70). Illicit lust on the one side and fruitless, unrequited longing on the other are alike to be condemned.

Turning to authorities on religious devotion roughly contemporary to Crashaw, we find that what some Christian writers thought to be true of secular love might also be true of sacred. There is no exact uniformity of opinion on the matter. St. Francis de Sales, for example, argues "that we are to have an insatiable desire of Loving God, adding continually love upon love."[22] But many authorities speak of an absence, or of a transformation, of desire in the higher stages of devotion. For example, Benet of Canfield writes, in *The Rule of Perfection*: "Not that one should forsake good desires, but he should forsake their imperfection; not that one should abandon them, but he should accomplish them; not forsake them, but purify and perfect them in God.... This flowing of burning desires into God is a transforming of working love into enjoying love."[23] Similarly, Augustine Baker writes that, since "Love is the Roote of all other passions," the first necessity in the spiritual life is to transform "desire to be possessed of, or to procure for our selves" any person or object, to an unselfish love that seeks only the good or glory of the person loved.[24] Perhaps the difference between these writers and St. Francis is chiefly semantic, since all agree that if desire is restless, perturbed, melancholic, self-centered, or possessive, it is not beneficial.

In Crashaw's case, desires were transformed into pleasures even before he turned away from writing and translating secular love poetry, as if he naturally enjoyed a comparative freedom from discontent and from the urge to possess what he lacked. We find also in his secular love poetry some of that characteristic ability to identify with the woman's point-of-view which was so strongly to typify his sacred verse. As I suggested some years ago, Crashaw was relatively uninterested in what were considered in his time to be active or "masculine" forms of devotion. In particular, he was relatively uninterested in meditation (whether Ignatian or "Protestant"), which involves rigorous intellectual analysis and active, even aggressive, searching for God.[25] Instead he gravitated naturally to a form of devotion usually recommended for women: sensible affection or affective devotion. This is a form of devotion that emphasizes feeling rather than intellect, and passivity rather than activity. The soul does not desire and search, but waits. That it should be a form of devotion recommended especially to women is, of course, connected with the prevalent view that women were more emotional and less intellectual than men. Although such an attitude appears patronizing and demeaning to us – and indeed doubtless it often was demeaning – it was not necessarily so. Until the Reformation, contemplation was traditionally thought to be a higher state of life than action. And in the long debate concerning which was the higher faculty, intellect or will (in the latter of which *caritas* was thought to inhere), it is far from clear that intellect was always the winner, particularly in spiritual affairs.

As St. Francis de Sales writes: "knowledge having produced holy love, Love doth not staie within the compasse of the knowledge which is in the understanding, but goes forward, and passeth farre beyond it; so that in this life we may have more love, then knowledge of God, whence great S. THOMAS. assures us that often tymes the most simple and women abound in devotion being more ordinarily capable of heavenly love then able and understanding people."[26] That women should be grouped with "the most simple" and men (by implication) with the "able and understanding" is at once both insulting to women and (in view of the context and of the Christian paradox that in the Kingdom of Heaven the last shall be first and the first shall be last) complimentary.[27]

On the subject of "feminine" love and devotion, St. Francis

de Sales also recounts an irresistible story about the first Franciscans:

The Blessed Brother Gilles, one of the first companions of S. FRANCIS, saied one day to S. BONAVENTURE, oh how happie you learned men are, for you understand many things, wherby you praise God: but what can we Idiotes doe? S. BONAVENTURE replied, the grace to love God is sufficient. No, but Father, replied Brother Gilles, can an ignorant man love God, as well as a learned? yes, saieth S. Bonaventure, yea more, a poore sillie woman may love God as well as a Doctour of Divinitie: with this Brother Gilles cried out, falling into a fervour, oh poore simple woman, love thy saviour, and thou shall be as great, as Brother Bonaventure; and upon it, he remained for the space of three houres in a RAPTURE.[28]

There is a nice balance here (as likely to offend feminist principles as to assuage them) between the usual opinion of society – that a woman is less than a man, and an uneducated lay brother less than a priest – and the point of the story (which sends Brother Gilles into a mystical rapture) that the love of God, which was thought to be the highest of human ends, does not depend on any of the usual human preparations or social distinctions.

Even those who practice Ignatian meditation do not practice intellectual analysis or aggressive meditation as ends in themselves, but use them to arouse their feelings and to motivate their wills toward some good resolution or change of heart and life. If women's feelings toward God were by nature already aroused and receptive – which was thought to be more commonly the case with them than with men – it would be unnecessary, even sterile and spiritually harmful, for them to undertake such intellectual exercises.[29] Augustine Baker writes: "It is a great mistake in some Writers, who thinke the *Exercise of the will* to be *meane* and base in comparison of *Inventive Meditation* and curious Speculation of Divine Mysteries." Some persons with affective natures, he continues, need not be "driven to the paines and expence of time in finding out Reasons and Motives to raise their affections to our Lord, but immediatly and without more a doe suffer the Affections to flow."[30]

Those naturally drawn toward sensible affection did not need to be women, but women provided the usual model. Some spiritual directors of women, such as St. Francis de Sales and Augustine Baker, were themselves inclined to a more emotional, less intellectual, form of devotion. In some cases they seem to have learned a great deal from, as well as taught, their charges. Such was clearly the case with Baker and Dame Gertrude More, with whom he was closely associated.[31] Such too would seem to have been the case with Crashaw, who was at least informally the spiritual director of several women. Earlier in this century, the "feminine" nature of his poetry was often vigorously attacked by critics (usually male) who accused him of aberrancy, foreign effeminacy, and bad taste.[32] More recently, it has been reinvestigated and praised.[33]

An extraordinary number of Crashaw's major devotional poems are concerned with women. His last collection, *Carmen Deo Nostro*, includes his epistle offering spiritual advice to the Countess of Denbigh; his poem "To the Queen's Majesty"; "Sancta Maria Dolorum," which views the Crucifixion through Mary's eyes; "In the Glorious Assumption of Our Blessed Lady"; "The Weeper," Crashaw's most vivid exercise in sensible affection; the three poems on St. Teresa, the affective-mystical Ode on a "Prayer-book given to a young Gentle-Woman" with its sequel; and the three complaints of Alexias, wife of St. Alexis. In all of these thirteen poems, to one degree or another, Crashaw not only addresses a woman but identifies with her emotionally or speaks directly through her. All of these poems educate the reader in what might be called "feminine spirituality" – except that Crashaw's point is that men can profit equally from such spirituality. At the center of this spirituality is Crashaw's central vision of sacred love, which conquers through weakness, suffering, passivity, and submission. Like the martyrs who welcome the Holy Name into the world, all of these spokeswomen exemplify (or are counselled to exemplify) a love that lets divine Love in through its wounds. If there is any element of parody based on the secular love tradition – which there must be, in a love so clearly couched in vivid sexual metaphors – it is a parody not of male but of female experience:

> She never undertook to know
> What death with love should have to doe;
> Nor has she e're yet understood
> Why to show love, she should shed blood
> Yet though she cannot tell you why,
> She can LOVE, and she can DY.
> ("A Hymn to ... Sainte Teresa," lines 19–24)

>   ...
> Leave her that; and thou shalt leave her
> Not one loose shaft but love's whole quiver.
> For in love's feild was never found
> A nobler weapon then a WOUND.
> Love's passives are his activ'st part.
> The wounded is the wounding heart.
> ("The Flaming Heart," lines 69–74)

The "she" of these lines is St. Teresa. Yet it might equally well be the poet's soul, also usually called "she." Crashaw makes it clear that he knows St. Teresa was no passive pushover; like Christ's (her own exemplar), hers is a conquering passivity. She is held up not only for our admiration but for our ardent imitation. Crashaw anticipates, in effect, a feminism that argues, not that women should be more like men and accumulate more power, but that men should be more like women, and learn to suffer, to serve, to give, and to love.[34] The same pattern may be found in a dozen of Crashaw's other major poems, which might be cited at length if they were not already so familiar. It is recognizably a pattern central to all of Crashaw's sacred poetry.

Authorities on devotion remarked that the proper end of sensible affection, as of meditation, was to rise out of the senses into the will and spirit, and ultimately to manifest itself as contemplation or mystical prayer. Indeed the mystics traditionally borrowed from the Song of Songs to describe their indescribable experience through the same kind of sensuous imagery as was commonly used in sensible devotion. Crashaw could find such a pattern in the mystical writings of St. Teresa, who was one of the strongest influences on his later work. Both forms of devotion, affective and mystical, emphasize passivity to the divine lover, both involve a similar use of rapturous, metaphorically sexual language. In Crashaw's "Prayer. An Ode," we may see how affective devotion reaches upward toward – or perhaps into – mystical devotion:

> O happy and thrice happy she
>   Selected dove
>   Who ere she be,
>   Whose early love
>   With winged vowes
> Makes hast to meet her morning spouse
> And close with his immortall kisses.
> Happy indeed, who never misses
> To improve that pretious hour,
>   And every day
>   Seize her sweet prey
> All fresh and fragrant as he rises
> Dropping with a baulmy Showr
> A delicious dew of spices;
> O let the blissfull heart hold fast
> Her heavnly arm-full, she shall tast
> At once ten thousand paradises;
>   She shall have power
>   To rifle and deflour
> The rich and roseall spring of those rare sweets
> Which with a swelling bosome there she meets
>   Boundles and infinite
>   Bottomles treasures
> Of pure inebriating pleasures.
> Happy proof! she shal discover
>   What joy, what blisse,
> How many Heav'ns at once it is
> To have her GOD become her LOVER.   (lines 97–124)

But if Crashaw's affective devotion aspires to contemplation, it also has its roots below, in secular love, the senses, and sexuality. It is influenced by St. Teresa but it also parodies secular love poetry. These connections may be clearly seen in a brief, comparatively less well-known poem, "A Song," which follows the three Teresa poems in the 1648 and 1652 collections:

> Lord, when the sense of thy sweet grace
> Sends up my soul to seek thy face.

Thy blessed eyes breed such desire,
I dy in love's delicious Fire.
O love, I am thy SACRIFICE.
Be still triumphant, blessed eyes.
Still shine on me, fair suns! that I
Still may behold, though still I dy.

Second part.
Though still I dy, I live again;
Still longing so to be still slain,
So gainfull is such losse of breath,
I dy even in desire of death.
Still live in me this loving strife
Of living DEATH and dying LIFE.
For while thou sweetly slayest me
Dead to my selfe, I live in Thee.

George Walton Williams suggests that this poem was "Perhaps inspired" by St. Teresa's *Interior Castle*.[35] If so, the debt is general rather than specific. To live by dying through the intensity of divine love is characteristic of St. Teresa's spirituality as it was also characteristic of St. John of the Cross's. A connection is equally clear to Crashaw's own Teresa poems. Even more obviously, as R. V. Young has suggested, the poem is a parody of a thousand Italian love songs and Elizabethan madrigals about dying from the intense experience of love – that is, from the ecstasy of sexual consummation.[36] In support of this parodic connection with secular love songs is an earlier version of Crashaw's text, which survives in manuscript, with a musical setting by an unknown composer. As Louise Schleiner notes, the composer rather heavy-handedly seizes the opportunity to emphasize the phrases "though still I die" and "so to be still slain" – just, I would add, as Italian composers so dearly loved to do with *io moro* in their love songs.[37] Thus the composer emphasizes what he finds in his text: Crashaw's emphasis on a powerful, killing "desire" that is – as in the passage from St. Francis de Sales's *Treatise on the Love of God* – not so much an empty longing for something absent as the intensely amorous experience of present, continuing, superabundant gratification. Here is the one place where Crashaw embraces desire: in "the insatiable desire of Loving God, adding continually love upon love," in the transformation of "working love" into "enjoying love."[38]

Therefore it is not entirely accurate to say that Crashaw abandons desire in his sacred poems. Rather, they are filled with something resembling St. Francis' transformed desire, which is neither a lustful longing – for possession of a person or object, for worldly success, or for sexual fulfillment – nor an empty longing for something absent; but rather a warm, sometimes fiery, longing for something already enjoyed, for a God who is not absent but, in some deeply satisfying fashion, already present.[39] We see such a desire exemplified in the Hymn to St. Teresa: "Her weake brest heaves with strong desire" (line 40); in "The Flaming Heart": "By all thy brim-fill'd Bowles of feirce desire" (line 99); and in "Prayer. An Ode": "setts the house on fire / And melts it down in sweet desire" (lines 73–74).

Returning to Crashaw's parody, "A Song," we find that there is only a hairline's difference between it and its secular exemplars, which in turn had borrowed earlier from the language of sacred devotion. If we change the first word "Lord" to "Love," the poem becomes entirely ambiguous. In that case, too, the speaker's sex becomes indeterminable. His basic stance is "feminine," to the extent that he is acted upon but does not act, dies but does not kill in return, suffers but does not inflict suffering. Aside from the opening word and the context of sacred poetry in which the poem is found, however, we could imagine the speaker to be a man addressing his mistress, a woman addressing her lover, or a suppliant addressing his or her God.

This sexual interchangeability is not generally true of English Petrarchan love poetry or, for example, of the devotional poetry of Donne, Herbert, and Vaughan. Although Donne often tries to assume the female role in relation to God – and thus to make use of a traditional devotional technique – he has great difficulties in doing so, and it would be hard to mistake his voice for a woman's. Herbert, who occasionally assumes the woman's role in the divine courtship, drops it for the child's role when that courtship would be consummated.[40] In "The Night," to take one instance, Vaughan assumes the traditional feminine role of the Beloved from the Song of Songs – but only at night in prayer. During the day he is a busy, distracted man. Of these poets, only Crashaw shows a natural, sympathetic, continuing identification with women – which we may fairly call *habitual*.

That Crashaw's religious poems were admired by some of his contemporaries, despite their differences on points of religion, is evidenced by the well-known comments of writers such as Abraham Cowley. Nevertheless, Crashaw did not have much direct influence with regard to love on the tone or the stance of other English devotional poets. His "feminine" way of thinking and feeling, in particular, has caused him to seem "foreign" to most observers (mostly masculine) over succeeding centuries. His introduction of figures like St. Teresa and St. Mary Magdalene as devotional intermediaries or mediators has seemed attractive to some English-speaking observers, but also rather quaint and foreign – something to wonder at and admire, perhaps, but not to imitate. His passiveness has been troubling. His emphasis on pleasure and on gratification of the senses has offended the sensibilities even of some of his stoutest defenders. He has fed our worst suspicions about the psychological linkages between sex and religion.

Our present time likes to think itself appreciative of good poetry wherever it finds it, almost regardless of its message. But not many of us are simultaneously and equally responsive to the pleasures of sexual gratification and of religious devotion. In general, those who admire sexual gratification without guilt and "androgyny" or "polymorphous perversity" without conventional restraint or prejudice may admire Crashaw from one restricted perspective. Those who, to put it equally bluntly, admire a pure and genuine but totally abstract and asexual religious devotion may admire him from another restricted perspective. (I am not thinking of particular critics, but invoking the straw men of two extremes.) Commerce between the two views is difficult, perhaps even impossible. I have tried to negotiate a complicated path, which I hope is responsive both to Crashaw's poetry and to his views about love as implied by that poetry.

The paradox may be that we are finally in a position, for the first time since the Reformation came into England and into the English-language literary tradition, to begin to understand and to sympathize with a "feminine" approach to love like Crashaw's. Yet we are less inclined than ever to follow that love in directions he would have wished it to lead us. Not unlike other ages – although the particulars change – we are more easily inclined to empowerment than to sacrifice, to vindication than to sympathy, to material welfare than to transcendence. At our most unselfish and self-congratulatory, we crave the empowerment, vindication, and material welfare of others who lack these perquisites – which are not, however, always wholly beneficial to their possessor. Crashaw preferred to wish that others should, like himself and the female saints he admired, cheerfully offer themselves up, in sacrifice, love, and suffering. It would be hard to argue that he has managed to introduce into our customary attitudes toward love anything that has permanently influenced succeeding ages – or is soon likely to do so. Yet he has often been admired. He has, seemingly, often been on the verge of being understood. And at least he remains a lasting and a remarkable provocation.

CHAPTER 6

Thomas Carew: "fresh invention"

Coming from the direction of the twentieth century, a reader might not notice what is perhaps the most radical quality in Thomas Carew's love poetry, since that quality consists in an absence: the virtual absence, for the first time since Wyatt, of the Petrarchan tradition in any of its moods and variations. True, from the beginning, English Petrarchists, like their Italian predecessors, indulged in mockery and undermined the tradition with cynical demurrals and pragmatic insertions. Even in the hands of iconoclasts like Donne, however, the basics persisted: distorted, mocked, fought against, yet ultimately still a determining force.[1]

As in politics Donne could rail against the patronage system, so in love he could protest Cupid's "vast prerogative," yet find no workable substitute for either of them, other than withdrawal from the world and society. Eventually, variations of Donne's solution – private love and the nuclear family as havens against a threatening world – would find wide acceptance, and privacy would, as it were, become socialized. But that outcome would have to wait at least a century before the right social, economic, and psychological conditions came into place to allow it wide expression. In Donne's time such conditions were not yet generally available to allow the version of idealized love expressed in the *Songs and Sonets* to take firm hold. As we have noted, even Donne himself, in his later poems and sermons, reverted to more traditional, conservative views.

Carew, however, coming on the scene roughly a generation later than Donne, took the seventeenth-century reinvention of love in a new direction. In his poetry the discourse of love and desire undergoes another fundamental change. Frequent traces of conventional Petrarchan imagery persist ("Aske me no more where *Jove* bestowes / When *June* is past, the fading rose"), but the basic posture, the fundamental relationship between mistress and lover, the framework itself of Petrarchism, finally dissolve. In place of the old Petrarchan lover, a new-model courtier, client, and lover appears on the scene. None of Carew's lovers stays faithful to a haughty, refusing mistress; none pines away with unsatisfied desire; none is killed, even in jest, by submission to superior disdain. The absence of a whole complex of originally feudal or courtly attitudes, although Carew was a consummate courtier, has its roots, as I shall argue, in his family situation and experience with the patronage system.

Like Donne, Carew learned by disgrace. A destructive confrontation with father, family, and culture forced him to find other forms of patronage and love, no longer feudal in principle. As I shall further suggest, more than such personally chastening experiences were necessary to allow Carew to develop and consolidate his new views. His immediate disgrace was very like Donne's. But unlike Donne, and many another malcontent who preceded him, he turned his personal experience not merely into a passing protest or withdrawal but a revolutionary shift in perception that found an immediate outlet in his social situation. He was enabled to do so by concurrent changes in the English economy and culture, changes taking place most notably in the field of agricultural reform.

The agricultural revolution of the modern age is closely connected with the passage of English society from a feudal to a market economy. The two developed together. This is not to say that the connection was uniquely inevitable, as is sometimes assumed. The early Medieval agricultural revolution in Europe, equally broad and important, was as closely associated with the development of monasticism and Christian corporatism.[2] More or less concurrent with early modern economic, political, and social changes was a change, or at least an important complication, in moral attitudes. New views became possible, and with them new parameters for moral evaluation. One cannot look long upon history without realizing that, in

societies where agriculture is central, basic moral assumptions
about human relationships and political theory are closely tied
up with agricultural practice. Chaucer's Plowman and the
apocryphal *Plowman's Tale*, More's *Utopia*, Latimer's *Sermon of
the Plow*, Winstanley's Digger tracts, are characteristic mile-
stones in English moral and political history. A central moral
and economic issue, over the course of several centuries, was the
enclosure movement, which may also be taken to stand for such
related developments as the movement from holding land in
common or by feudal tenure to private ownership, or from
service to a feudal landlord to labor for hire. We may readily
think of numerous writers who bitterly cursed enclosure as
selfish and destructive: that is the position assumed in works
ranging from *Utopia* to *The Deserted Village*, and indeed it
continues to find expression today among many historians and
literary critics. But since the seventeenth century other views
have been possible.

The great divide in the movement from feudal corporatism to
liberal individualism came to its crisis in the mid-seventeenth
century. Up to that time, the general assumption was that
enclosure could profit an individual landowner only at the
expense of his tenants and neighbors. Around 1650, however, as
Joyce Oldham Appleby has shown, writers began for the first
time to argue explicitly that private ownership, self-interest,
and self-enrichment were, or could be, beneficial to the common
good or commonwealth.[3] This view, so inconceivable in terms of
earlier moral, economic, and political principles, yet so basic to
later developments in British and western history and economic
thought, was first offered in certain British writings of the mid-
seventeenth century advocating agricultural reform.

The idea that enclosure and other aspects of private land
improvement are as much to the benefit of society as a whole as
to the individual landowner was first strongly proclaimed in a
tract written by Gabriel Plattes, an associate of the reformer
Samuel Hartlib, which was published anonymously in 1641.[4]
Its breathless revolutionary fervor on behalf of a combination of
moral, political, and scientific reforms – all presumed to result
from undertaking certain practical agricultural improvements

– is summed up quite accurately in its full title: *A Description of the Famous Kingdome of Macaria; Shewing its Excellent Government. Wherein The Inhabitants live in great Prosperity, Health, and Happinesse; the King obeyed, the Nobles honoured; and all good men respected, Vice punished, and vertue rewarded. An Example to other Nations*. For the most part, this little tract is as apocalyptically hopeful and vague as its title. It is not at all well or clearly written (indeed one comes away from it with the impression of an author who has undergone a powerful conversion experience of a kind that he himself does not fully understand), but it puts forward one very significant new proposition: "if any man holdeth more land than he is able to improve to the utmost, he shall be admonished, first, of the great hindrance which it doth to the Commonwealth. Secondly, of the prejudice to himself; and if hee doe not amend his husbandry within a yeares space, there is a penalty set upon him, which is yeerely doubled, till his lands be forfeited, and he banished out of the Kingdome, as an enemy to the common-wealth" (p. 4).

Two important principles are implicit in this fictional legislation. First is the assumption that public good follows directly from private profit. People may best help their country or commonwealth by helping themselves. Second is the insistence that landowners may hold their land only so long as they observe certain social and moral obligations, which are fulfilled not by seeing to the direct welfare of their own farmers, tenants, and dependents (as Thomas More's traditional, still essentially medieval spokesmen would insist) but rather by the maximization of production and profit, which will redound, indirectly yet inevitably, to everyone's welfare. Ownership of land was already undergoing a process of change, from the old aristocratic practice and corresponding ideal of feudal tenure (an ideal eagerly accepted by many brand-new Tudor aristocrats who imitated their predecessors and suppressed their origins) to a new meritocracy of owners who improved their land, increased their rents, and raised productivity. The central thesis of *The Famous Kingdome of Macaria* is that this transfer of ownership or change in management from a feudal to an individualistic style is a good thing, indeed that from it will flow prosperity, good government, willing obedience to authority, general health and happiness. On the model of Macaria, private land ownership and improvement can solve all of England's social, moral, and political, as well as economic, problems, making the country's inhabitants all wealthy, contented, and virtuous. Thus the ideals of Christian charity and of aristocratic *noblesse oblige* toward inferiors are partly yet broadly displaced by a new ideal of "improvement," which, by mandating greater efficiency in agricultural practice, will increase the general wealth and welfare.

Following the execution of King Charles, agricultural change began to move more rapidly. Several tracts advocating the virtues of enclosure appeared at this time. Among them were Silas Taylor's *Common Good: or the Improvement of Commons, Forests and Chases by Enclosure* (1652); Joseph Lee's *Considerations Concerning Common Fields and Enclosures* (1654); and Lee's *A Vindication of a Regulated Inclosure* (1656). Another tract by Adam Moore, Gent., *Bread for the Poore. And Advancement of The English Nation. Promised By Enclosure of the Wastes and Common Grounds of England* (1653), may be taken to speak for the rest. Moore early shows his agreement with Plattes's underlying political-moral rule: "An idle Member in a Common-wealth...is either actually cast out by justice, or at least suffereth a divorce from generall affection... Neither may we account him a droan only that sitteth still and is idle, but him also (and worse) that is busie in hindring commodity" ("To the Reader," Sig. в1ʳ). That is, it is now immoral to attempt to hold on to the old "moral economy," so called, and to obstruct progress.

Many Royalists complain in the 1650s that England, which they remember as formerly an Eden, now has fallen into ruin and is overrun metaphorically by thorns and brambles. To the contrary, Moore, who is among a very few writers since the end of the Middle Ages to take seriously God's command to unfallen Adam and Eve to keep Eden and to dress it (Genesis 2:15), argues that England will only become an Eden by means of agricultural improvement and rural labor: "No, as *Adam* in *Eden*, so are we by that all-Creator placed in this Garden, *To keep it and dresse it*, for the comfort, encrease, and preservation of his people committed unto it" (p. 2). Milton holds the same view, based on the same key text, in *Paradise Lost* and *Paradise Regained.*[5]

This new Eden of the improvers is not something recollected from the near or distant past, to be longed for nostalgically, but rather something in the future to be brought into being. The revised vision literalizes Milton's proclamation at the beginning of *Paradise Regained* that the mission of the Son is to bring into being a new *"Eden* rais'd in the wast Wilderness" (1.7). As Adam Moore argues, there is only one way to bring this improving vision into existence: "The principall and onely means to ripen the fruit of new hopes is *Enclosure*, and distribution of the Lands to private owners, which being appropriated to their particular uses, will then be cleansed and purged of the former deformities, and so fully improved by their carefull industry, that it will undoubtedly yield to them Such advancement thereby, and consequently relief to the *Republike*, as hereafter ensueth" (p. 13).

This Eden, as we might expect, also specifically requires the displacement of old-fashioned landed aristocrats, whose false ideals gaze backward toward an unreal and an idle Eden, by forward-looking, new-model improvers. The change is to be brought about either by transfers of property or by an almost religious conversion of those readers and landowners willing to follow the new principles: "Yet (some may say) it will seeme strange or unpleasing to Lords of *Wastes* or Tenements to see their Lands and inheritances disposed perpetually from their own possession into the tenure and occupation of other persons. But I answer, that a work being in hand for the generall good, we must either follow the current of generall acceptance, or sit down hopelesse of successe" (p. 36).

The final element in this transformation of values, as I have suggested in *The Georgic Revolution*, is the revaluation of labor. Work, which in the consensus of many old-fashioned moralists represented the curse on fallen Adam and his sons, condemned to earn their bread in the sweat of their faces,[6] now to the contrary represents the very means of restoring Eden in this present world:

And touching imployment for the poor (wherewith this land so infinitely aboundeth) such means thereof would be for them in the manurance of each sort of these *Wastes* enclosed, (as by *Diking, Hedging, Fencing, Setting, Sowing, Reaping, Gleaning, Mowing, Making hay* and what not? which is all *Bread for the Poor*) that from the noisome and deboist courses of *Begging, Filching, Robbing, Roguing, Murthering*, and whatsoever other Villanies their unexercised brains and hands undertake, they would (even gladly) be reclaimed and refined to loyall and laudable courses, as well for their own contenting relief, as the unspeakable comfort and honour of the whole State, who now (as a wretched and needy mother) is enforced to make continuall Massacres of them, for those misdoings which even their want of bread urgeth them to commit.   (p. 30)

The poor, since Elizabethan times increasingly seen as little better than idle vagabonds and criminals, subject to punishment, have been expelled from the estates to which their ancestors were attached by dwindling, old-fashioned landlords, weakly unable to manage their estates properly. These same poor, having been expelled by economic change, now in turn may be usefully brought back into the new system as laborers for hire, happy, in their bitter circumstances, to find work with the new, more efficient breed of improving landlords. It is hard to recapitulate these arguments for progress without falling into some degree of irony. The simple hopefulness of such seventeenth-century improvers as Taylor, Lee, and Moore is for us almost irrecoverable. Yet the more one considers the whole process of agricultural change in England, the more one is driven to see in it an inextricable mixture of curse and blessing. One might wish that events had happened differently, but could one wish them not to have happened at all?

Just as the ideal model of the landowner or master began to change, so the ideal of the worker or servant changed correspondingly. Mobility, which had been judged by most Elizabethan writers to be a serious crime, or at least a social evil, now began under certain circumstances to seem a virtue and even a social good. In a market economy the availability of mobile workers-for-hire is increasingly desirable. Indeed, as we see more clearly by extrapolating into later industrial times, a total market economy works most efficiently (in some respects) if workers and masters alike are more mobile, free of feudal obligations, free of family ties, and ready to move into whatever part of the system most needs their services. These changes in value naturally have an impact – indeed a variety of impacts – on attitudes toward love and family. The connection between cultural and individual change is observable, as we shall see, in Carew's development of a new kind of English love poetry.

Carew's youthful expectations were high. His family on both sides were successful city people who moved among circles at the porous border between trade and gentility. Although his instincts were aristocratic, he could not have been altogether ignorant of city trades and professions. His mother and grandmother both were daughters of Lord Mayors; his father practiced law, proceeded Master in Chancery in 1576, and was among the notorious crowd of successful new men knighted by King James in 1603. Carew's family by blood and marriage also included members of the government and the nobility. But just as he left Oxford for the Middle Temple in 1612, pursuing the usual course of a younger son hoping to rise in the world, his father, Sir Matthew, suffered financial reverses and, as a letter of 1613 reveals, had to turn to his prominent nephew-by-marriage, Sir Dudley Carleton, Ambassador to Venice, for assistance:

My very honorable good Lord,
    There hathe passed many a drearye and sorowfull daye over my head sence my last writeng unto your lordship, many griefes, mich sorrow, and great mishaps ... my self to be cozened and deceaved, of all my land, wheruppon I had levyd my whole estate, and brought my self in debt for it. Where I was in hope to have left my son a thowsand pound land per annum, I am not lyke to leave him anye.[7]

Sir Matthew had two sons whom he hoped to launch in life: the elder to receive his land in accordance with the usual principles of primogeniture, the younger, Thomas the future poet, to be given a good start up the ladder of a professional or public career. But things were not working out as he had hoped. Sir Matthew's financial reverses were compounded by the perverse refusal of either son to cooperate with his plans: "[My] twoe sons, the one roneth up and downe after houndes and hawkes, the other [Thomas] is of the midle temple, where he hath a chamber and studye, but I feare studiethe the lawe very litle, so as I am neither happye in my self nor my children" (p. xviii).

Thomas Carew's case was apparently resolved when Sir Dudley agreed to employ him. Since Carleton held a government post, by taking service with him Carew assumed his first position in the complex of patronage networks, formed by personal relationships and political allegiances, that ascended ultimately to court and throne.[8] As his father's fortunes waned, his own future brightened. He served with Carleton in Venice, Florence, and Turin, and accompanied him to the Netherlands in March 1616. There, shortly after reaching his majority, he slipped. Like Donne, he offended his patron mortally and, through him, the whole system. His sin was to set down in his private writings something severely offensive to Sir Dudley and Lady Carleton.

At first, Carleton kept the matter quiet. He sent Carew back to England under pretext of seeking better service. There Carew courted his cousin Lord Carew, recently of the Privy Council, and the Earl of Arundel, whom he had met in Florence. In September 1616, Carew wrote probably his earliest surviving compositions: three "suitors' letters" to Carleton, to use Frank Whigham's term.[9] Though they seem to have many purposes – reporting on Carew's suits for employment, paying his respects, passing on bits of news and gossip – it is fair to say that all three letters are among the most careful of all his writings and that they are subordinated entirely to a single end: the all-important pursuit of advancement and place in the world to which he belonged by birth. The concluding rhetoric of the first letter, in which he reports his failure to elicit a definite response from Lord Arundel, may best indicate his terrible predicament. Carew does not yet know that Carleton's promised recommendation will never arrive and that he is already irredeemably disgraced in the eyes of past and future patrons, but he clearly suspects that something has gone badly wrong. A single long, graceful, beautifully crafted but increasingly desperate sentence

ends the letter and tails into a complimentary close and
signature:

Your Lordships letters to my Lord of Arrondell, because it was
necessarie for me to wayte uppon my Lord Carew, and could at no
time see him but with the King from whose side he seldome moveth,
I left with Master Havers to be delivered to him, of whome I learned
that he was as yet unfurnished of a Secretarie, wherefore according to
your Lordships instructions my fathers councell and my owne
inclination I will labour my admittance into his service, wherein I
have these hopes, the present vacancie of the place, the reference my
father had to his Grandfather and the knowledge which by your
Lordships meanes he had of me at Florence, wherein if neede be and
if Master Chamberlane shall so thinke good I will engage my Lord
Carew, and whereunto I humbly beseech your Lordship to add your
effectuall recommendation, which I knowe will be of more power then
all my other pretences, which yow will be pleased with your most
convenient speede to afforde me, that I may at his returne hether
(which will be with the Kings some *20* dayes hence) meete him with
your Lordships letters and that I may in case of refusall returne to your
service the sooner, from which I profess (notwithstanding all these
fayre shewes of preferrment) as I did with much unwillingness depart,
so doe I not withowt greate affliction discontinue; my thoughts of their
proper and regular motion not aspiring higher then the orbe of your
Lordships service, this irregular being caused by your self whoe are my
primum mobile, for I ever accounted it honour enough for me to *correre
la fortuna del mio Signore* nor did I ever ayme at … greater happiness
then to be held as I will allways rest / Your Lordships / Most humbly
devoted / to your service / Thomas Carew.   (pages 202–03)

Carew's impending disgrace throws a sharp light on his
words. We notice his awareness of intricate and demanding
family linkages. So many people must be placated. He
approaches Arundel at the behest of his cousin-by-marriage and
his father, invokes a connection between his father and
Arundel's grandfather, thinks of bringing to bear (if prudent
advice permits) the influence of his other noble cousin. In
another letter to Carleton he writes that, while waiting for the
promised recommendation, he has "had leysure to see my sister
Grandmother and other my frends in Kent, whoe remember
their most affectionate services to your Lordship and my Lady"
(p. 206). But all depends on the arrival of Sir Dudley's letter;

without it (for it is as much a release as a recommendation) he cannot shift allegiance from one member of his extended family circle to another. True, he bravely asserts that he acts at "my owne inclination." We may doubt this assertion, however, by the evidence of the letter itself – except insofar as any loyal servant must conform his will to his master's, as closely as a devout man conforms his will to God's. Carew's language increasingly approaches religious fervor as he professes a chivalric desire faithfully to reattach himself to his former master and to follow him into any danger, attributing to Sir Dudley the Godlike power of a *primum mobile*.

Such was the pitch to which Carew rose; but he failed. Called to a meeting with his father and confronted with his offense, he stubbornly refused to apologize in acceptable form. As a result he was cut off permanently from his own extended family. Lady Carleton was Sir Matthew's niece by blood. The connection that got Carew his position now worsened his guilt. Sir Matthew died two years later, at the age of eighty-five, still grumbling of ungrateful sons; Dame Alice, the poet's mother, lived two more decades yet omitted all mention of the prodigal from her will. He was by then a worldly but still not a filial success. The evidence suggests a complete and lasting break between Carew and his family. The immediate result of his slip was to drop him clear out of the patronage network.

Although the patronage system in England in the Renaissance and seventeenth century was not, strictly speaking, feudal, it preserved many of the essential features of feudalism, including loyalty and service to a person rather than a governmental office or business corporation. The system also mixed concerns that would later be perceived as theoretically separate: government service and private employment, public work and family obligation. In most patronage relationships family connections and alliances played a central role. A man who betrayed or repudiated such natural obligations might widely lose his reputation for employability. So, after his disastrous slip with Carleton, and especially after his refusal to seek a reconciliation in due form, Carew was in effect a man without a family, without reasonable hopes for employment, and, therefore, without good prospects for a life suitable to a man of his birth and upbringing.

His disgrace proved critical to his career and poetry. As Kenneth Burke often observed, writers are affected by their cultures, times, historical situations, family and individual circumstances, in ways both social and psychological. A particular poet shares characteristics with his contemporaries but possesses, or is possessed by, others peculiar to himself. Carew's development of a radically new kind of love poetry in England – libertine, anti-authoritarian, almost wholly disconnected from the Petrarchan traditions that even Donne felt obliged to parody and dispute – was closely related to the crisis of his career and the psychosocial forces it unleashed.

Of course, Carew later became a successful courtier, able to look down from a secure position at still struggling young friends like Suckling. He rose by assuming an attitude and a style of living diametrically opposed to what his family intended for him. Preferment in the service of Carleton or Arundel represented filial obedience and dutiful use of the kinship network. His refusal to apologize severed those connections. It is risky to psychologize on slight evidence; still it seems the break in Carew's career represents a typically youthful revolt against father, family, and social system, all combining to represent authority to him.

This scenario of mutually destructive intergenerational warfare, familiar alike in Freud, history, and our experience, might have ended the story had it not been for later public events. In 1625 James's court gave way to Charles's. There was a distinct change in tone and a repudiation of former styles and values. Whether the new court was better or worse than the old is arguable. At any rate, it thought itself different and offered opportunities for a fresh start. In 1630, against strong competition, Carew was named Gentleman of the Privy Chamber Extraordinary and Sewer in Ordinary to the King. He obtained these posts and the honor and security they represented by finding his own patrons, unconnected with his family: chiefly Kit Villiers, younger brother of the Duke of Buckingham, who represented *par excellence* not the use but the abuse of favor.

Arundel, whose favor his family had urged him to court, was a bitter opponent of Buckingham's, so Carew's transfer of allegiance could hardly have mended his bad relations with his natural friends.[10] Christopher Villiers, Carew's new patron, got as far as he did, despite his frequent drunkenness and other scandalous behavior, only because his brother was the most successful *parvenu* in all of British history since Piers Gaveston offended the nobility of an earlier age. Carew wrote several poems for this patron and his family and further helped Villiers, who had small wit or polish, to court and win a rich wife. From a position in the patronage network that was filial and duteous, Carew moved to a position of mutual advantage, as, in effect, a hired employee of the brother of the King's favorite.

This transformation in Carew's stance toward the world, resulting in his invention of a new manner in poetry, went through three observable stages. First he rebelled utterly against his family and against any hope of regaining family patronage. His father, in a series of letters to Carleton intended to repair the breach, but which must only have made matters worse, vividly describes the nadir of Carew's career. Thomas, he writes, "haveng geven over al studye here eyther of lawe or other lerning, vagrantlye and debauchedlye takethe no maner of good but al lewde courses, with the which he will weary me and al his other frendes, and run hym self into utter ruyn." He further reports that his son "lieth here syck with me of a new disease" (p. xxvii), which, Rhodes Dunlap and others speculate, was that syphilis about which Carew's friend Suckling was to jest so indelicately in his poem "Upon T. C. having the P." Then Carew evidently pulled himself together sufficiently to accompany Sir Edward Herbert to France, an arrangement that may be interpreted either as a temporary exile or as a somewhat tentative step toward rehabilitation.[11] That rehabilitation could not have proceeded smoothly, however, for Carew's next certainly documented action in pursuit of his career was to turn to his family's political enemies for advancement.

Carew may have had other help. Rhodes Dunlap recounts the scandalous tale about Henrietta Maria: "Thomas Carew, Gentleman of the Privy Chamber, going to light King Charles

into her chamber, saw Jermyn Lord St. Albans with his arm
round her neck; – he stumbled and put out the light; – Jermyn
escaped; Carew never told the King, and the King never knew
it. The Queen heaped favours on Carew" (p. xxxv). The tale,
as Dunlap notes, may be apocryphal, for it seems almost too
good to be true; yet at least it tells us the kind of image a
contemporary attached to Carew. He arrived by using his wits
and his new friends, not his family connections. He learned that
insolence, rebellion, and libertine behavior, gracefully indulged,
might be not impediments but actual helps to advancement and
honor.

Carew's central image for the ideal courtly stance, in his
poem comforting Kit Villiers' widow on the death of her
husband, is not a Jonsonian circle with a firmly fixed center, as
we might expect of a Son of Ben, or of a loyal, steadfast courtier
of the old Sidneian school, but an eddy dancing in a stream:

> He chose not in the active streame to swim,
> Nor hunted Honour; which, yet hunted him.
> But like a quiet Eddie, that hath found
> Some hollow creeke, there turnes his waters round,
> And in continuall circles, dances free
> From the impetuous Torrent; so did hee
> Give others leave to turne the wheele of State,
> (*Whose restlesse motion spins the subjects fate*)
> Whilst he retir'd from the tumultuous noyse
> Of Court, and suitors presse; apart, enjoyes
> Freedome, and mirth, himselfe, his time, and friends,
> And with sweet rellish tastes each houre he spends.
>   ("To the Countesse of *Anglesie*," lines 57–68)

As Michael Parker notes, an eddy "moves contrary to the
direction of the tide or current." To model one's life on such a
motion "demands an unceasing awareness and an 'active
grace.'"[12] These are qualities suggestive of Carew, not Villiers.
To be an eddy is to give oneself to the stream and take one's
energy from it yet at the same time to move, covertly, to a
counter impulse. In this apparent surrender to the social
current, a skillful courtier gains "freedome," and, with that
freedom or space for independent movement, he enjoys

"mirth," "time," "friends," and (above all) "himselfe." We see in this image a triumph of courtly flexibility, not of noble faithfulness to an ideal. Its implications extend far beyond courtly behavior, to the general society: for it is an early adumbration of the growth of modern individual subjectivity, of the impulse to establish an identity within, yet independent of, the social matrix.

No doubt Carew felt real gratitude to the man who restored his career: "But all his actions had the noble end / T'advance desert, or grace some worthy friend" (lines 55–56). Still, in describing such a "new-model courtier," to borrow Parker's apt phrase (p. 102), Carew bases his ideal principally on his own experience and not on that of his unfortunate friend. The eddy is his own solution to the social and family impasse in which he had earlier been caught. He projects his ideal courtly stance onto the figure of his dead benefactor, who was notorious for his lack of courtly finesse and outward delicacy and who – when he suffered disgrace and banishment for having, like Carew, offended his patron – never recovered.

In another poem, "To my Mistris sitting by a Rivers side. AN EDDY," Carew employs the same basic image as a persuasion to his mistress to leave the main current of the stream, which again represents tradition and society, and – more specifically – conventional attitudes toward love:

> Marke how yond Eddy steales away,
> From the rude streame into the Bay,
> There lockt up safe, she doth divorce
> Her waters from the chanels course,
> And scorns the Torrent, that did bring
> Her headlong from her native spring.
> Now doth she with her new love play,
> Whilst he runs murmuring away.   (lines 1–8)

The mainstream will run on to lose its identity in the ocean, but the eddy, by detaching itself, will preserve itself:

> Let him to the wide Ocean hast,
> There lose his colour, name, and tast;
> Thou shalt save all, and safe from him,
> Within these arms for ever swim.   (lines 23–26)

Carew's image recalls the conventional usage, in which life is a river and life's ultimate goal – eternity – the sea. Part of this conventional meaning of the sea, however, is excluded. It represents dissolution only, unaccompanied by transformation into a higher state of existence. Like Donne, Carew draws back from Christian eternity and substitutes a precarious clinging to life and love. But his image, an eddy rather than Donne's little world, though (Donnelike) he pretends that it offers them entire and eternal safety from death or change, confesses much more candidly by its very nature its inherent lack of stability.

For a man of Carew's time, personal identity was largely a product of social position, and personal psychology closely depended on one's place in the patronage network and experience in getting there. So a convergence of psychological and cultural forces importantly affected his life and poetry. We see just such a convergence in the image of the eddy, which reveals, to a postmodern reader, how the independent subject may grow, or seem to grow, out of the social self. In different, less forgiving historical circumstances, Ralegh and Sidney learned the politics of desire for an unobtainable object, desire that was an inextricable mixture of frustrated religious, political, and amatory ambitions.[13] The political experience of these earlier courtier-poets reverberated with and reinforced a Petrarchan stance in their love poetry. Carew's psychosocial circumstances, to the contrary, taught him a politics and an amatory strategy based on cynicism, libertinism, and scorn for authority. The stream of authority and society, he evidently recognized, was too pervasive to escape, too strong to be wholly resisted, but consummate courtly abilities could enable a skillful practitioner to dance in it and thus to achieve a precarious but real degree of personal freedom and pleasure.

The result is a new kind of English love poetry. In "To A. L. Perswasions to love," the lover represents a new-model amatory servant, ready to abandon his mistress for another who will reward him better. If she plays hard to get, he warns her, she will only defeat herself:

> And what will then become of all
> Those, whom now you servants call?
> Like swallowes when your summers done,
> They'le flye and seeke some warmer Sun.   (lines 45–48)

The right sort of patron, he learned from painful experience, needs supportive clients just as clients need a generous patron. So, he tells A. L., choose a suitor who will be useful and reward him appropriately:

> Then wisely chuse one to your friend,
> Whose love may, when your beauties end,
> Remaine still firme: be provident
> And thinke before the summers spent
> Of following winter; like the Ant
> In plenty hoord for time of scant.
> Cull out amongst the multitude
> Of lovers, that seeke to intrude
> Into your favour, one that may
> Love for an age, not for a day;
> One that will quench your youthfull fires,
> And feed in age your hot desires.   (lines 49–60)

Thus Carew implicitly presents himself as a client who can help his patroness to what she wants, giving a new twist to the age-old *carpe-diem* theme on which he bases the poem. He also offers a cynically pragmatic version of the perennial desire for eternal love, which here becomes sexual gratification drawn out by mutual convenience into old age. Seize the day – and prolong it.

"Ingratefull beauty threatned" takes Carew's new-found knowledge that the patronage relationship cuts both ways and creates a triple equivalence between the poet and his subject, the lover and his mistress, the client and his patron:

> Know *Celia*, (since thou art so proud,)
>   'Twas I that gave thee thy renowne...
> That killing power is none of thine,
>   I gave it to thy voyce, and eyes:
> Thy sweets, thy graces, all are mine;
>   Thou art my starre, shin'st in my skies;
> Then dart not from thy borrowed sphere
> Lightning on him, that fixt thee there.

> Tempt me with such affrights no more,
>   Lest what I made, I uncreate.   (lines 1–2, 7–14)

He has "made" her as he made Villiers. If ill treated he will simply go elsewhere and make someone else, letting her sink back into nonentity. As becomes more evident in a context of social mobility and clientage for hire, no mistress has "killing power" over a lover prepared to leave her service if provoked.

Carew's behavior as client and lover almost certainly was influenced not only by the difficult particulars of his family circumstances and the better fortune of changing court fashions and personalities, but also by the more general rise at midcentury of a market economy. Everywhere feudal service was giving way to labor for hire, a fundamental change that was beginning to produce an increasingly mobile society more responsive to individual financial reward, or wages, than to extended-family loyalty. A similar mobility is found in Carew's "Good counsell to a young Maid":

> When you the Sun-burnt Pilgrim see
>   Fainting with thirst, hast to the springs,
> Marke how at first with bended knee
>   He courts the crystall Nimphe, and flings
>   His body to the earth, where He
> Prostrate adores the flowing Deitie.
>   But when his sweaty face is drencht
>   In her coole waves, when from her sweet
> Bosome, his burning thirst is quencht;
>   Then marke how with disdainfull feet
>   He kicks her banks, and from the place
> That thus refresht him, moves with sullen pace.
>
> (lines 1–12)

"So," he continues, "shalt thou be despis'd, faire Maid, / When by the sated lover tasted" (lines 13–14). The politics of desire and ambition in a situation of too much stasis, characteristic of both love and politics in an earlier age, give way to a politics of satiation and disillusionment in a situation of too much change.

Even rejection by the mistress takes a new direction (though with some precedent in Wyatt and the French). In "A

deposition from Love," Carew tells us that he "was foretold"
(presumably by Petrarchan authorities) and long believed that
all the "plagues" of love are at its entrance. If only the lover can
win his mistress, his troubles are over. Experience teaches
otherwise. Although he has managed to "enter, and enjoy, /
What happy lovers prove," to "kisse, and sport, and toy, / And
tast those sweets of love" (lines 11–14), these pleasures only
increase his unhappiness later when his mistress abandons him.
They are the beginning, not the end, of sorrow and loss. The
Petrarchan lover, Carew concludes, loses what was never his,

> But he that is cast downe
> From enjoy'd beautie, feeles a woe,
> Onely deposed Kings can know.   (lines 28–30)

Thus opportunism cuts two ways and undermines the very basis
of the political and amatory orders. If clients are now
empowered to seek out new patrons with impunity, and lovers
new mistresses – or (ominously) even subjects new kings – then
all victors in the game of preferment risk being dropped if a
better client or an apter lover appears on the scene.

As the psychologies of amorous and political disenchantment
converge, constancy of service becomes less a reliable ideal than
a rhetorical weapon, to be wielded and dropped at will. "*True
love can never change his seat,*" Carew urges, in "Song. Eternitie of
love protested," but his other poems belie that ideal. The
chivalric vow he once addressed to Sir Dudley, "to *correre la
fortuna del mio Signore,*" is now recognized for what it always was:
a polite foreign anachronism. In "Boldnesse in love," Carew
again applies his new experience, hard-learned in the wars of
patronage, to love:

> Marke how the bashfull morne, in vaine
> Courts the amorous Marigold,
> With sighing blasts, and weeping raine;
> Yet she refuses to unfold.
> But when the Planet of the day,
> Approacheth with his powerfull ray,
> Then she spreads, then she receives
> His warmer beames into her virgin leaves.   (lines 1–8)

Petrarchan sighs and tears, begging and dutiful subservience, only fail. To succeed, the suitor must drop old pieties, boldly lie, and seek his own advantage. As the title even of the apparently old-fashioned poem "Song. Eternitie of love protested" suggests, the Petrarchan ideal of unconditionally faithful love, like the feudal ideal of loyalty until death, becomes more a protestation or a piece of rhetoric than something put into practice once the mistress is persuaded. Eternity is no more than a word the successful lover speaks, not a commitment to be put into practice. If service to one mistress yields insufficient payment, then it is time to seek out another, like a worker exchanging a too-stingy employer for one who gives better wages.

Of course there is more to Carew's love poetry than mere opportunism. Since I have focused on the crisis of his early career, which forced him into an alternative route to prosperity and a reinvention of himself, I have focused on the related employment in his poetry of libertinism, pragmatism, and self-interest in the pursuit of love. Sometimes love has for Carew a more positive side. Along with the general stripping away of dead Petrarchan conventions, which no longer suit the new age and his new experience in courting patrons, come the blessings of less of that crawling or enforced subservience that results when love, patronage, and family go wrong, of greater mutuality and equality between lovers, of more recognition that love is a two-way transaction.

But the benefits of mutuality are arrived at by a route that is painful and disillusioning, dependent more on bringing the other person down in estimation than on raising oneself. Patron and client, mistress and lover, employer and employee, are valued for their usefulness, for what they can do, rather than for their intrinsic merit and honor, for what they are. Perhaps these glum results follow naturally from Carew's having begun the revision of his career by anticipating that root modernist practice, in some ways encouraged by the new economics, of repudiating tradition and "killing the father." Still, in "To A. L.," cynical though Carew's address is, we find a connection between his new-found irreverence and the possibility of mutuality and equality in love:[14]

> Did the thing for which I sue
> Onely concerne my selfe not you,
> Were men so fram'd as they alone
> Reap'd all the pleasure, women none,
> Then had you reason to be scant;
> But 'twere a madnesse not to grant
> That which affords (if you consent)
> To you the giver, more content
> Then me the beggar; Oh then bee
> Kinde to your selfe if not to mee.   (lines 17–26)

Again Carew's redefinition of love and patronage relates to economic change. Love is reduced to a "thing," to sexual "pleasure," which in turn is a commodity to be reaped, given, or begged. This achievement of mutual benefit through the pursuit of mutual selfishness reminds us of the familiar paradox of the profit motive in the early modern political economy, which, though not yet fully worked out, was already implicit in the changing agricultural marketplace that Carew's reaping metaphor calls to our attention.[15] Self-interest and individualism, like enclosure and labor for hire, are just beginning to be seen in progressive circles not as violations of the general welfare but as efficient ways of increasing the total stock to the ultimate good of all. For Carew, the new ethic is as applicable to love as, for Plattes, it is to agriculture.

The question remains: Where might Carew have learned these ideas? His experience pointed him toward such a solution, but, as we have suggested, that was not enough for an earlier generation of equally ingenious young men whose advancement was also blocked. Change of allegiance was not unknown to feudal times or to the English patronage system, but it was not admired as a practice. Similarly, the idea that women have sexual desires equal to or greater than men's was not new, but traditionally it had been viewed as a threat even more dangerous than male lust, not as an advantage to be bargained with. It was the new agricultural economics that first made such apparently self-serving notions respectable.

The Famous Kingdome of Macaria, which represented the earliest and by no means the most explicit argument for a new morality based on new economic circumstances, was not published until 1641, while Carew's love lyrics belong to the late 1620s and 1630s. Nor is it likely that Carew would have been an avid reader of such tracts had they been available to him. The new ideas that they popularized were arising among such innovators as belonged to the Hartlib circle – mostly men who would take the Parliamentary side in the Civil War – whereas, had Carew lived into the next decade, it is virtually certain that he would have remained a Royalist. The answer, I think, is that such ideas are "in the air" before they see print, and that they are available to anyone with eyes to see and ears to hear, regardless of his basic ideological persuasion. A true poet is usually a person who is alive to such ideas, whether he likes them or not. By no means do we get the impression from Carew's poems that he was literally an "improver." Rather, he took more immediately and perhaps somewhat ironically to the notion of mutual benefit through self-service, which represented the practical rather than the idealistic component of the typical improvers' argument – the hook they used to appeal to people's self-interest, not the visionary end toward which they directed the imagination of true believers.

Nevertheless, as early as 1633, in "An Elegie upon the death of the Deane of Pauls, Dr. John Donne," we find Carew employing agricultural practice as a metaphor for poetic innovation:

> The Muses garden with Pedantique weedes
> O'rspred, was purg'd by thee; the lazie seeds
> Of servile imitation throwne away;
> And fresh invention planted ...   (lines 25–28)

His subject is poetry, not love or politics, yet his admiration for "fresh invention" and his dismissal of "servile imitation" clearly suggest that he was ready to associate rural labor with the ideal of change as improvement. "Invention," which as a technical term had long meant selection of an image or a trope from one of the standard rhetorical places (and which we might rather call the "discovery" or "deployment" of something already existent), may here be seen just in the process of assuming its Romantic and modern sense of creating something wholly new.

In a second passage of the elegy on Donne, Carew continues the metaphor:

> As in time
> They had the start, so did they cull the prime
> Buds of invention many a hundred yeare,
> And left the rifled fields, besides the feare
> To touch their Harvest, yet from those bare lands
> Of what is purely thine, thy only hands
> (And that thy smallest worke) have gleaned more
> Then all those times, and tongues could reape before.
>
> (lines 53–60)

Gleaning is not notably an activity associated with the new agriculture. It more immediately calls to mind the timeless shifts that impoverished marginal workers are forced to practice in order to survive. Yet, by going beyond ordinary reaping to harvesting from "bare lands" more crops than earlier owners could bring home from traditional, well-guarded fields (even though he refers to reaped fields rather than barren commons), Carew's imagery once more suggests that he had caught hold of some of the essential aspects of the improving vision.

It is, I think, also significant that, for the central theme of *Coelum Brittanicum* (1634), his most fervent praise of the splendors and sexual virtues of the Caroline court, Carew drew on Bruno's *Lo Spaccio della Bestia Trionfante* (1584), one of the originary texts for the whole movement toward scientific, economic, and cultural reform in the seventeenth century. Momus's remark concerning the replacement in Carew's masque of all the old gods and values by new ones – "hence springs all this inno-vation" (p. 159), he says – is peculiarly apt, since the fictive transformation in which Charles and Henrietta Maria took such great satisfaction is, in fact, an adaption of Bruno's notably progressive and scientific vision. Thus Carew appropriates the energies of economic and political reform for other purposes, but his gesture of adaption and containment may be seen in retrospect as more than a little ironic.

Further evidence that an unsympathetic Royalist could pick up and incorporate into his love poetry the latest happenings in agricultural progress may be found in a poem by Richard Lovelace, written at some time before its publication in *Lucasta* (1649), and therefore before any of the tracts defending enclosure except Plattes's *Macaria* had appeared. "Elinda's Glove" is, in effect, a translation of the old courtly love relationship between haughty mistress and abject servant into a new language reflecting the new economic practices, like old wine decanted into a new bottle.

> I.
> Thou snowy Farme with thy five Tenements!
>   Tell thy white Mistris here was one
>   That call'd to pay his dayly Rents;
> But she a gathering Flowr's and Hearts is gone,
> And thou left voyd to rude Possession.
>
> II.
> But Grieve not pretty *Ermin* Cabinet,
>   Thy Alablaster Lady will come home;
>   If not, what Tenant can there fit
> The slender turnings of thy narrow Roome,
> But must ejected be by his owne dombe?
>
> III.
> Then Give me leave to leave my Rent with thee;
>   Five kisses, one unto a place:
>   For though the *Lute's* too high for me;
> Yet Servants knowing Minikin nor Base,
> Are still allow'd to fiddle with the Case.

As I have noted in speaking about this poem in *The Georgic Revolution*, it is filled with images of horror based on Royalist experience of land expropriation and expulsion in the 1640s.[16] But it may also be observed that it has the same relation to the new economy as courtly love poems had to the old. It sees an inexorable social or economic reality against which the lover struggles in vain, in this instance not against the prototypical disdain of a proud feudal superior but the heartless cruelty of a greedy new-style landlord.

The lover, who comes not to pay his compliments, but his rents, finds a glove that emblematizes the economic relations between a landlord and his tenant farmers in their undersized cottages, who will be roughly expelled if they cannot produce. There is even a danger that the absent owner might be displaced by an interloper: by a new owner or by the potentially insubordinate lover himself. Only the smallness of her glove prevents such "rude Possession." About this poem the same thing may be said that was said earlier about courtly love poems. The lover need not like the system to feel himself caught in it, and to feel obliged to deal with the difficulties of his personal situation within the constraints his culture imposes on him. That Lovelace's tone is light and graceful by no means effaces these darker implications.

It is not always the case that a courtly lover simply elevates his mistress onto a "pedestal," as the saying goes.[17] Such elevations often rather imply a polite form of protest, a venting of uncomfortable feelings of humiliation or chagrin, aptly expressed in the familiar feudal conventions. Lovelace, in the absence of a mistress who has gone off "gathering Flowr's and Hearts," finds the abuses of heartless landlords apter and more powerful than the abuses of feudal masters to express his feelings and situation. There is more than a suggestion of sexual jealousy in the middle stanza, as the lover entertains the thought that his mistress may, after all, not return home from her expedition, as indicated by his nervously insouciant little phrase, "If not." As the imagery implies, a rival lover may be expected to suffer the same fate as he has: ejection by the glove's owner as well as by the glove. Her delicacy and her alabaster beauty serve to expel any rough, would-be intruder who has sought to possess her. But it is small comfort to the resentful lover that his mistress may be out gathering and ejecting new victims. In the meantime, he enjoys what little pleasure a sulky servant can, by taking the opportunity at least to "fiddle with the Case."

As with Lovelace, so with Carew: however aristocratic the poet, however impenetrable his air of careless *sprezzatura* or defensive irony, he must, if he is a poet of any ability, still deal with the world as he finds it. For Carew, situated as he was at court, the best image is his own. He is like an eddy, dancing in the stream of society, skillfully making for himself a fragile refuge while the main current runs to the sea. But he draws also on the energies of another stream, a growing one, already well on its way toward replacing the current in which he chooses to remain. This precarious and perpetual balancing act between a dying culture and a rising one allows him the satisfactions of a difficult task well done and a pleasurable degree of freedom.

Libertinism or free love is analogous to the free market just as the extended family is analogous to feudal politics. Indeed, they are more than analogous. Politics and family in a feudal or an early Renaissance patronage system are inextricably interdependent. A man without family – by marriage or by formal or informal adoption if not by blood – cannot expect to gain patronage. As family feelings, obligations, and loyalties shape the political network, that network in turn shapes courtship, marriage, and family. But in a free-market economy (and, even more, in the industrialized society that results) extended family ties become impediments rather than helps to the smooth working of the system and to individual success. Mobility and utility rather than stability and loyalty, mutual advantage rather than mutual giving, become the prime virtues. Impartial trade replaces the intense give-and-take of familial relationships. People move where they are most needed and where they can find most advantage, in a constantly shifting social system that encourages no more than temporary allegiances between masters and servants, patrons and clients, mistresses and lovers. At the same time lover and mistress, or, as we would now call them, lover and lover, meet on terms of greater equality, in a general breakdown both of patriarchal social authority and the now waning courtly authority of the etherialized lady-mistress. Equality is gained, permanence lost. These are, of course, only tendencies, which, several hundred years later, are still spasmodically working themselves out.

CHAPTER 7

John Milton: *"Because wee freely love"*

Throughout much of the modern period, from the late nineteenth century until past the middle of the twentieth century, Milton suffered a series of attacks from famous critics and was generally out of favor. The story is familiar.[1] Yet, even though we may have grown tired of hearing it, it still has a lesson to teach us. Although the attack was on multiple grounds, both substantive and stylistic, one may conclude that religion and politics had much to do with stimulating it. When Sir Walter Raleigh proclaimed that *Paradise Lost* was a monument to dead ideas, he meant that there could be no serious place for Christianity in the modern world. When Ezra Pound assailed Milton mainly on stylistic grounds, he revealed similar motives at the point where he excoriated him for "his asinine bigotry, his beastly hebraism." Milton was not a Jew, but for many critics, of whom Pound was only among the frankest, his particular brand of Christianity was imbued with a disturbing zeal, which they associated with Matthew Arnold's category of "Hebraism," and which they found less attractive than Arnold's more rational and balanced category of "Hellenism."[2]

T. S. Eliot had very complicated reasons for attacking Milton, among them a desire to clear the ground for a new kind of modern poetry, but surely another important reason was his lack of sympathy for Milton's particular brand of revolutionary politics and enthusiastically non-conformist religion. These characteristics were, in part, what made the fiercely religious Dante, but not Milton, acceptable to Eliot as a true "classic." (I am inclined to concur, too, with those who find Eliot's second essay on Milton not much of a retraction.) In the same way, one may make a case that although F. R. Leavis attacked Milton chiefly on grounds of style, Milton's particular brand of morality was also incompatible with what Leavis thought to be moral – and Leavis's version of political morality was an important determinant in all of his influential decisions about which works should remain in the "great tradition" and the "line of wit" and which should be ousted. Similarly, although A. J. A. Waldock attacked Milton for incompetence in his handling of narrative, it turns out that this incompetence results from Milton's having in the first place foolishly chosen a biblical myth, which was bound to fail as the groundwork for an epic. And the anti-Christian bias of William Empson was so forthright as almost to neutralize itself: "I think the traditional God of Christianity very wicked, and have done since I was at school, where nearly all my little playmates thought the same."[3]

Even among the writings of some of Milton's foremost defenders, one finds evidence of a strong distaste for Milton's "bigotry," as the plain-speaking if bigoted Pound termed it. Tillyard, who is generally sympathetic to Milton's Protestant and democratic tendencies, nonetheless expresses the feelings of many fellow critics when he admits there has "always been a vein of ferocity in Milton." In most of Milton's poetry, Tillyard argues, this ferocity is mitigated by his better qualities, but it shows, to the embarrassing full, in the "ironical gloating" and "tedious butcheries" that typify *Samson Agonistes*.[4]

As we know, Leavis announced to the world in 1933 that Milton had been dislodged from his preeminent position "with remarkably little fuss."[5] As we also know, that "dislodgment" did not stick. Indeed, in one of time's curious reversals, some of the very qualities that made Milton such an object of suspicion among the Modernists eventually endeared him to some of the Postmodernists. Milton's first defenders against the concerted Modernist attack were relative moderates, exemplified by C. S. Lewis and Douglas Bush, not to mention Northrop Frye and Christopher Ricks.[6] But more recently Milton has been admired as a violent revolutionary, as a philosopher of contradictions, and as a purveyor of demolitions – in short, as a kind of political Samson. Marvell's initial suspicions, that in *Paradise Lost* Milton might intend a work of destruction, have been proclaimed correct after all. As Marvell tells us, he feared that the bold, blind poet

> would ruine (for I saw him strong)
> The sacred Truths to Fable and old Song,
> (So *Sampson* groap'd the Temples Posts in spight)
> The World o'rewhelming to revenge his Sight.[7]

What Marvell once feared, however, is now frequently welcomed. For some time Milton has been seen as much more congenial to modern times than Donne, who seemed so "modern" just a generation ago.[8] Milton is now acclaimed as the great forerunner of our times, as a destroyer of custom and tradition, as a revolutionary who would willingly pull down the whole of society out of fervor to replace it with something better.[9] His violence is sometimes still deprecated – yet at the same time admired, as a source of poetic energies and a necessary, if brutal, stage in the evolution of humanity.

One cannot write usefully about Milton and love without first reconsidering his work in the light of all those many charges of bigotry and violence that were raised against him by earlier generations of critics, or without also reconsidering it in the light of the (sometimes ambivalent) praise more recently accorded him for his masterful exposition of revolutionary political, cultural, and religious violence. Is love compatible with hate? Is Milton's ever truly a poetry of love? In contemporary eyes, religious love – or zeal – is likely at first glance to seem either anachronistic or dangerous. It may seem dangerous, in particular, if it is "fundamentalist" (a liberal code-word for any religion that threatens to overleap its bounds and tell *you and me* what we would rather not hear). Deeply influenced by western democratic liberalism and by post-Romantic individualism, we are especially suspicious of religious conformity. We value our freedom, and we suspect that religious conformity may somehow encroach on it. But we may be less aware of certain other dangers, which are sometimes to be found in religion that does *not* conform. These are dangers especially relevant to Milton.

In *Paradise Lost*, Raphael restates an ancient formula when he describes the religious love of the angels:

> freely we serve,
> Because wee freely love, as in our will
> To love or not; in this we stand or fall.   (5.538–40)[10]

This view of love as free service, which is recapitulated in the familiar collect of the Book of Common Prayer, in the assertion that the service of God is "perfect freedom," goes back at least to St. Augustine's formulation in the *Enchiridion*: "For only he is free in service who gladly does the will of his Lord."[11] In the old Christian view, absolute freedom is impossible to a contingent being. In the modern, pragmatic view, it might also seem impossible, since the demands of each free individual compete against those of every other free individual, as well as against those of the family and the public interest. In Milton, however, the balance of freedom and service, which he sees as underlying the love of God, is unconstrained by the normative influence of Church or community, or by more than a notional solidarity with others.

For this reason, a good place to begin analyzing divine love in Milton is with his handling of the biblical marriage trope, which we also found useful earlier in helping us to understand the human flavor and the particular qualities of the loves that Donne, Herbert, and Crashaw felt toward their God. These were the loves that reflected their ultimate allegiances and that reordered their priorities, both public and private. Religious love – or its replacement by some other kind of paramount love, from the altruistically political to the selfishly material – is fundamental. Tell me what you love above all other things, and I will tell you what you are.

Donne and Herbert, like others belonging to the Anglican confession, accepted the biblical image of the Church as the Bride of Christ. Although both might sometimes wonder where that true Bride could be found, amid the corruptions of the world and the violent disputes of Christian Churches and sectaries, neither doubted that such a true Church existed, in spite of all her superficial divisions and blemishes. With Milton it was quite another matter. Most of his voluminous writings about the Church are concerned with matters of church governance, as suggested by the title of his early tract, *The Reason of Church-Government* (1642). In practice Milton viewed the institutional Church as having been, throughout most of its history, a sink of wicked superstition and an impediment to the enlightenment of individual souls by God's spirit of truth and prophecy. From about 1638 onward, in his eyes the Anglican Church was no better than the Roman Catholic Church – only more "privy" in its depredations. His is the extreme version of the view of history first adumbrated by Wyclif, who identified the Church of his day with Antichrist and called for its destruction in order to recover the holiness of a long-lost primitive Church. Martin Luther gave Wyclif's view irresistible new energy and set it loose to sweep through the western world and through the thinking of all who lived under the Christian dispensation.[12] The Church of a thousand years was the Whore of Babylon. The true Church had not been seen among men since the days of Christ and the Apostles.

Ordinary Anglicans of Milton's day generally concurred with the opinion that the Roman Catholic Church was the Bride, not of Christ, but of Antichrist. But only the extreme sectarian reformers, of whom (in this regard) Milton was one, took this opinion to its logical conclusions. We see in Donne's "Show me deare Christ" and in Herbert's "The Church Militant" some of the possible damage such an opinion could do to the institutional Church, Anglican as well as Roman Catholic. Donne's sonnet leaves the reader very unclear whether the Church of England escapes the general censure. Herbert's long poem about his well-beloved Church, although it begins by declaring her, in her early days, the Bride of Christ, ends notoriously with the speculation – which many American Puritans and later revolutionaries took up and popularized as prophetic – that Christ's true spiritual Bride was about to abandon wicked England and its corrupt institutional Church. England, Herbert mourns, brims with "malice, and prodigious lusts, / Impudent sinning, witchcrafts, and distrusts." True religion – and therefore the true Church – stands poised, ready to

"flee" England for "the *American* strand" (line 236–48). Yet, in
the ways Donne and Herbert went about their lives as
clergymen in the Church of England and continued ordinarily
to speak lovingly about their Church, they (and their fellow
Anglicans generally) ignored the full consequences of such
thoughts. Not Milton.

For a man as interested as Milton was in the Church, in
personal religion, and in marriage, he invokes the biblical
marriage trope surprisingly seldom, and even less often with
approval. In *Colasterion* (1645), the last of his divorce tracts, he
confronts his "nameless" opponent's argument for the permanence of marriage, based on Ephesians 5:29: "*If the husband
ought to love his Wife, as Christ his Church, then ought shee not to bee put
away for contrariety of minde.*[13] Responding to this argument,
Milton does not attempt to separate the case of human marriage
and divorce from its ideal exemplar, the divine marriage of
Christ and his Church, as he might easily have done. Rather he
follows the logic of his radical views on the imperfect nature of
the Church:

This similitude turnes against him. For if the husband must bee as
Christ to the Wife, then must the wife bee as the Church to her
husband. If ther bee a perpetual contrariety of minde in the Church
toward Christ, Christ himselfe threat'ns to divorce such a Spouse, and
hath often don it. If they urge, this was no true Church, I urge again,
that was no true Wife.   (2:732)

Donne preached that God uses the word "divorce" only twice
in the Bible, and does so only in order to repudiate it. He begins
with a rhetorical question, to which he leaves no doubt whatever
that the answer is negative: "And would GOD pretend to send
thee a *gracious messadge*, and send thee a *Divorce*?"[14] For Donne
and for traditional Christians up to his time, to be once married
to God is to be married forever. On the model of Israel in the
Old Testament, Donne and his fellow Anglicans argue, the
external Church can fall away from her husband and sin with
strangers, but she always remains God's spouse, and as such He
will always gladly receive her back again. This marriage may be
blemished or deeply troubled on its human side, but God will

never end it.[15] In Christ's words: "thou art Peter, and upon this rock I will build my church; and the gates of hell shall not prevail against it" (Matthew 16:18). Milton's Christ, however, stands ready to divorce his Church if she proves an improper helpmeet. Indeed, as Milton proclaims with obvious relish, he "hath often don it."

Milton expresses a similar view of the divine marriage in *The Judgement of Martin Bucer* (1644). He argues that a husband is the "head and preserver not only of his wife, but also of his children and family, as Christ is of his Church." Therefore, if a man's wife becomes "tainted with ignominy," he should divorce her for the sake of the children for whom he is also responsible (2:467). Although Milton does not explicitly say so, the logic of his unusual comparison is that Christ, too, should divorce his Church, if she offends against the good of her children – that is, against individual Christians. Thus if Christ's role as Head comes into conflict with his role as Husband, the first role always takes precedence.

Not for nothing had Tyndale preferred to translate the Greek New Testament word *ekklesia*, transliterated in the Latin Vulgate as "ecclesia," into English as "congregation" or "assembly" rather than "Church" – just as Luther translated it into German as *Gemeinde* rather than *Kirche*.[16] In later English Bibles, such as the Geneva and the Authorized Version, Tyndale's translation did not generally prevail on this point (owing in part to the ridicule of Sir Thomas More), but it symptomized a perennial suspicion among Reformers of the "Church" in its Catholic sense as the Mystical Body and the Bride of Christ, a suspicion which never entirely disappeared. Henry VIII banned the Tyndale New Testament. He and his successors preferred an Established Church that was unified and apostolical, and that would be perceived by the people as more than a merely human institution – for obvious political as well as doctrinal reasons. In King James's succinct phrase, No bishops, no king. A Marxist might add, no mystification, no popular responsive love. Separatists and independents like Milton attacked that kind of traditional view of the Church for precisely opposite reasons. Milton often complained that kings and bishops used religious mysteries only to control the people's minds.

Milton plays ironically upon the marriage trope in *The Reason of Church-Government*, where he wittily jokes, at the expense of church traditionalists: "So that in stead of finding Prelaty an impeacher of Schisme or faction, the more I search, the more I grow into all perswasion to think rather that faction and she as with a spousall ring are wedded together, never to be divorc't" (1: 782). Here the episcopal ring signifies a new parodic marriage. In *The Doctrine and Discipline of Divorce* (1643, 1644), Milton lends some credence to the marriage trope when he calls the Beloved in the Song of Songs "the Spouse of Christ" (2:251). But in *Tetrachordon* he addresses this traditional reading more skeptically: "wisest *Salomon* among his gravest Proverbs countenances a kinde of ravishment and erring fondnes in the entertainment of wedded leisures; and in the Song of Songs, which is generally beleev'd, even in the jolliest expressions to figure the spousals of the Church with Christ, sings of a thousand raptures between those two lovely ones farre on the hither side of carnall enjoyment" (2:597). Whether Milton concurs with the general belief he does not say. As Milton was presumably aware, there is a tradition that interprets the Song of Songs literally as well as allegorically.

But investigation shows that Milton rarely evokes the divine marriage trope apart from divorce.[17] In *Animadversions* (1641) he reveals most clearly that he did not put his unconventional view of the Church forward in *Colasterion* only in the heat of polemic.[18] In what appears, remarkably, to be the only truly positive reference in all of his works to the biblical marriage trope, Milton nonetheless strikes a familiar note. He tells us that after God "had decreed to purifie and renew his Church that lay wallowing in Idolatrous pollutions," he first sent his messenger Wyclif "to touch softly our sores, and carry a gentle hand over our wounds." That was God's way of preparing for the Lutheran Reformation, which came into England with a divine violence: "How else could they have been able to have receiv'd the sudden assault of his reforming Spirit warring against humane Principles, and carnall sense, the pride of flesh that still cry'd up Antiquity, Custome, Canons, Councels and Lawes[?]" (1:704). As he approaches the end of this section, Milton grows increasingly apocalyptic: "seeing the power of thy grace is not past away with the primitive times, as fond and faithless men imagine, but thy Kingdome is now at hand, and thou standing at the dore." For the climactic close of his apocalypse, Milton invokes the image of Christ as the Royal Bridegroom: "Come forth out of thy Royall Chambers, O Prince of all the Kings of the earth, put on the visible roabes of thy imperiall Majesty, take up that unlimited Scepter which thy Almighty Father hath bequeath'd thee; for now the voice of thy Bride calls thee, and all creatures sigh to bee renew'd" (1:707). Milton speaks warmly and enthusiastically here, as nowhere else, of the Church as the Bride of Christ. He does so, however, only in the context of the last and final Reformation, that "reforming of Reformation it self" (*Areopagitica*, 2:553), which he expects will shortly be brought into England by Christ's Second Coming. Either Milton expects Christ to renew his marriage with his Church after a long divorce or series of divorces, as he suggests in *Colasterion*, or (despite traditional biblical interpretations) he thinks that the wedding has not yet taken place. Christ will marry his Church, but only when he takes up his scepter at the end of time.[19]

Milton's treatment of the Church is very different even from that of most radical Protestants of his day, who coupled the Church as the Bride in the Song of Songs with the Church as the Woman Clothed with the Sun in the Book of Revelation,[20] but who spoke of a Church oppressed and exiled, not divorced. Daniel Featley, for example, much like Herbert in "The Church Militant," pictures the Church as the "The Spouse of Christ" reduced to "a pilgrime," flying "from place to place, from Citie to Citie, from Kingdome to Kingdome."[21] Featley's Church, like Herbert's, is a Church in the wilderness persecuted by Satan and Antichrist, not, as Milton implies, a Church consenting to be a helpmeet of Antichrist – therefore a Church that has been deservedly divorced by her divine Spouse many times over.

The Church as a loving Mother does not fare much better at

Milton's hands. "[I]f any man be dispos'd to use a trope or figure, as Saint *Paul* once did in calling her the common Mother of us all," Milton tells Bishop Hall and his fellow prelates in *Animadversions* (1641),

> let him doe as his owne rhethorick shall perswade him. If therefore we must needs have a mother, and if the Catholick Church onely be, and must be she, let all Genealogie tell us if it can, what we must call the Church of *England*, unlesse we shall make every English Protestant a kind of poeticall *Bacchus*, to have two Mothers: but marke Readers, the crafty scope of these Prelates, they endeavour to impresse deeply into weak, and superstitious fancies the awfull notion of a mother, that hereby they might cheat them into a blind and implicite obedience to whatsoever they shall decree, or think fit. And if we come to aske a reason of ought from our deare mother, she's invisible, under the lock and key of the Prelates her spirituall adulterers. (1:727–28)

So much for the Church's motherhood.[22] And so much for the concept of a true, "invisible" Church that transcended the imperfections of churches in this world. Milton needed no instruction in modern methods of demystification, or in modern deconstructive iconoclasm, the breaking down of religious and political imagery.

As Milton grew increasingly disillusioned with the progress of the Reformation in England during the course of the Civil War and Protectorate, he became more and more radical in his views. As is well known, when he came to write the closing books of *Paradise Lost*, he simply omitted any mention of Luther, Calvin, and the Protestant Reformation from his account of Church history. After Christ ascends into Heaven, his work is continued by the Spirit of God, working internally within the hearts of the first generation of Christian faithful:

> Hee to his own a Comforter will send,
> The promise of the Father, who shall dwell
> His Spirit within them, and the Law of Faith
> Working through love, upon thir hearts shall write,
> To guide them in all truth, and also arme
> With spiritual Armour. (12.486–91)

The first, apostolic generation of the Church is filled with the Spirit's "wondrous gifts" (12.500). This Church is a Church entirely individuated and internalized: its members are at one with the Holy Spirit, who dwells within each individual heart and writes on that heart, guiding and arming each person spiritually against the assaults of Satan. Through evangelization and baptism the Apostles and other disciples prepare the way for the Spirit's coming. This spreading conquest of the Spirit, however, seemingly lasts for only a single generation:[23]

> Thir Ministry perform'd, and race well run,
> Thir doctrine and thir story written left,
> They die; but in thir room, as they forwarne,
> Wolves shall succeed for teachers, grievous Wolves.
>
> (12.505–08)

From the second generation onward, the leaders of the Church serve not God but only "thir own vile advantages" of wealth and power. "[A]ppropriating / The Spirit of God," they "force the Spirit of Grace it self" (12.518–25). They persecute the few remnants of the faithful and lead the rest, the vast majority, into superstitious practices, away from receptivity to the Spirit into "outward Rites and specious formes" (12.534).

This, Milton concludes, is the whole story of the Church – not just until the Protestant Reformation should restore the primitive holiness that was lost, but until the Last Judgment, which will bring all history to its end:

> so shall the World goe on,
> To good malignant, to bad men benigne,
> Under her own waight groaning till the day
> Appeer of respiration to the just,
> And vengeance to the wicked, at return
> Of him ...
> Last in the Clouds from Heav'n to be reveald
> In glory of the Father, to dissolve
> *Satan* with his perverted World, then raise
> From the conflagrant mass, purg'd and refin'd,
> New Heav'ns, New Earth, Ages of endless date
> Founded in righteousness and peace and love
> To bring forth fruits Joy and eternal Bliss.   (12.537–51)

From this compressed retelling of Church history it is clear that, after having experienced the failure of the Puritan Revolution,

Milton concluded that Satan would continue to rule over England and the world, and that Antichrist and his servants would rule over the corrupted Churches, Catholic and Protestant alike. The fulfillment of God's Reformation, for which Milton had hoped and worked so long, would never occur beyond the hearts of a few individuals, until God destroyed the world and remade it at the end of days, as Adam explicitly recognizes:

> How soon hath thy prediction, Seer blest,
> Measur'd this transient World, the Race of time,
> Till time stand fixt: beyond is all abyss,
> Eternitie, whose end no eye can reach. (12.553–56)

The end of the world may yet come soon – no one knows the day or the hour (Matthew 25:13) – but Milton no longer expects to see the Apocalypse realized in earthly history or in English politics.[24] In Milton's eyes, the Church of this world is not, and never can be, an object worthy of love – either of God's love or of man's.

What are the practical consequences of Milton's unusually relentless and unforgiving attitude toward the Church as the Bride of Christ and the Mother of Christians? Whether we take it to be a cause or a symptom of other, related attitudes, it manifests his severe and uncompromising vision of love. For Milton, either an object or a person is good or it is evil; likewise either a wife is good or she is evil. Depending on her goodness or lack of goodness, a man should either embrace her or put her away. Love must make no compromise with weakness. With Milton's putting the Church essentially out of the picture as a mediator or as a normative influence on the interchange of divine and human love – out of the picture, too, as a middle term between the vision of the spotless heavenly Bride and the errant religious communities of this world – there remains, on the ultimate stage of things to love, only God and the individual, who must work out his salvation alone and respond to proffered grace with fear and trembling.

It is a commonplace that in their religion the first Protestants substituted a confrontation between the individual soul and

God for the institutional Church with its mediating hierarchy
and system of authority, liturgy, and sacraments. But the story
of Protestantism is largely a story of compromise, often of
oscillation, between radical vision and what is politically and
humanly possible. In Milton, who in his last years belonged to
no sect and attended no church, the Protestant anti-institutional
tendency was carried to its extreme. Seeing the entire wreckage
and subversion of the Church in all her manifestations, he
concluded that Christ's original message, and the means to a
loving relationship with God, was "Left onely in those written
Records pure, / Though not but by the Spirit understood"
(12.513–14).[25] Just once in the course of history, for a brief
generation, the Spirit spoke to the Church broadly, and many
of those who heard the gospel message responded with enthusiasm. From that time onward the Spirit would continue to
call specially elected leaders and to offer grace to all[26] – to each
heart and soul individually. But governments and institutional
Churches would largely block and confuse that call. Only
scattered individuals or small gatherings of the elect would
respond with true faith and love, in the spirit of that "Law of
Faith / Working through love" which Milton finds widely
realized only in the primitive Church.

Such radical religious individualism has consequences. No
one can read much of Milton's prose, especially the nine early
tracts on divorce and on the evils of the prelacy, without being
both delighted and appalled by the spirit of his fierce diatribes.[27]
Few writers exceed Milton in satirical savagery. Fierce zeal,
mocking laughter, and withering scorn are often the strongest
and most prevalent notes in his prose, but the writing sweeps us
away, even against our better judgment, with its ferocious
energy and its unerring rhythms. The imagery is unsettling,
often scatological. Hatred, disgust, division, and rejection
abound. The notorious double ending with which he trium-
phantly closes *Of Reformation* typifies his terrible spirit:

Then amidst the *Hymns*, and *Halleluiahs* of *Saints* some one may
perhaps bee heard offering at high *strains* in new and lofty *Measures* to
sing and celebrate thy *divine Mercies*, and *marvelous Judgements* in this
Land throughout all AGES ... Where they undoubtedly that by their

Labours, *Counsels*, and *Prayers* have been earnest for the *Common good* of *Religion* and their *Countrey*, shall receive, above the inferiour *Orders* of the *Blessed*, the *Regall* addition of *Principalities*, *Legions*, and *Thrones* into their glorious Titles, and in supereminence of *beatifick Vision* progressing the *datelesse* and *irrevoluble* Circle of *Eternity* shall clasp inseparable Hands with *joy*, and *blisse* in over measure for ever.

But they contrary that by the impairing and diminution of the true *Faith*, the distresses and servitude of their *Countrey* aspire to high *Dignity*, *Rule* and *Promotion* here, after a shamefull end in this *Life* (which *God* grant them) shall be thrown downe eternally into the *darkest* and *deepest Gulfe* of HELL, where under the *despightfull controule*, the trample and spurne of all the other *Damned*, that in the anguish of their *Torture* shall have no other ease then to exercise a *Raving* and *Bestiall Tyranny* over them as their *Slaves* and *Negro's*, they shall remaine in that plight for ever, the *basest*, the *lowermost*, the *most dejected*, most *underfoot* and *downe-trodden Vassals* of *Perdition*.   (1:616–17)

The Yale editors urge that Milton was not alone in "the heat of his pamphleteering zeal." Prynne, they note, calls the bishops a "dunghill generation of Lordly Peacockes."[28] But this and the other examples they proffer are quite feeble compared with Milton's lordly abuse. Even Bunyan's similar double ending of the first book of *The Pilgrim's Progress* seems, by comparison, grim but regretful:

[T]he King...commanded the two shining Ones that conducted *Christian* and *Hopeful* to the City to go out and take *Ignorance* and bind him hand and foot, and have him away. Then they took him up, and carried him through the air to the door that I saw in the side of the Hill, and put him in there. Then I saw that there was a way to Hell, even from the Gates of Heaven, as well as from the City of *Destruction*. So I awoke, and behold it was a Dream.[29]

One finds in Bunyan none of the "relish" for which Milton has so often been criticized.

This doubleness is, of course, biblical. It has to do with the fundamental nature of God's Judgment, which at the Apocalypse will bring "respiration to the just, / And vengeance to the wicked" (12.540–41). It has to do with the principle that makes Milton's Christ the embodiment of Love at one point and the embodiment of "hate" at another.[30]

> Beyond compare the Son of God was seen
> Most glorious, in him all his Father shon
> Substantially express'd, and in his face
> Divine compassion visibly appeerd,
> Love without end, and without measure Grace. (3.138–42)

In this description we already hear Joseph Summers' "voice of the Redeemer," "the speech of redemptive love."[31] Yet the Son also appears and speaks in another voice:

> Thou shalt be All in All, and I in thee
> For ever, and in mee all whom thou lov'st:
> But whom thou hat'st, I hate, and can put on
> Thy terrors, as I put thy mildness on,
> Image of thee in all things. (6.732–36)

The putting-on of terrors precedes the Son's entry into the War in Heaven at his Father's command. However much we may agree with Arnold Stein's argument that the War in Heaven is often comical and parodic, rather than always straining after the heights of sublimity, as most earlier critics had thought,[32] there is nothing comical about the Son's entry into battle on the third day. As John Shawcross may have been the first to suggest, Milton marks the ascent of the Son into the Chariot of Paternal Deity as a central event of *Paradise Lost* by placing it at the very center of the poem.[33] Few would question the sublimity of Milton's description of Christ's expulsion of the rebel angels – introduced by another change in the Son's countenance, which visibly expresses the divine anger:

> So spake the Son, and into terrour chang'd
> His count'nance too severe to be beheld
> And full of wrauth bent on his Enemies. (6.824–26)

As it turns out, only in a limited sense does the Son stage a military attack on Satan and his followers, since the main cause of their inglorious rout is simply the sight of him and his terrible equipage. Not even the first sight of hell is more terrible:

> the monstrous sight
> Strook them with horror backward, but far worse
> Urg'd them behind; headlong themselves they threw
> Down from the verge of Heav'n, Eternal wrauth
> Burnt after them to the bottomless pit. (6.862–66)

This, we might say, is the truest version of the Fall of Satan, staged and recounted so many times and described from so many viewpoints throughout *Paradise Lost*. Satan threw himself from Heaven, impelled by his inability to look upon the face of God. The beatific vision has become for him the face of wrath.

In part, this hatred and anger of God, visibly expressed in the Son's countenance, is simply a matter of the beholder's state of mind, of his perception. Milton himself suggests as much when he shows how the faces of angels change in the sight of Adam and Eve after the Fall. Adam cries out:

> How shall I behold the face
> Henceforth of God or Angel, earst with joy
> And rapture so oft beheld? those heav'nly shapes
> Will dazle now this earthly, with thir blaze
> Insufferably bright.   (9.1080–84)

More subtly, Milton has the guilt-stricken Adam wish for oblivion, so God's "dreadful voice no more / Would Thunder in my ears" (10.779–80). This is Adam's revision of an event that Milton a short while earlier pictured quite differently, in what must be among the mildest versions of the judgment in Eden:

> Now was the Sun in Western cadence low
> From Noon, and gentle Aires due at thir hour
> To fan the Earth now wak'd, and usher in
> The Eevning coole when he from wrauth more coole
> Came the mild Judge and Intercessor both
> To sentence Man: the voice of God they heard
> Now walking in the Garden, by soft windes
> Brought to thir Ears.   (10.92–99)

Just as I have suggested elsewhere concerning Milton's depiction of the background of the Father's first appearance in the Heavenly Council scene,[34] the background of the Judgment scene is an essential part of Milton's description of his central figure. Who else but this Creator-Intercessor-Judge made the cool evening and the gentle airs, which carry the mild voice of God to the ears of the guilty pair? Yet we can easily understand Adam's mistake. To the guilty, judgment always seems to come – or is heard with cringing anticipation – as a voice of thunder. "The wicked flee when no man pursueth" (Proverbs 28:1). If this is so, the divine hatred may be less substantive than first appears.

But such a thought, comforting to those who may yet repent, can be of no comfort to the damned. For them, for those confined to Hell,

> hope never comes
> That comes to all; but torture without end
> Still urges, and a fiery Deluge, fed
> With ever-burning Sulphur unconsum'd:
> Such place Eternal Justice had prepar'd
> For those rebellious.   (1.66–71)

If, for Satan, Hell is a state of mind, which he brings with him even into Paradise, it is also a place and a punishment, inescapably real.

Not surprisingly, it is Satan who, from knowledge gained by terrible experience, gives us another important bearing on the nature of divine "hatred." In his first soliloquy, as he contemplates how he has reached his present fallen state, he asks the question Adam will later ask: Whose fault?

> Hadst thou the same free Will and Power to stand?
> Thou hadst: whom hast thou then or what to accuse,
> But Heav'ns free Love dealt equally to all?
> Be then his Love accurst, since love or hate,
> To me alike, it deals eternal woe.   (4.66–70)

This comes close to the heart of a mystery that is central to *Paradise Lost*. Satan admits that his damnation has resulted from his rejection of divine love. After he has freely rejected God's love, that very love deals him "eternal woe": a woe that in turn consists, most fundamentally, in the absence of God and love.[35] This – the perpetual internal echoing of rejected love – is the descending spiral, with its "lowest deep" opening to reveal a still "lower deep" (4.76), into which the damned have thrown themselves. In Satan's eyes, love and hatred have become effectively interchangeable, because they are equally painful to a being who has cut himself off from all heartfelt relationships with any other being.[36]

Dante makes precisely the same point in his inscription over the gate of Hell:

> PER ME SI VA NE LA CITTA DOLENTE,
>   PER ME SI VA NE L'ETTERNO DOLORE,
>   PER ME SI VA TRA LA PERDUTA GENTE.
> GIUSTIZIA MOSSE IL MIO ALTO FATTORE;
>   FECEMI LA DIVINA PODESTATE,
>   LA SOMMA SAPIENZA E 'L PRIMO AMORE.
> DINANZI A ME NON FUOR COSE CREATE
>   SE NON ETTERNE, E IO ETTERNO DURO.
>   LASCIATE OGNE SPERANZA, VOI CH'INTRATE.

> (Through me you enter the woeful city,
>   Through me you enter eternal grief,
>   Through me you enter among the lost.
> Justice moved my high Maker:
>   The divine power made me,
>   The supreme wisdom, and the primal love.
> Before me nothing was created
>   If not eternal, and eternal I endure.
>   Abandon every hope, you who enter.)[37]

The severity of divine justice – manifested in a trinity of power, wisdom and love that together founded Hell – is the terrible underlying axiom that makes the *Inferno* the uncompromising work that it is. Love founded Hell. Within the poem Dante faints at his first sight of the damned (3.133–36), and Virgil turns pale: "L'angoscia de le genti / che son qua giù, nel viso mi dipigne / quella pietà che tu per tema senti"; "The anguish of the people here below paints my face with the pity that you take for fear" (4.19–21). Yet in the end Dante does not flinch from inscribing over the gates of Hell his terrible words about God's love.

If anything, Milton is more uncompromising than Dante. Where Dante is in danger of bearing too much allegiance to a political faction, the imperial party, Milton is in danger of bearing allegiance to no faction. Milton, supremely self-confident, is not one to faint at the thought of God's love turning to hate in the perception of the damned. He cheers on the trampling down of the prelates into the lowest depths of hell, "after a shamefull end in this *Life* (which *God* grant them)."

What is a modern reader to make of such an attitude? As we
have seen, many have simply condemned Milton for bigotry.
This is what (to vastly simplify) I would call the Enlightenment
attitude toward Milton – that we are more rational and more
tolerant than he was; that we no longer have any use for
religious zeal.[38] From this attitude comes the primary Modernist
impulse to "dislodge" Milton. Alternatively we can try to
secularize Milton's fierceness and to recuperate from his
religious bigotry elements acceptable to contemporary ideologies. What we are no longer willing to accept as religious zeal we
may still find palatable if we transform it into a more purely
political zeal, into philosophical innovation or poetic strength.
This is what I would call a typically Postmodernist attitude
toward Milton.[39] For Milton's peculiar impatience with traditions, with institutions, and with the great sweep of the
historical past, his desire to begin all things anew and to do them
perfectly, is something we as Moderns or Postmoderns alike can
share. We can understand his hatred of oppressive institutions
and of unacceptable social practices.

There are obvious difficulties with both attitudes. As for
Enlightenment scorn of Milton, there is no reason to believe
that our century has been any less cruel and savage than
Milton's – in fact, quite the opposite. Religious zeal may be
displaced – politicized or secularized – but (I would argue) history shows that it cannot be entirely suppressed. As for
Postmodernist revisions of Milton, too often they are wishful
misreadings, tending toward empty recuperative pieties. Granted that Milton was a political reformer, he was always a
religious reformer first. It might seem, therefore, given Milton's
own position and turning to the normative assumptions of his
time for guidance, that a Christian reading would be truest to
his vision. What such a reading must notice, however, is that
the state and the Church played less and less of a role in Milton's
thinking, as he suffered progressive disillusionment with what
he viewed as the broad failure of the Reformation as well as the
collapse of the Puritan Revolution. In the end, Milton
mistrusted all human institutions and all forms of community.
He became that impossible paradox, a Christian without a

Church, answerable only to his God.[40] Milton's ultimate allegiance was to God alone, without mediation, without secure normative influence, without obvious mitigating connections with the persons and things of this world.

Perhaps, then, the Enlightenment and Postmodernist views of Milton find something in his work to justify them after all, for in Milton's uncompromising religious vision the seeds of future secularism are plain to see. A vision which sweeps everything else away teaches us to sweep it away too. We can, to a degree, admire Milton's love for a pure God from whose skirts the Church and everything sinful have been brushed away; but we are also right to fear such a love, unguided by precedent and tradition, utterly free to reform its divine object in its own image. Considering the limitless freedom Milton demands for divine love, we can only grant that he handles it supremely well in *Paradise Lost*. We might almost believe in his insistent claim that such an epic could not have been written unless the poet, like a second Moses, were directly inspired by the Spirit of God.[41] Nonetheless, precisely this individuated freedom to reject the past and the communal wisdom makes the religious love of *Paradise Lost* not just an archaic product of "dead ideas" but something importantly new: a poem whose visionary power makes it a potent hinge between the old radical religious enthusiasms and the new ideological enthusiasms they later engendered.[42] Milton's epic hangs poised between two worlds. It brings ancient Christian love into the modern world. More ominously, by cutting that love loose from prior restraints, it portends the ever-mutating instigations of modern ideological zeal.

CHAPTER 8

John Milton: "Haile wedded Love"

It is well known that Milton had an immense influence on the thinking of later poets, and indeed on that of politicians, opinion leaders, and people generally, on the subject of love and companionate marriage.[1] During the eighteenth century, his hymn to marriage in *Paradise Lost*, "Haile wedded Love," was repeatedly detached from its context: to be quoted, paraphrased, set to music, and variously alluded to, by numberless people. Even Voltaire, who was scornful of *Paradise Lost* on the whole, speaks well of Milton as a benign authority on the subject of love, praising him for removing "with a chaste Hand the veil which covers everywhere the enjoyments of that Passion. There is Softness, Tenderness and Warmth without Lasciviousness, the Poet transports himself and us, into that State of innocent Happiness in which *Adam* and *Eve* continued for a short time."[2]

At the same time, Milton the tender advocate of marriage suffered an equally wide-ranging notoriety as "the Great Divorcer." On the Continent especially, but also among his English political opponents, he was widely known, or misknown, as a divorcer, a polygamist, and a frightening advocate of unlimited libertinism.[3] According to Robert Baillie (1645), Milton "in a large Treatise hath pleaded for a full liberty for any man to put away his wife, when ever hee pleaseth, without any fault in her at all, but for any dislike or dyspathy of humour."[4] A century later, even those who as a matter of modesty or prudence avoided reading Milton's divorce tracts still knew of their reputation, as Lady Bradshaigh reveals in a letter to Samuel Richardson (1752): "I never read Milton's

Treatise upon Divorces, but have heard it much condemned, as a thing calculated to serve his own private ends."[5] The original Oxford English Dictionary gives as its only definition of "Miltonist," "A follower of Milton in his views on divorce." The editors cite Symmons (1810): "A party, distinguished by the name of Miltonists, attested the power of his pen, and gave consequence to his pleading for divorce"; and Southey (1835): "Hayley... had reasons for being what in the days of the Commonwealth was called a Miltonist."[6] The word first appeared in this sense in Milton's lifetime, was evidently well established by the nineteenth century, and only recently was superseded in contemporary American usage by "Miltonist" as a critic of, or authority on, Milton.[7]

Although Milton never actually divorced Mary Powell or either of his two other wives, he certainly gave rumor plentiful opportunity for malice on the subject of his divorce tracts. As John Halkett has shown, in the most detailed study of Milton and marriage against the background of contemporary opinion, Milton was far ahead of his time in calling for divorce on grounds of what we would now call incompatibility. To his bewildered and scandalized contemporaries, Milton seemed rather to be arguing for divorce on the basis of mere personal whim. The Anglican Church allowed separation from bed and board (not full divorce and remarriage) only on grounds of adultery. Some Continental Reformers advocated divorce on grounds of both adultery and desertion. Nevertheless, according to Halkett, "no Reformed church allowed divorce on the basis of incompatibility."[8] It would take religion and the law in England and America some three hundred years to catch up with Milton's views.

Still the argument can easily be made that Milton's views on divorce are simply the necessary obverse of his highly idealistic views on marriage. Once again, we may say that Milton was following Protestantism to what he deemed to be its logical conclusions, anticipating "the reforming of Reformation it self."[9] Or perhaps rather, as it turned out, he was unwittingly anticipating the full consequences of post-Protestant Modernism, that is, the end results of the ongoing Protestant revision of the relations among God, the Church, and the individual. On this issue, once again, Milton's peculiar use of the marriage trope provides us with revelatory insights. As we have already remarked, Milton alludes to the Pauline comparison between man and wife, God and Church, most often when speaking about divorce. In the divorce tracts he argues that just as Christ often divorced the Church for spiritual incompatibility, so men had every right to divorce their wives on similar grounds. For Milton the argument "that was no true Wife" is coordinate with the corresponding argument "this was no true Church" (2:732).

Halkett cites numerous texts to disprove the assertion, common in studies of "Protestant marriage," that Puritans of Milton's time put companionship above the other traditional ends of marriage, procreation and assuagement of lust. Certainly seventeenth-century Protestant writers included loving companionship as *one* of the three important ends of marriage, but seldom, if ever, did they argue that it was the prime end. Most of them continued to put procreation first. Halkett quotes a passage from Jeremy Taylor as simply "the most perspicuous" in explaining what nearly all Anglicans and Puritans agreed to be the proper ends of marriage:

The preservation of a family, the production of children, the avoiding fornication, the refreshment of our sorrows by the comforts of society; all these are fair ends of marriage and hallow the entrance: but in these there is a special order; society was the first designed, "It is not good for man to be alone"; – children was the next, "Increase and multiply"; – but the avoiding fornication came in by the superfoetation of the evil accidents of the world. The first makes marriage delectable, the second necessary to the public, the third necessary to the particular ... but of all these the noblest end is the multiplying of children.[10]

Many writers, Anglican and Puritan alike, make the point that procreation is the prime end of marriage, not for its own sake but because it is the means of increasing membership in the Church. Thus the marriage trope turns back upon itself and becomes literalized, as may be seen in a comment of William Guild's on the Song of Songs as a divine allegory of the marriage between Christ and his Church:

The cause wherefore the holy Ghost represents this love and union between these two in all this Song, by the similitude of matrimoniall conjunction, is, because in all other bonds of love or friendship, there is not either so sacred a ground of so holy and particular intire affection, nor such a communion of so deere things, as hearts, bodies, and goods, nor so strait a conjunction of parties, becoming thereby one flesh, not so durable for time, being dissolvable only by death, and the effect divine rather than humane, God using men thereby but as instruments to propagate his Church.[11]

As Halkett argues, "Most divines – both Puritan and Anglican – consider the spread of the church through the begetting and education of children to be the primary function of marriage" (pp. 16–17). Bartholemew Parsons, an Anglican, writes that "The maine end and scope then that persons entring into this covenant of God, the mariage band must aime at, is that they may build Israel that out of their loynes may issue seed to be profitable members of the church and commonwealth."[12] Among Calvinists, William Perkins writes that "Wedlock must be used to suppresse, then to satisfie that corrupt concupiscence of the flesh, and especially to enlarge the church of God. Rom. 13.14"[13] Samuel Hieron writes that marriage "is the foundation of a family, and a family ought to bee a modell of a Church."[14] William Ames writes that "in marriage [is] first sought an holy seed. Malac. 2.15"[15] Richard Bernard writes that married couples should desire children "for the enlargement of Gods Church."[16] And Benjamin Needler gives, as God's chief reason for creating Eve, the spread of the Church.[17] Although Donne does not explicitly mention the Church in this context, he makes it plain that procreation must go beyond mere physical begetting to involve socialization and inculturation of children, as aspects of the training needed to prepare them for final salvation: "For this world might be filled full enough of children, though there were no mariage; but heaven could not be filled, nor the places of the fallen Angels supplied, without that care of childrens religious education, which from Parents in lawfull mariage they are likeliest to receive."[18]

Certainly Milton shared with his fellow Christians the view that procreation is one of the important ends of marriage, and that in turn procreation should be directed toward God. At the moment of their embrace after remembering their first meeting, Milton names Adam and Eve – as he does so often elsewhere in *Paradise Lost* – "our general Mother" and "our first Father" (4.492–94). After their own duty to worship God and to love each other, the first couple's chief purpose in life is to "multiply a Race of Worshippers / Holy and just" (7.630–31). But Milton is far less inclined than his fellow Protestants to see the Church or the commonwealth as the proper intermediary means for bringing this end about. Until it has been thoroughly transformed at Christ's Second Coming – which in *Paradise Lost* will not occur until after history has come to an end – the Church is much more likely, in Milton's view, to corrupt and frustrate the process of multiplying fit worshippers than to guide and further it.

What the universal corruption of the Church means, inevitably, is that for Milton it can no longer be the great spiritual analogy or example of ideal marriage, or even the best available support for married couples in easing their loneliness and bringing up their children. The Church is no fit helpmeet or mother. Rather, it is the Whore of Babylon, the chief inciter in this fallen world to idolatry and lust. The pattern of sinful lust that Satan has planted at the very heart of the Church has its typological roots in the Old Testament. Milton shows the fallen angels entering and corrupting the very Temple itself:

> the Love-tale
> Infected *Sions* daughters with like heat,
> Whose wanton passions in the sacred Porch
> *Ezekiel* saw, when by the Vision led
> His eye survay'd the dark Idolatries
> Of alienated *Judah*.   (1.452–57)

Here, exemplified in the Temple as a type of the Church, is no opposition of true and false religions, but a corrupted religious establishment, to which the only counterbalancing force is a single outsider, more an onlooker than a member, a prophet directly inspired by God.

Similarly, the figure of Belial exemplifies for Milton the

perennial propagation of lust not only in Sodom and at the Restoration court, as many critics have observed, but also throughout history and at the heart of all the English Churches in his own day. Before the part usually quoted, Milton observes:

> To him no Temple stood
> Or Altar smoak'd; yet who more oft then hee
> In Temples and at Altars, when the Priest
> Turns Atheist, as did *Ely's* Sons, who fill'd
> With lust and violence the house of God.   (1.492–96)

Similar images to these of Milton's, of the Church as a center for licentious corruption and of spiritual fornication, are familiar enough in other Protestant writers, such as Spenser. But there is one significant difference. In Milton, there is as yet no Una – no true Church – to be found in this world; there is only a bevy of Duessas.

In addition, by the time he began serious work on *Paradise Lost*, Milton had come to think that there should simply be no connection between the Church and marriage. As he points out in *The Likeliest Means to Remove Hirelings* (1659), although Protestant divines "denie [marriage] to be a sacrament," yet they have illogically "retaind the celebration." They have done so, he charges, only because it is "material to thir profit." Such at least was the corrupt situation in England "till prudently a late parlament recoverd the civil liberty of marriage from thir incroachment; and transferrd the ratifying and registring therof from the canonical shop to the proper cognisance of the civil magistrates" (7.300). As William Riley Parker points out, Milton once put this belief into practice. He wed his second wife, Katherine Woodcock, in a civil ceremony. "They were married on Wednesday, 12 November [1656], by Sir John Dethicke, alderman and one of the justices of the peace for the city of London."[19] Thus Milton's quarrel with the traditional connection between marriage and the Church went well beyond his dissatisfaction with the Church's present imperfect condition. Even if God were to come down into England and perfect his Church, marriage should still, in Milton's view, be divorced from its ancient ecclesiastical connection. Considered as a religious matter, marriage is the proper business only of the husband, his wife, and God.[20]

As we have seen, because of his scorn for the Church, Milton was always in danger of falling into isolation and individualism in religious matters – and therefore in all matters. But although he helped open the way to pure religious individualism for others, he did not quite fall all the way into it himself. Indeed, he not only well understood the attractive pull of individualism but its dangers. Therefore he made Satan its most extreme spokesman and exemplar in *Paradise Lost*. Satan cannot bear to admit dependence on anyone, even God. "Better to reign in Hell, then serve in Heav'n" (1.263). As a number of critics have argued, Satan is an incestuous self-lover, a narcissist who is unable to break out of an inwardly directed self-regard to love God or another being.[21] The narcissistic nature of Satanic love is especially evident in his daughter Sin's vivid description of her birth:

> Out of thy head I sprung: amazement seis'd
> All th' Host of Heav'n; back they recoild affraid
> At first, and call'd me *Sin*, and for a Sign
> Portentous held me; but familiar grown,
> I pleas'd, and with attractive graces won
> The most averse, thee chiefly, who full oft
> Thy self in me thy perfect image viewing
> Becam'st enamour'd, and such joy thou took'st
> With me in secret, that my womb conceiv'd
> A growing burden.   (2.758–67)

This inward turn of love is completed by Death, the third member of the infernal trinity, who incestuously rapes his mother and engenders the breed of hellhounds, who return inside to feed upon her womb.

Toward the outer world, and for beings other than himself, Satan can feel only an empty, ravenous desire, which tortures him with terrible envy of the love enjoyed by others, such as Adam and Eve:

> Sight hateful, sight tormenting! thus these two
> Imparadis't in one anothers arms

> The happier *Eden*, shall enjoy thir fill
> Of bliss on bliss, while I to Hell am thrust,
> Where neither joy nor love, but fierce desire,
> Among our other torments not the least,
> Still unfulfill'd with pain of longing pines.   (4.505–11)

Such is the inevitable end of unresolved narcissistic desire, in sterility, loss, and longing.

After her creation, Eve, too, narrowly skirts the dangers of self-destructive individualism and of insatiable desire, when she is momentarily, but still innocently, held enthralled by her reflection in the smooth lake:

> As I bent down to look, just opposite,
> A Shape within the watry gleam appeerd
> Bending to look on me, I started back,
> It started back, but pleas'd I soon returnd,
> Pleas'd it returnd as soon with answering looks
> Of sympathie and love; there I had fixt
> Mine eyes till now, and pin'd with vain desire,
> Had not a voice thus warnd me, What thou seest,
> What there thou seest fair Creature is thy self,
> With thee it came and goes: but follow me,
> And I will bring thee where no shadow staies
> Thy coming, and thy soft imbraces, hee
> Whose image thou art, him thou shall enjoy
> Inseparablie thine, to him shalt beare
> Multitudes like thy self, and thence be call'd
> Mother of human Race.   (4.460–75)

Even a perfect, unfallen human being feels a need to love someone else and to be loved in return. Merely to love oneself means to turn away from the real world into an inward world of reflections and of shadows, not of substance, where the seeming return of mutual love proves an illusory echo, and the initial impulse to love, good in itself, is inevitably transformed, as the eyes become endlessly "fixt," into a Satanic pining away toward death in "vain desire." Only in another loving person can the joys of "soft imbraces" and of mutual companionship be found, and only in this love of, and being loved by, another can spiritual fruition and procreation of children take place.

As Adam recognizes soon after his creation, and tells a gently questioning God, only God is self-sufficient. By his very nature, man needs companionship, to give and to receive solace from loneliness:

> Thou in thy self art perfet, and in thee
> Is no deficience found; not so is Man,
> But in degree, the cause of his desire
> By conversation with his like to help,
> Or solace his defects. No need that thou
> Shouldst propagat, already infinite;
> And through all numbers absolute, though One;
> But Man by number is to manifest
> His single imperfection, and beget
> Like of his like, his Image multipli'd,
> In unitie defective, which requires
> Collateral love, and deerest amitie.   (8.415–26)

For Milton, the mutual love found in marriage is an absolute requirement for human nature to realize its full potential.[22] The isolated individual is, by his very nature, "defective."

Despite the efforts of many critics in recent years to make Milton into a modern feminist, however – or to repudiate him for *not* having been a modern feminist – the "collateral love" between Adam and Eve is not entirely equal. Adam and Eve, Milton says, are

> Not equal, as thir sex not equal seemd;
> For contemplation hee and valour formd,
> For softness shee and sweet attractive Grace,
> Hee for God only, shee for God in him.   (4.296–99)

Adam's outward appearance declares his "Absolute rule"; Eve's implies her "Subjection, but requir'd with gentle sway" (4.301, 308). The whole action of the poem, as well as many similar passages, confirms that Adam excels in the manly graces, Eve in the womanly.[23] Adam is more rational, Eve more loving. Adam is prone to uxoriousness, Eve to self-love. Both are fully human; both possess enough free will to stand or to fall. But they are neither identical nor, in Milton's view, wholly "equal." After the Fall, the curse pronounced on the woman is to obey her husband, whether he be just or unjust. Before the Fall – and, Milton urges, even after, when aided by grace in a well-adjusted Christian marriage – she obeys freely by her own loving choice.

But the inequality of Adam and Eve in *Paradise Lost* is relatively slight – almost notional, almost an accedence to Pauline convention rather than an obvious disparity. For every strength of Adam's there is an equivalent strength of Eve's, just as for every potential weakness of his there is a corresponding potential weakness of hers. Each of them alone is "in unitie defective"; each needs the other. As Diane McColley has pointed out, before the Fall it is always Eve who willingly raises the issue of Adam's marital headship, never Adam. She typically addresses him:

> O thou for whom
> And from whom I was formd flesh of thy flesh,
> And without whom am to no end, my Guide
> And Head. (4.440–43)

Adam addresses Eve with equal love and reverence, if not submissiveness. Until the temptation puts new ideas into Eve's mind, Adam's headship is not a problem for her. Adam, of course, far from asserting his headship, is only too prone to forget it.

As many critics have further pointed out, it is Adam who, in his pleasant talk with God before Eve's creation, makes the strongest statement in the poem for the impossibility of true mutual love between "unequals":

> Among unequals what societie
> Can sort, what harmonie or true delight?
> Which must be mutual, in proportion due
> Giv'n and receiv'd; but in disparitie
> The one intense, the other still remiss
> Cannot well suite with either, but soon prove
> Tedious alike: Of fellowship I speak
> Such as I seek, fit to participate
> All rational delight. (8.383–91)

There can be little doubt in the mind of anyone who has read much of Milton's work that his heart is fully invested in Adam's plea for an equal, whom he can love collaterally – even though, at second glance, Adam's remarks on the difficulties of "unequal" love raise other interesting problems – coming, as they do, in a conversation between two distinctly unequal beings, man and God.

But what Adam is looking for is indicated in some of the key words of his speech: society, harmony, delight, mutuality, proportion, intensity, fellowship, and "All rational delight." Society and fellowship suggest that Milton looks in marriage for a communality that he does not find either in the Church or in the other social institutions of the fallen world. Delight reminds us that he seeks not only an interchange of views and ideas with another person, but also a relaxation of seriousness and of that ambitious laboring that characterize a man's role in the larger world. What Milton means is clearer in a long passage in *Tetrachordon*, from which I can quote only a small part:

No mortall nature can endure either in the actions of Religion, or study of wisdome, without sometime slackning the cords of intense thought and labour ... We cannot therefore alwayes be contemplative, or pragmaticall abroad, but have need of som delightfull intermissions, wherein the enlarg'd soul may leav off a while her severe schooling; and like a glad youth in wandring vacancy, may keep her hollidaies to joy and harmles pastime: which as she cannot well doe without company, so in no company so well as where the different sexe in most resembling unlikenes, and most unlike resemblance cannot but please best and be pleas'd in the aptitude of that variety.[24]

We can recognize in this passage something we have already seen in Donne's *Songs and Sonets*: a plea for marriage, or for mutual love, as a relief and a shelter from the everyday working world. Harmony, proportion, and mutuality further suggest that the married relationship should be one of giving and taking – but not one of exact equivalence, or even, necessarily, of strict equality. Harmony comes from the blending of different musical notes in due proportion or, as the passage from *Tetrachordon* suggests, in the "most resembling unlikenes" of "different sexe."

Adam requires a relationship that should not be so unequal that it would be "intense" on one side and "remiss" on the other. The disparity may remind us of Milton's complaint in *The Doctrine and Discipline of Divorce* of the horrors of being "bound fast to an uncomplying discord of nature, or, as it oft happens, to an image of earth and fleam" (2:254). We may assume that Adam is complaining of the remissness of the hypothetical inferior partner and not of the intensity of the superior one, for an almost dangerous intensity is one of the chief characteristics of the ideal Miltonic marriage. After Eve's creation, Adam wakes "To find her, or for ever to deplore / Her loss, and other pleasures all abjure" (8.479–80). And he confesses to Raphael that, when he sees Eve,

> transported I behold,
> Transported touch; here passion first I felt,
> Commotion strange, in all enjoyments else
> Superiour and unmov'd, here onely weake
> Against the charm of Beauties powerful glance. (8.529–33)

Adam is surely wrong to put the blame for this weakness on his created nature.[25] Raphael promptly responds, "Accuse not Nature, she hath don her part; / Do thou but thine" (8.561–62).

But the intensity of Adam's feelings, as he further explains to Raphael, is not due to mere animal lust or sexual desire. It is due to the intensity of his love for Eve. The rebuke was narrowly deserved, but it goes slightly askew. Adam says that he honors two of the ends of marriage with "mysterious reverence": these are the two ends related to "the genial Bed," sexual intercourse and procreation (8.595–99). But for him, as for Milton, the chief end of marriage is found simply in the loving relationship itself. Nothing else in marriage

> So much delights me as those graceful acts,
> Those thousand decencies that daily flow
> From all her words and actions mixt with Love
> And sweet compliance, which declare unfeign'd
> Union of Mind, or in us both one Soule;
> Harmonie to behold in wedded pair
> More grateful then harmonious sound to the eare.
>
> (8.600–06)

Indeed, it almost appears that Adam has a more "spiritual" view of love than Raphael, who responds to Adam's question about the love of angels for one another with his famous description of a perfect, unfrustrated mode of sexual intercourse (8.615–29). Perhaps with angels the spiritual element may be presumed; or perhaps they enjoy a more universal sense of community than is to be found on earth, as Milton suggests in his images of angelic harmony.[26] Therefore they would seem to have less need of paired community as a cure for loneliness.

Presumably Miltonic angels have no need to procreate, since the Father's plan is to make up for the lost third of the angelic host by creating the human race. One cannot be absolutely certain, since Milton is silent on this specific point and is, of course, nowhere more heterodox than on the matter of angelic materiality.[27] Indeed, for the angels, sexual intercourse would seem to have as its *raison d'être* only one of the three ends appropriate to human marriage: that is, it has some equivalence to the assuagement of burning – though presumably without the fallen element of "superfoetation" that Jeremy Taylor, following St. Paul, attaches to this end. Raphael puts it simply that the angels "enjoy / In eminence" (8.623–24). Indeed the whole matter of angelic sexuality in *Paradise Lost*, although pleasing and amusing to the modern mind, is vexed, and difficult to account for except as Milton's dream of what human sexuality might have been had not Adam fallen and prevented the gradual conversion of human bodies "all to Spirit, / Improv'd by tract of time" (5.497–98). Raphael's speech undercuts the traditional Christian view of the angels – a result that Milton would not have minded, any more than most modern readers. It also undercuts the traditional Christian view that sexuality is unnatural when separated from procreation – which Milton, unlike most modern readers, would have minded. And finally it seems to undercut Milton's own dearest opinion, centrally important in *Paradise Lost* and pervasive in the divorce tracts, that sexuality in marriage – in itself and as a means of procreation – is subordinate to mutual love and companionship.

It is a truism of Milton criticism that much of the power of *Paradise Lost* comes from Milton's having set one high form of

love against another: married love against the love of God.[28] As
Halkett puts it: "Adam loves in Eve precisely what the angel
tells him to. One of the central paradoxes of *Paradise Lost* is that
Milton has so constructed his argument that it is exactly the
perfection of his marriage with Eve which acts upon Adam as
the greatest incentive to the temptation to disobey" (p. 122).
The anguished intensity of Adam's love is evident in his decision
to join her in eating the forbidden fruit:

> How can I live without thee, how forgoe
> Thy sweet Converse and Love so dearly joyn'd,
> To live again in these wilde Woods forlorn?
> Should God create another *Eve*, and I
> Another Rib afford, yet loss of thee
> Would never from my heart; no, no, I feel
> The Link of Nature draw me: Flesh of Flesh,
> Bone of my Bone thou art, and from thy State
> Mine never shall be parted, bliss or woe.　　(9.908–16)

Adam draws on the great biblical marriage text to justify his
decision to join Eve in the Fall. He draws on the bond of "sweet
Converse and Love," on the mystical union of flesh, bone, and
spirit – and not on mere sexual desire.[29] It is easy to understand
why so many readers have since agreed with him.

One common reaction of readers to Adam's decision is to
wonder what might have happened if he had chosen otherwise.
Of course, Adam cannot choose otherwise, because his story is
already written in Genesis. But Milton himself encourages us to
consider the alternatives. We know that Adam has already
fallen, but we know that, in Milton's view, he fell freely. C. S.
Lewis raises the possibility that Adam might have resisted the
temptation, "scolded or even chastised Eve, and then inter-
ceded with God on her behalf."[30] More recently, a number of
critics have suggested that Milton really thought that Adam
should have divorced Eve, left her to her fate, and married
again.[31] But I do not think such an argument can be supported
by Milton's divorce tracts. True, Eve makes a horrible mistake.
She drags Adam – and all of their progeny to the end of
time – down into a state of universal subjection to sin and death.
But she repents. And – more important in Milton's eyes, oddly

enough – it cannot easily be argued that she and Adam are truly incompatible, for it was God himself who created them for each other and brought them together in marriage.

The difficulty with the usual arguments for Adamic divorce is that Milton's doctrine of incompatibility is not really compatible with Christianity – whether Catholic, or Protestant, or extreme Puritan – though it is, perhaps, understandable as a kind of drawing out of Protestantism to its ultimate limits. The underlying problem, as Halkett notes, is that Milton's views leave no room for a wife to reform over a period of time or to make difficult adjustments. Among orthodox Reformers, "It was never suggested that a lack of wifely virtue – unless manifested by adultery – could provide grounds for divorce. Matrimonial difficulties, however intense they might be, were to be met by prayer, forbearance, and an attempt to reform the offending partner" (p. 39). As Halkett notes, Milton's contemporary opponents readily saw this weakness in his case. "Milton apparently seeks to forestall the objection which was in fact put forward by his opponents and answered with scorn in *Colasterion* – that the condition of unfitness was alterable" (p. 49). In traditional Christian thinking, no human being may be judged incapable of salvation or reformation before his or her death.[32] "Judge not, that ye be not judged" (Matthew 7:1). This is all the more true for Milton, who throughout *Paradise Lost* gives such primacy to the universality of offered grace and the freedom of every human will to reform itself.

What Milton meant by incompatibility, then, was not simply lack of virtue, or even persistence in a habitual state of sinfulness. Rather it is some mysterious, unchangeable quality of the soul, which is simply not subject to the will or to any effort of reform, even if aided by appeals to divine grace. Milton's unforgiving view seems, as Halkett's analysis suggests, to be associated with two ancient systems that lived in uneasy conjunction with Christianity in the seventeenth century, Platonism and astrology.[33] We are all familiar with the popular idea that two people may be incompatible in marriage because their birth signs are incompatible. It is odd to find that Milton subscribed to a similar theory. Conjugal love, he argues, "requires not only moral, but natural causes to the making and maintayning; and may be warrantably excus'd to retire from the deception of what it justly seeks, and the ill requitals which unjustly it finds." That is, a man may divorce his wife, not on account of any moral failure on her part, or any lack of virtue, but simply because he discovers that they were not compatible to begin with in some vaguely astrological manner:

For Nature hath her *Zodiac* also, keepes her great annual circuit over human things as truly as the Sun and Planets in the firmament; hath her *anomalies*, hath here obliquities in ascensions and declinations, accesses and recesses, as blamelesly as they in heaven. And sitting in her planetary Orb with two rains in each hand, one strait, the other loos, tempers the cours of minds as well as bodies to several conjunctions and oppositions, freindly, or unfreindly aspects, con-senting oftest with reason, but never contrary.

This in the effect no man of meanest reach but daily sees.

(2:680–81)

Thus the incompatibility Milton is chiefly interested in is an incompatibility of "Nature," similar to that of the stars, and not a matter of morality. It is the discovery that two married people were naturally incompatible to begin with, but did not immediately realize it. God, it turns out, did not make them for each other. Therefore, as Halkett logically concludes, "Divorce was possible only between those who were initially unfit to marry each other" (p. 50).

Milton's contemporary John Selden, in *Uxor Ebraica*, offers some comments that suggest where Milton might have found such ideas:

Regarding the unrestricted practice of divorce and right of divorce among the most ancient pagans in the East, there is a famous passage in Claudius Ptolemy that derives from the astrological works of the Chaldeans and Egyptians and that deals with marriage and divorce. The words are as follows: "The cohabitation of spouses shall be permanent when it would happen that each of their natal luminaries were harmoniously configured ... They are dissolved on trivial grounds and are mutually separated when the ordained positions of the heavenly bodies should happen to be either in unconnected signs or in a diagonal or square to each other" ... The transmission among the ancients of a very liberal law and practice of dissolving matrimony, or divorce as they call it, can be especially seen in the most ancient art, such as it was, of astrology ... The attitude of eastern people thus becomes clear. From these people Julius Firmicus reports that "if Venus is in the house or decan of Mars, they will reject their wives or cruelly murder them."[34]

Milton's doctrine of natural incompatibility also resembles, as Halkett notes, "certain Platonic assumptions." It depends "on a theory of soul relationships, divorced from most considerations of bodily or religious 'fitness'. It seems to have reference to a preordained universal order whose rule extends into private relationships as deeply as into the social and cosmic framework" (pp. 56–57). As James Turner points out, Calvin himself unexpectedly invokes Plato when commenting on the Genesis text concerning the nature of the marriage bond: "in the conjunction of human beings, that sacred bond is especially conspicuous by which the husband and wife are combined in one body and one soul, as nature itself taught Plato."[35] But Calvin is here speaking of the Platonic concept of an inseparable unity through love of two persons, soul and body, not the quite distinct concept of the preordained fitness of one particular person for another. The first concept is readily compatible with Christianity. The second is compatible only with considerable forcing.

Many authorities wrote about the matter of marital incompatibility. But the topics discussed were, typically, more down-to-earth than Milton's arguments. According to Perkins, for example, the "fitness" of a couple for marriage depends on such "essential" signs as opposition of sex, absence of forbidden degrees of consanguinity, ability to perform intercourse, and freedom from a previous marriage contract. Perkins also mentions important – but nonessential – "accidental" signs of fitness, such as compatibility of religion, age, rank, and reputation.[36] The "essential" signs were traditionally recognized to be grounds for annulment, in both the Protestant and Catholic Churches. If, for example, a man should already be validly married, a second "marriage" would be simply invalid. The "accidental" signs, however, would not ordinarily be grounds for annulment or divorce in any Church. They are matters that a prudent couple are advised to consider carefully before marrying. After marrying is too late. Anyone who has read Chaucer or Boccaccio, for example, knows that to enter into a May-December marriage may be unwise, but such rashness is not itself grounds for divorce.

As one may easily see, Milton's theory of a mysterious "natural" incompatibility has no place among the agreed signs of marital fitness. Indeed, quite oddly for him, it is neither a practical impediment nor a religious one, but tenuous and rather mystical. Millions of readers today would disagree with such an evaluation, but that is because much has changed and we live in a post-Romantic age. Although Milton had little patience with vague superstition or with nebulous forms of paradox and transcendence, it is hard not to conclude that, when it came to conjugal love, he joined in company with Donne in helping to invent a new kind of intense, private, mutual relationship, which excluded the social and institutional worlds and which threatened to separate from Christianity and become a substitute religion. In Adam's case, it did for a while become such a substitute.

Ultimately, Milton solves the mystery of why there should be incompatible marriages by laying it to the will of God, which the couple before their marriage have neglected or misunderstood: "And when he forbids all unmatchable and unmingling natures to consort, doubtles by all due consequence, if they chance through misadventure to be miscoupl'd, he bids them part asunder, as persons whom God never joyn'd" (2:272). Indeed, such divisions of unlike from unlike have been a fundamental principle of nature since God's creation of the world, and, furthermore, they will continue to be so at the promised reformation of nature at the end of time: "as God and nature signifies and lectures to us not onely by those recited decrees, but ev'n by the first and last of all his visible works; when by his divorcing command the world first rose out of Chaos, nor can be renew'd again out of confusion but by the separating of unmeet consorts" (2:273). In a strange parody of Revelation, divorce is the alpha and omega of God's power over nature.[37] But if God has the ultimate authority over marriage and divorce, Milton is, nonetheless, willing to permit a kind of intermediation or intervention – of the planets, of mysterious unchangeable qualities of soul, of God's deputy Nature, of what amounts to a kind of "fate" or "necessity" – to come between God and the individuals concerned. This intermediation is unlike anything Milton permits in any other area of human experience.[38] And it intervenes on sacred marital grounds, where (against all tradition) he will not allow the Church to tread. Milton's natural incompatibility takes no account of Christian virtue, divine grace, or remediable free will. In short, it radically anticipates the Romantic and Modern habit of grounding ideal sexual love in a kind of mysterious "natural supernaturalism," which is beyond all hope of human understanding and beyond our ability to change or control.

A result of Milton's doctrine of incompatibility may be seen in *Samson Agonistes*, in the parting of Samson and Dalila. All of Dalila's pleas come to nothing. Samson is adamant; their separation is final. "No, no, of my condition take no care," he tells her, "It fits not; thou and I long since are twain" (lines 928–29). A little later, he dismisses her for the last time: "At distance I forgive thee, go with that" (line 954). This is a cold forgiveness. As I have argued elsewhere, Dalila's love is a parody of the real thing, but with tragic depth it movingly echoes the heroic strain of the great romances. As I have also argued, Samson cannot yet forgive her, because she does not, like Eve, yet truly repent.[39] But is she lost to all hope of future amendment? Can there be no further chance, as there will be for Samson? That is precisely the question Milton's contemporaries raised in opposition to his divorce tracts. Several critics have argued that Dalila, an evil wife, deserved a divorce.[40] But, in a moving argument, John Ulreich has accused Samson – and through him (though not intentionally) Milton – of a failure of charity.[41] Samson cannot forgive Dalila until she repents. But should he not give her further opportunity to change? Is this (like the case of the lost sinners in *Wuthering Heights*) her 491st transgression?[42] No doubt Dalila is an evil woman, but one fears that the real reason for their separation is Miltonic incompatability. Of course, Milton is tied to the denouement in Judges, so there can be no reconciliation; but Milton himself unbearably sharpens the dilemma by choosing to follow a minority tradition that makes Dalila Samson's wife.

The fissures that gape so widely in Milton's arguments in the divorce tracts are for the most part only implicit or potential in *Paradise Lost*. Yet some carryover may be discerned. Milton reasserts the Augustinian principle that lesser loves must be subordinated to greater, and therefore that Adam's love for Eve must be subordinated to his love for God. Such is the gist of Raphael's parting advice to Adam:

> Be strong, live happie, and love, but first of all
> Him whom to love is to obey, and keep
> His great command; take heed least Passion sway
> Thy Judgement to do aught, which else free Will
> Would not admit; thine and of all thy Sons
> The weal or woe in thee is plac't; beware.   (8.633–38)

Such too is the judgment of the Son after the Fall:

> Was shee thy God, that her thou didst obey
> Before his voice, or was shee made thy guide,
> Superior, or but equal, that to her
> Thou did'st resigne thy Manhood, and the Place
> Wherein God set thee above her...
>   Adorn'd
> Shee was indeed, and lovely to attract
> Thy Love, not thy Subjection.   (10.145–53)

Milton clearly endorses this principle of hierarchical priorities, not only in comments by the narrator but in his management of the action. Indeed, the immediate result of Adam's choosing to pursue his love for Eve before his love for God shows that it was no choice at all: he loses both. His later reconciliation with Eve is likewise impossible until they have first agreed jointly to reconcile themselves with God.

Yet no doubt Milton pitches the conflict between the two loves, human and divine, remarkably high. And in doing so he sets a new standard for idealized marital love. In *Paradise Lost*, neither the isolated human being nor the married couple together can be absolute, can escape contingency. Yet the immeasurably appealing relationship between Adam and Eve comes nearly as close to claiming absoluteness for married love, despite the narrator's disclaimers, as Satan does to claiming it for individual autonomy. Who can doubt that Adam and Eve would have stood, had they stayed together? Separately, each is free, "sufficient to have stood" (3.99), but vulnerable. Together, they become something "abler," although they are also so intensely and dynamically interactive that they seem always to be at risk.[43] No normalizing, institutionalized stability, of Church, society, or family, is available to aid them.

Of course – the reader may protest – Adam and Eve naturally conduct their married life without reliance on the Church or on other socializing institutions. No such institutions, no such wider society or extended family, no children, yet exist in Eden. Just so. Milton has chosen the ideal couple to portray the ideal Miltonic marriage: isolated, self-sufficient, alone with their God. A reader sufficiently trained in theology to be aware of the *difference* between Adam and Eve and ourselves will be cautious. Lewis, in *A Preface to Paradise Lost* and again in his revision of the temptation story in *Perelandra*, indicates how wide and perilous the distance is between the unfallen couple and us as fallen readers. So too does Fiore, though with more application of theology and less of fictive imagination.[44] But the temptation before us as readers is to forget or ignore these barriers – and, of course, we often have, since the eighteenth century and even before. With disregard for fine distinctions, Adam and Eve have been welcomed into the domestic relations of love in the eighteenth century, into the Romantic elevation of love as religion in the nineteenth century, and into the construction of Freudianism and the shaping of feminism in our own century.[45] Even "no-fault" divorce and the doctrine of sexual "privacy" as put forward by the Supreme Court in Griswold and Roe v. Wade owes something indirectly to Milton's views.[46]

After all, how can we resist Milton's attractive ideals and images? Not even the skeptical Voltaire chose to resist them. In Adam's description to Raphael of his own marriage, we hear Milton's voice speaking through Adam's, inviting our fallen participation in the unfallen perfection of Adam and Eve, soliciting too our participation in Adam's praise of

> those graceful acts,
> Those thousand decencies that daily flow
> From all her words and actions mixt with Love
> And sweet compliance, which declare unfeign'd
> Union of Mind, or in us both one Soule;
> *Harmonie to behold in wedded pair*
> *More grateful then harmonious sound to the eare.*
>
> (8.600–06; italics added)

Who might the imagined being be, whom Adam, suddenly becoming an external witness to his own marriage, invites to "behold" the "harmonie ... in wedded pair"? Who but Milton, together with his lucky readers? Adam and Eve are not just one, uniquely unfallen, harmonious pair; they are the representative ideal, the attractive model, of all harmonious pairs.

Even after their fall and reconciliation, Adam and Eve are a model couple, as closely united with each other as they are cut off and isolated from other companionship. "[B]ut now lead on," Eve tells Adam, toward the close of the poem:

> In mee is no delay; with thee to goe,
> Is to stay here; without thee here to stay,
> Is to go hence unwilling; thou to mee
> Art *all things under Heav'n*, all places thou,
> Who for my wilful crime art banisht hence.
>
> (12.615–19; italics added)

From now on, each member of the pair – and all of their descendents – must relinquish the pleasures of living in the lost paradisal garden for the "paradise within" them – nonetheless "happier farr" (12.587). As a couple, they must also relinquish their marriage bower, that central mystery of the garden – a paradise within a paradise – for a renovated paradise of mutual comfort and love within marriage, which has no fixed place and relies on nothing under heaven for support. No other comfort to approach this one may be looked for in this world.

Milton, never a simple man, was at times an urbane poet of friendship and community.[47] He found ways around his hatred of communal forms. We recall his poems and letters to Diodati, his sonnets to Lawrence and Skinner, and other tokens of a remarkable ability to make and sustain friendships. But (Diodati excepted) most of that urbanity pales beside the zealous exclusivity of his love for God and the intensity of his feelings about conjugal love. As the fallen and reconciled Adam and Eve move into history and the wide wilderness of Eden, the only truly vital solace they may expect from isolation is from each other. And so we see them last, alone together:

> They hand in hand with wandring steps and slow
> Through *Eden* took thir solitarie way.   (12.649–50)

More intensely and continually than the love of God, love in marriage is Milton's cure in *Paradise Lost* for the perils and sorrows of loneliness.

Indeed, married love is the only form of human love the mature Milton is really interested in. In *Paradise Lost*, the courtly love of the heroic romances is restricted to a parodic role in the turbulent – sometimes even melodramatic – interval between Eve's Fall and her reconciliation with Adam.[48] Ever-desirous Petrarchan love – now diminished to little better than a comical cousin of incestuous narcissism – is mocked by Satanic posturing in the temptation of Eve and reduced to a scornful subordinate clause in the marriage hymn: "Or Serenate, which the starv'd Lover sings / To his proud fair, best quitted with disdain" (4.769–70). Kerrigan and Braden build a strong case to the effect that Milton resolved, or killed, the Petrarchan tradition.[49] As I have argued, however, it might be preferable to say that he gave it a final, decisive blow, at the end of a longer struggle that began with Sidney. He did so, in *Paradise Lost*, by almost ignoring it; by putting both courtly and Petrarchan love entirely in the shade of the loving relationship between Adam and Eve. In some of the youthful poems, which I have not considered here, courtly love and Petrarchism play a much larger part. Milton had to prove all things for himself and liked to slay his own dragons. In his capacious personal development as a poet, he recapitulates the literary tradition, just as ontogeny once was thought to recapitulate philogeny. But we have been through the story once, from Sidney to Carew, and there is no need for us to recapitulate it yet again. When Milton had reached maturity, Petrarchism was already effectively dead. His great accomplishment was to put in its place a love that still looks far more attractive to us, and far more "natural," because it has grown like a substitute Petrarchism for our time. It may well prove in the end to be more obsessive, longer-lasting, more capable of variation and mutation, than its predecessor. For thus (to simplify crudely) it gives us, as bourgeois romantics in an alienated modern world, the lasting satisfactions for which we seek, much as Petrarchism did for humanist aristocrats. If it fails, we shall surely miss it.

For Milton, mutual conjugal love performs all of the offices traditionally expected of the Church, commonwealth, parish, congregation, local community, or extended family. The only normative influence he allows over it is the direct spiritual intervention of God in the hearts of the married couple. It is a shelter from the working world, a cure for alienation. In *Paradise Lost*, as in the *Songs and Sonets*, expectations are almost infinite. Here, too, marriage is either paradise or paradise lost, and its first minute after noon is night. Milton insists that married love ultimately depends on the love of God – in the case of Adam and Eve, as they wander into exile, on "Providence thir guide" (12.647). Nevertheless it was easy, with the increasing secularization of the general culture, for Milton's readers to omit that fundamental – yet by him radically isolated – axiom. Then there was no stable foundation at all. Disappointed – as how could such an idealized love not often fail to be, under so much weight of expectation, incapacity to reform the partners' fixed "natures," and lack of earthly external support – it finds its resolution in dreaming, in despair, and in divorce. Just as Milton's Satan spawned (or gave "a local habitation and a name" to) a century and more of Romantic individualism – of Blakean, Shelleyan, and Byronic heroism – Milton's portrayal of ideal marriage produced an equivalent outpouring of fascination for the infinite mysteries, the intense pleasures, and the affectionate consolations of mutual, private conjugal love. No one, not even Shakespeare or Goethe, has had more influence on love in the modern world.

Conclusion

If I have spent more time in this book on the problems of love than on its glories, that may be partly owing to my focus on the ways that cultural change and responding psychological adjustments exert pressure on us. Change is difficult. But an additional reason may be that, in tracing shifts in attitudes and assumptions about love as revealed in a selection of poems spanning a century of transformation, I have sometimes deliberately leaned toward sympathy with earlier rather than later attitudes. We ourselves are the (largely unconscious) products of many of the changes I have discussed, so that our natural bias is toward the present rather than the past. That is more true now than ever, as political deconstruction and the hermeneutics of suspicion have largely replaced the nostalgic admiration for past customs and practices that characterized many critics of an earlier generation.

As I noted in the introduction, readers are inevitably free to prefer their present viewpoints to those of anyone in the past – and, of course, they are overwhelmingly likely to do so. So I have chosen sometimes to swim against the tide of post-modernist culture and criticism. That is, I have sometimes remarked on what is valuable in assumptions we have lost sight of as our attitudes toward love have changed, as well as on – what will be more obvious to most readers today – what we may have gained by those changes. If, for example, courtly attitudes toward love now seem quaint and foreign to us, so too romantic, modern, and postmodern attitudes may – indeed surely will – seem equally strange, each in its turn, to the perceptions of succeeding generations. Nevertheless, I hope that this book also recognizes and celebrates the remarkable energies of the poetry I have discussed: the splendors and the miseries of love, the fierce desires, the frustrated searchings, the fiery or tender satisfactions, and (above all) the creative responses to cultural stress. Such powerful pleasures and bewilderments alike disclose the nature of man as he was perceived to be at that time: a sinfully paradoxical creature, but capable of loving heroically and of responding passionately to salvation.

Concerning the divine love of the Holy Spirit, Sir Thomas Browne remarks:

This is that gentle heate that brooded on the waters, and in six dayes hatched the world; this is that irradiation that dispells the mists of Hell, the clouds of horrour, feare, sorrow, despaire; and preserves the region of the mind in serenity: whosoever feels not the warme gale and gentle ventilation of this Spirit, (though I feele his pulse) I dare not say he lives; for truely without this, to mee there is no heat under the Tropick; nor any light, though I dwelt in the body of the Sunne.[1]

But even divine love may, as we have seen, be a dividing sword as well as a "warme gale." In Milton, to misappropriate his own phrases from *Areopagitica* (2:514), love and divorce are "as two twins cleaving together," in this case not just "from out the rinde of one apple tasted" at the Fall, but from the very moment of creation, when God first began bringing order out of chaos by separating them.

Secular love, too, came in a bewildering multiplicity of forms. "'Tis a happy state this indeed, when the fountain is blessed," says Robert Burton, in his disquisition on love-melancholy:

But this love of ours is immoderate, inordinate, and not to be comprehended in any bounds. It will not contain itself within the union of marriage, or apply to one object, but is a wandering, extravagant, a domineering, a boundless, an irrefragable, a destructive passion ... No cord or cable can so forcibly draw, or hold so fast, as love can do with a twined thread. The scorching beams under the equinoctial, or extremity of cold within the circle Arctic, where the very seas are frozen, cold or torrid zone cannot avoid or expel this heat, fury, and rage of mortal men.[2]

One cannot help but observe that love has its constant problems in any age. Yet we would be nothing without it.

Indeed perhaps we *are* somewhat diminished, since, when it comes to love, by all extant signs the nineteenth century has been the only one since the end of the Middle Ages to challenge the inventiveness and enthusiasm of the period we are studying. From the writing of *Astrophil and Stella* to the publication of *Paradise Lost* was a time of great, as well as influential, love poetry. At certain times, people seem to be suffused with zealous and extravagant loves of all kinds, to an extent that might make a prudent man both envious and fearful. But as for us, we live mostly among the remnants of earlier discoveries about love. We are the diminished heirs of our immoderate predecessors, wondering if we can still make use of their old furnishings. Our claim to analyze love is often stronger than our ability to express or to live it. In our serious inquiries, we prefer to talk about sexuality and desire. We undertake gender studies. We anatomize power relationships. We trace the origins of pornography. In our literature – as well as in our popular culture – we have exchanged Sir Philip Sidney's passionate examinations of desire and guilt for the cynical, ever-dwindling expectations that typically characterize the Postmodernist representation of sexual relationships. In short, for all our innovations, the past may still have something to teach us.

Some recent studies of marriage and family, which have claimed to show that loving, companionate marriage was unknown before the seventeenth century, are not wholly persuasive to anyone who has read the Bible, the classics, and history. The faithful, loving couple is an ageless phenomenon, as Burton again reminds us:

As Seneca lived with his Paulina, Abraham and Sarah, Orpheus and Eurydice, Arria and Paetus, Artemisia and Mausolus, Rubenius Celer, that would needs have it engraven on his tomb, he had led his life with Ennea, his dear wife, forty-three years eight months, and never fell out. There is no pleasure in this world comparable to it, 'tis *summum mortalitatis bonum* [the highest good of humanity], *hominum divumque voluptas, Alma Venus* [the delight of men and gods, bountiful Venus]; *latet enim in muliere aliquid majus potentiusque omnibus aliis humanis voluptatibus*, as one holds, there's something in a woman beyond all human delight; a magnetic virtue, a charming quality, an occult and powerful motive. The husband rules her as head, but she again commands his heart, he is her servant, she his only joy and content: no happiness is like unto it, no love so great as this of man and wife, no such comfort as *placens uxor*, a sweet wife ... when they love at last as fresh as they did at first, *caraque caro consenescit conjugi*, [still dear companions as the years go on], as Homer brings Paris kissing Helen, after they had been married ten years, protesting withal that he loved her as dear as he did the first hour that he was betrothed.[3]

Burton's mixture of mythical and historical couples may seem odd to us, and many authorities in his day would have demurred at his inclusion of Helen and Paris, whose destructive love brought down Troy. But these were some of the famous exemplars who were admired by the ancients and by most succeeding ages. We are inclined these days to fix our eyes on the processes of cultural change and to deny any continuity in human feelings; but the parameters of viable change in so central a matter as love are not totally boundless. What Donne and Milton did, then, was not to invent companionate marriage but to give it a fresh set of perceptual underpinnings, those we have been discussing. They established the little world of privacy and of magical transcendence, and they separated married love from its classical connections with civic virtue and from its Christian connections with the Church, the local community, and society, and even (sometimes) from those with God.

With the dimensions of their accomplishment thus qualified, to what extent might it yet be said that poets from Sidney to Milton actually "reinvented" love and (in Carew's phrase) passed their "fresh inventions" on to aftertimes? Or to what extent were they rather just victims or "products" of impersonal historical forces? As I have said in the introduction, I prefer not to attempt a definitive answer to this question, when our greatest cultural historians have yet to agree on the ground-rules. But I think there is ample evidence to support the assumption that influence flows two ways. It is clear, at least, that Milton has been an overwhelming presence, directly and indirectly, even down into the Age of Television. The chief Modern poets, such as Pound and Eliot, found him still a formidable force to deal with – although, as Harold Bloom has often shown, he had already been subjected to centuries of borrowing, imitation, revision, theft, and all the various forms of creative misreading and filial struggle – not to mention the enfeebling efforts of straightforward, pious veneration. Still, Pound and the early Eliot thought that they should kill Milton again, should perform the archetypal modernist ritual of slaying the father. But so far he has proved unkillable. He remains with us, as pervasive as ever.

We continue to admire Sidney, who stands at the threshold of the early modern transformation of love. We are more likely to pity his tale of Astrophil, however, than to imitate his frustrated courtly Petrarchan mode of loving. Sidney seems modern – as he is also perennial – chiefly as the embodiment of unquenchable desire. We share his desire, even though we no longer suffer his time's peculiar way of manifesting it. The part played by a poet like Donne, who preceded Milton in the momentous invention of private mutual love, is more equivocal. He was a major poet, but not of Milton's overwhelming force and stature. Certainly he affected many writers and intellectuals in the earlier part of our century, and they in turn affected many readers. For instance, Donne taught Dorothy Sayers' Harriet Vane and Lord Peter Wimsey how to love. He has taught several generations of college faculty and their students how to love. But Donne worked on posterity through fewer channels than Milton. Like Shakespeare, Milton became almost a force of nature, influencing us as much through the broad movements of culture and through the formation of laws and of public institutions, as he does in our private imaginations when we sit and read *Paradise Lost*. Thus what begins as a strong individual affecting culture may in time become an aspect of culture affecting individuals, in a never-ending process of change and transformation.

It may be, of course, that the youthful Milton himself learned something vital from Donne, a poet whom he was certain to have read, although publicly he almost ignored him. Both poets, although greatly different in most other ways, shared some of the essential – and for their times unusual – attitudes that have come to define Romantic and Modern love. As I have argued, they shared an intensely spiritual yet peculiarly non-Christian twist precisely at the mystifying nodal point where their versions of mutual love aspire most strongly toward the ideal, the infinite, the transcendental. The growth of natural supernaturalism, which unfolded historically as a long-wave phenomenon of two centuries and more, may already be found, *in germine*, at the heart of their visions of love. In both cases – although for very different reasons – these poet-lovers were in retreat from society, from the demands of institutional conformity, and from the strains of working and of ambitiously striving in the world. While Donne most often looked with longing toward the past, Milton hoped to bring on the future. Donne was conservative, Milton radical. Donne put religion aside while he loved, or reduced it to a metaphor; Milton fiercely if inconsistently invoked his God to support his views. Yet, in responding to the evolving psychosocial forces of their times, each of them helped crucially to re-form the future of love.

Carew found an alternative solution to some of the same problems Donne and Milton confronted, a solution that may be more comfortable than Donne's to Postmodernists. He invented a kind of love that does not try to set up barriers against society or to enclose itself within magical *limina*, but that survives in contrary fashion by immersing itself in society, like an eddy in a stream. Donne and Milton sought privacy by their resistance to society, by divorcing love from all impediments, and even by calling for revolution; Carew sought it through constant, skillful manipulations and negotiations in the business of daily life. While Donne and Milton made for themselves private retreats, little worlds of faithful mutual love, shelters to console their loneliness and alienation, Carew devised an appearance of aristocratic integrity that paradoxically accommodated itself to the crass ways of a new world. He became a flexible and opportunistic client of increasingly cynical patrons, in a society beginning to base its ethics on the marketplace. Thus he also solved problems of aristocratic love and service that destroyed both Ralegh and Sidney.

For Carew, privacy is first an attribute of individuality. The pleasures of mutual love arise from the consensual agreement of two skilled, worldly, nearly autonomous individuals. The libertinism that fascinated but sickened Donne in the *Elegies* gained new legitimation from Carew's revised view of social relationships. Just as Donne anticipates Descartes, Carew anticipates Adam Smith. Responding to many of the same intensifying cultural pressures as his fellow poets, Carew chose a materialist solution and learned how to live with the new condition of the world. In their different ways, Donne and Milton chose a new form of idealism. But Donne's was a fragile and desperate solution, which he later abandoned, although that has not discouraged many since from repeating the experiment. Milton's version of marital love, despite its renowned tenderness and "softness," was, to the contrary, ruthlessly resolute, as strong as steel, divinely sanctioned.

Even among these chief representatives of England's major age of religious poetry, we witness a diminishment or a marginalization of religion. Donne neglected his God to court his mistresses; then in his middle years, when he turned to writing his *Holy Sonnets* and hymns, he found that his God was neglecting him. In his poems, Donne's love and Christ's are ever at cross-purposes. Herbert vowed to convert sinful secular love into sacred love, but at the point of consummation turned away, preferring the trusting love of a child. This is not to say that Herbert prudishly censored himself, for the voice of his love always reverberates with moving authenticity. Still he left to his successors and to English hymn writers a legacy of unsexed devotion, which could express its love only in limited ways. Crashaw was more successful than either Donne or Herbert in finding a way to love God with a sense of fulfillment and of joyful return. His "feminist" devotion may now seem as admirable as it once seemed perverse. But in his own day he was forced into exile and had to marginalize himself from his native English culture in order to pursue his goal of sacred love. Perhaps he will always stand somewhat apart from the English tradition; if so, the loss is mutual.

How we think about love, marriage, and divorce inevitably

depends on our situations and above all on our ultimate allegiances – which, in the seventeenth century, usually manifested themselves as the love of God. The churchless and potentially violent love of God that underlies *Paradise Lost*, even though it is usually admirably ameliorated in Milton's own poetic practice, was the form of sacred love that best anticipated the direction modern history would take: toward the divorce of religious love from its ancient roots in corporate worship and liturgy into private devotion, and at the same time toward novel, sometimes unrecognizably mutated, secular ideologies and political passions. Had he not been so centrally involved in the transformation of love, both human and divine, Milton would not have been the major poet that he was. Had he not been so great a poet, he could never have had the enormous influence he has had on the modern world. In the seventeenth century, thousands of zealots burned with a fierce and sometimes murderous zeal. Most of them are now forgotten. Only Milton could transform that zeal into poetry which we still read today with admiration, with real pleasure, and with only an initial stumble of anachronism.

Some years ago, a non-denominational minister rented the house next to ours. One day, while I was pruning some bushes outside my house, he came running across the lawn, crying out in a loud voice much like Christian fleeing from the City of Destruction: "It was Milton who made Christianity and the world what they are today!" I did not know him well and have not seen him since. I imagine that he must have heard I was a Miltonist (that is, a teacher of Milton, not a divorcer) and that he held me partly responsible for the sorry state of things. I don't even know whether he thought Milton too radical or not radical enough. I wish I had asked him: for now I think that, whatever he meant, he may have been right.

But let us end this book with a return to mutual love, which Milton portrays for us with all its transporting pleasures and hidden dangers:

> Here in close recess
> With Flowers, Garlands, and sweet-smelling Herbs
> Espoused *Eve* deckt first her nuptial Bed,

> And heav'nly Quires the Hymenaean sung,
> What day the genial Angel to our Sire
> Brought her in naked beauty more adorn'd,
> More lovely then *Pandora*, whom the Gods
> Endowd with all thir gifts, and O too like
> In sad event, when to the unwiser Son
> Of *Japhet* brought by *Hermes*, she ensnar'd
> Mankind with her faire looks, to be aveng'd
> On him who had stole *Joves* authentic fire.   (4.708–19)

Few poets have understood better than Milton the perils of giving and receiving love in such an intensely private and mutually passionate conjugal relationship. Few have better understood that, regardless of these inherent dangers, such a love and its attendant sexuality can only with greater loss be disparaged or refused – "Defaming as impure what God declares / Pure" (4.746–47).

All loving human relationships, Milton argues, flow from this one "true source" (4.750). In it "all the Charities / Of Father, Son, and Brother first were known" (4.756–57). To view marriage as the foundation stone of society and of the state was, of course, a commonplace. Thomas Becon puts the case even more sweepingly: "Out of it as oute of a moste riche and golden floud all other orders and degrees of life issue and flow forth: yea as a moste fruteful mother bringeth it forth such as may worthely lyve ... without whom ... whole Realmes, whole king-domes, whole Common weales fal to ruine."[4] Some feminists object to Milton's seemingly exclusionary reference to "Father, Son, and Brother," implicitly omitting mother, daughter, and sister from the network of society. I am inclined to exculpate him on this point, since what he argues here is not male supremacy but rather the priority and superiority of married love to all other bonds within society – even those bonds that men might regard as most dignified and important.

Still, the practical, real-world connections between marriage and the state are far less obvious in Milton than they are in Becon or in most other writers of his time. Unlike Becon, Milton would not much have minded if "whole Realmes, whole kingdomes, whole Common weales" fell into ruin. If married love had for Milton an essential civilizing power, that power was enacted in isolation. It did not spread out through intermediary institutions and communal groups, which might pragmatically have bridged the gap between individual couples and society as a whole. As Raphael tells Adam, his love for Eve is, or should be, "the scale / By which to heav'nly Love thou maist ascend" (8.591–92). That is, love and marriage give each individual soul – or individual couple – a means to raise itself by an inner Platonic process, even a mystical process, much as the Holy Spirit lifts individual souls – not whole nations, churches, or congregations – toward heaven.

For Milton everything rests on marriage. Marriage is necessarily so intense as to be dangerous. It is potentially as disruptive as it is civilizing. Even the perfect woman, Eve, is vulnerable to becoming Adam's Pandora or Proserpina. But still later she will reconcile with Adam, to realize her more positive potential, which is to become our first Mary and Ruth. She will also become the "Mother of Mankind" (5.388) and (most important to Milton) the mother of "that destind Seed," who will "achieve / Mankinds deliverance" (12.233–35) and reestablish – largely through the precise means of human love and marriage – "a paradise within thee, happier farr" (12.587).

Notes

1 All biblical quotations are from the Authorized Version. Although his interests are quite different from mine, a similar view of the underlying importance of Genesis is put forward by James Grantham Turner, *One Flesh: Paradisal Marriage and Sexual Relations in the Age of Milton* (Oxford: Clarendon Press, 1987).

2 Thomas S. Kuhn, *The Structure of Scientific Revolutions*, 2nd edition (University of Chicago Press, 1970).

3 Useful entry into the subject of women writers in the Renaissance is provided by "Recent Studies in Women Writers of Tudor England," compiled by Elizabeth H. Hageman and Josephine A. Roberts, *English Literary Renaissance* 14 (1984): 409–39; "Recent Studies in Women Writers of the Seventeenth Century (1604–1674)," compiled by Elizabeth H. Hageman *ELR* 18 (1988): 138–67; essays excerpted from these issues are reprinted in *ELR: Women in the Renaissance*, ed. Kirby Farrell, Elizabeth H. Hageman, and Arthur Kinney (Amherst, University of Massachusetts Press, 1990). See also Barbara Kiefer Lewalski, "Writing Women and Reading the Renaissance," *Renaissance Quarterly* 44 (1991): 792–821. The most significant woman writer of lyric love poetry may have been Mary Wroth. Lewalski cites a forthcoming article (which I have not seen) by Nona Fienberg, "Mary Wroth and the Invention of Female Poetic Subjectivity," in *Reading Mary Wroth: Representing Alternatives in Early Modern England*, ed. Naomi Miller and Gary Waller (Nashville: University of Tennessee Press, 1992), forthcoming.

4 As I have found in negotiating the language of articles with the copyeditors at *PMLA*, gender style is quickly reduced to individual instances. If, for example, I say "poet…he," it is not because I think all poets are men (untrue even in the male-dominated seventeenth century) but because at that point I am talking about

male love poets. If I say "the true Church was not seen among men for a thousand years," I do so because I am representing the voice of a seventeenth-century writer whose views are not mine – with regard to women *or* the Church.

5 See especially *The Allegory of Love* (London: Oxford University Press, 1936); also *Studies in Medieval and Renaissance Literature* (Cambridge University Press, 1966); and *Spenser's Images of Life*, ed. Alastair Fowler (Cambridge University Press, 1967).

6 In addition to Lewis, see especially Thomas P. Roche, *The Kindly Flame* (Princeton University Press, 1964); and Carol V. Kaske, "Spenser's *Amoretti* and *Epithalamion* of 1595: Structure, Genre, and Numerology," *English Literary Renaissance* 8 (1978): 271–95; but nearly every study of Spenser has something useful to say about love.

7 See Lewis, again; also C. L. Barber, *Shakespeare's Festive Comedy* (Princeton University Press, 1959); Northrop Frye, *Anatomy of Criticism* (Princeton University Press, 1957); Barbara L. Parker, *A Precious Seeing: Love and Reason in Shakespeare's Plays* (New York University Press, 1987); and innumerable studies of other facets of love in Shakespeare – on fathers and daughters, fear of replacement by one's progeny, possible homosexuality in the sonnets, and so forth.

8 Foucault and Stone are the social historians best known to literary critics working in the Renaissance and seventeenth century, but their views are not undisputed among other historians. For some sense of the different views of such social historians as E. P. Thompson, Alan Macfarlane, Susan Amussen, Ralph Houlbrooke, Martin Ingram, Linda Pollock, and Jim Sharpe, see David Cressy, "Foucault, Stone, Shakespeare and Social History," *English Literary Renaissance* 21 (1991): 121–33.

9 Lauro Martines, *Society and History in English Renaissance Verse* (London: Basil Blackwell, 1985), p. 18. Indeed, as Christopher N. L. Brooke eloquently argues in *The Medieval Idea of Marriage* (Oxford University Press, 1989), pp. 157–59, 174–76, historical documents and "facts" must be studied with as much care and consideration for their "diplomatic" (that is, their historical circumstances, cultural context, presumed purpose and audience, etc.) as we bring to poems.

10 These notions are now so prevalent as to be almost commonplaces; but for a variety of notable approaches see, *inter alia*, the works of Fredric Jameson, Stephen Greenblatt, Richard Helgerson, Stanley Fish, Norman Holland, Jonathan Culler.

11 From "No Is the Father of Yes," in Samuel Hazo, *Nightwords*: 50

Poems (Riverdale-on-Hudson, NY: Sheep Meadow Press, 1989), p. 83; quoted with the kind permission of Samuel Hazo.

12 Owen Barfield, *Saving the Appearances: A Study in Idolatry* (London: Faber & Faber, 1957). This book proposes a final (Anthroposophist) thesis few readers will accept; but it usefully and definitively, it seems to me, undermines the nineteenth-century "materialist" assumptions on which so many current "historicist" readings are based, by an appeal to recent science – which has only gone much further in directions Barfield noted thirty years ago. Foucault has proposed a similar view of the contingently objective nature of "things," arguing from another (in my view more gnomic and therefore less useful) set of assumptions.

1 SIR PHILIP SIDNEY: "HUGE DESYRE"

1 As Margaret W. Ferguson points out in *The Trials of Desire: Renaissance Defences of Poetry* (New Haven: Yale University Press, 1983), p. 137: "In all of these works [*The Lady of May, Astrophil and Stella*, and *The Old* and *New Arcadia*], Sidney portrays young male heroes who seek to justify their desires for amorous or political action of a type not allowed by social conventions." This was also, of course, the pattern of Sidney's own life. I take desire, or Freudian *eros*, to be the major subtext of Ferguson's chapter on Sidney, but in the event she says little specifically about it.

2 David Kalstone, *Sidney's Poetry: Contexts and Interpretations* (Cambridge, MA: Harvard University Press, 1965), p. 106. A. C. Hamilton writes: "In his major sonnet sequence, Sidney treats a love that may be neither satisfied nor rejected. At the end ... he still seeks his 'only light' in her while he remains hopelessly bound in the 'dark furnace' of unsatisfied desire" (*Sir Philip Sidney: A Study of His Life and Works* [Cambridge University Press, 1977], p. 79). Likewise Richard C. McCoy writes: "Sidney is distinctive ... in his emphasis on the troubling aspects of sexual desire" (*Sir Philip Sidney: Rebellion in Arcadia* [New Brunswick: Rutgers University Press, 1979], p. 71). Dorothy Connell views love in Sidney more optimistically (*Sir Philip Sidney: The Maker's Mind* [Oxford: Clarendon Press, 1977], especially pp. 9–33), as does Neil L. Rudenstine (*Sidney's Poetic Development* [Cambridge, MA: Harvard University Press, 1979], especially pp. 222–38).

3 Hamilton, *Sir Philip Sidney*, pp. 104–05.

4 According to William A. Ringler, Jr., "Thou blind man's marke" and "Leave me ô Love," attached to *Astrophil and Stella* by most previous editors, were actually written earlier – and thus the classic

retraction preceded the sequence seemingly most in need of one. See *The Poems of Sir Philip Sidney*, ed. Ringler (Oxford: Clarendon Press, 1962), pp. 423–24. All quotations from Sidney's poems are from this edition. The deathbed confession is reported in an anonymous manuscript, *The Manner of Sir Philip Sidney's Death*, discovered and transcribed by Jean Robertson in "Sir Philip Sidney and Lady Penelope Rich," *Review of English Studies* 15 (1964): 296–97, and reprinted in *Miscellaneous Prose of Sir Philip Sidney*, ed. Katherine Duncan-Jones and Jan van Dorsten (Oxford: Clarendon Press, 1973), pp. 161–71.

5 Whether or how convincingly Petrarch recants or transcends his love of Laura in the *Rime* (as opposed to the *Secretum*) is a matter for interpretation and emphasis. His myriad followers have assuredly kept the principal focus on desire. On Sidney's Petrarchism, which she sees as more revisionary than I do, see Marion Campbell, "Unending Desire: Sidney's Reinvention of Petrarchan Form in *Astrophil and Stella*," in *Sir Philip Sidney and the Interpretation of Renaissance Culture: The Poet in His Time and Ours: A Collection of Critical and Scholarly Essays*, ed. Gary F. Waller and Michael D. Moore (London: Croom Helm, 1984), pp. 84–94.

6 On the growth of the Sidney myth from his life see, *inter alia*, F. J. Levy, "Philip Sidney Reconsidered," *English Literary Renaissance* 2 (1972): 5–18; Louis Adrian Montrose, "Celebration and Insinuation: Sir Philip Sidney and the Motives of Elizabethan Courtship," *Renaissance Drama* 8 (1977): 3–35; Alan Hager, "The Exemplary Mirage: Fabrication of Sir Philip Sidney's Biographical Image and the Sidney Reader," *ELH* 48 (1981): 1–16.

7 As Raphael Falco explains in his forthcoming book, *The Conceived Presence: Literary Genealogy in Renaissance England*, succeeding poets did much retroactively to invent the heroic figure of Sidney as their poetic precursor, as the noble founder of their line, in order to validate their own writings.

8 Inseparable from this question are questions of how to relate Sidney's moral commitment to the Protestant cause and the exemplary theory so strongly urged in his *Defence of Poetry* to his practice in the *Arcadia* and in *Astrophil and Stella*. On these matters see, for example, Andrew D. Weiner, *Sir Philip Sidney and the Poetics of Protestantism: A Study of Contexts* (Minneapolis: University of Minnesota Press, 1978). Among studies stressing the separation of Sidney and Astrophil largely on moral grounds, see Ann Romayne Howe, "*Astrophil and Stella*: 'Why and How,'" *Studies in Philology* 61 (1964): 150–69; Alan Sinfield, "Astrophil's Self-Deception,"

Essays in Criticism 28 (1978): 1–18; Jean Robertson, "Sir Philip Sidney and Lady Penelope Rich."

9 James J. Scanlon, "Sidney's *Astrophil and Stella*: 'See what it is to Love' Sensually!" *Studies in English Literature* 16 (1976): 65–74. The *fons et origo* of such interpretations is D. W. Robertson, Jr., *A Preface to Chaucer* (Princeton University Press, 1962); and see Robertson, "The Concept of Courtly Love as an Impediment to the Understanding of Medieval Texts," in *The Meaning of Courtly Love*, ed. F. X. Newman (Albany: State University of New York Press, 1968), pp. 1–18. For a survey of earlier opinion on the Sidney-Astrophil problem, see J. G. Nichols, *The Poetry of Sir Philip Sidney* (New York: Barnes & Noble, 1974, especially pp. 52–79.

10 Alan Sinfield, "Sidney and Astrophil," *Studies in English Literature* 20 (1980): 25–41; 27. This is only one point in a subtle and complex essay, which stresses (as I do here) both sides of the case but finally comes down on the Protestant-moralist side. See also Sinfield's "Sexual Puns in *Astrophil and Stella*," *Essays in Criticism* 24 (1974): 341–55.

11 Sinfield, p. 40. One could also read *Astrophil and Stella* along lines made familiar by Stanley Fish's *Surprised by Sin* (New York: Macmillan, 1967). But it is hard to find an incremental education of the reader in the sequence, or a weaning from false passions to self-control. If anything, our sympathy for Astrophil grows with our awareness that he is destroying himself.

12 Arthur F. Marotti, *John Donne, Coterie Poet* (Madison: University of Wisconsin Press, 1986).

13 According to the *O. E. D.*, "confusion" meant primarily "Discomforture, overthrow, ruin, destruction, perdition." It first began to move toward its present meaning in the sixteenth century. Sigmund Freud, "The Relation of the Poet to Day-Dreaming" (1908) in *On Creativity and the Unconscious* (New York: Harper & Row, 1958), pp. 44–54. "If phantasies become over-luxuriant and over-powerful, the necessary conditions of an outbreak of neurosis or psychosis are constituted" (p. 49). The writer "softens the egotistical character of the day-dream by changes and disguises" and "bribes us by the offer of a purely formal, that is, aesthetic, pleasure in the presentation of his phantasies" (p. 54). Freud's followers have, of course, extended these tentative observations.

14 Sidney's rhetorical technique here also closely resembles that of the *Defence*, where he puts poetry in a better light by mocking the "sullen gravity" and rude manners of two unattractive straw men whom he puts forward to represent literalistic history and moralizing philosophy (see Ferguson, *Trials of Desire*, p. 142).

15 *Miscellaneous Prose*, p. 169.

16 See *A Concordance to the Poems of Sir Philip Sidney*, compiled by Herbert S. Donow (Ithaca: Cornell University Press, 1975), s.v. "desire."

17 See, for example, sonnet 143, which uses infant imagery similar to Sidney's, or sonnet 147.

18 Henry Howard, Earl of Surrey, *Poems*, ed. Emrys Jones (Oxford: Clarendon Press, 1964), pp. 1–2.

19 *Collected Poems of Sir Thomas Wyatt*, ed. Kenneth Muir (Cambridge, MA: Harvard University Press, 1950), p. 4.

20 Not even the noblest Elizabethans were immune from such pursuits; see Richard C. McCoy, *The Rites of Knighthood: The Literature and Politics of Elizabethan Chivalry* (Berkeley: University of California Press, 1989). In an earlier period, Henry VIII beheaded Surrey for what he judged an impermissible addition to his coat of arms.

21 Here we are talking about mindsets or inward habits more than legal requirements. A feudal superior to whom an oath has been sworn may dissolve it, but even then a follower may feel honor bound. The obligation has been internalized, where it can no longer be undone. The image Wyatt and Surrey use – of abandoning a superior in battle – calls to mind many instances, outwardly futile but always spoken of admiringly, when followers refuse to abandon a defeated lord even at his urging. The conflicting obligations of honor and of Christian virtue are, of course, another major preoccupation of the age.

22 See, for example, Raymond Southall, *The Courtly Maker: An Essay on the Poetry of Wyatt and his Contemporaries* (Oxford: Basil Blackwell, 1964).

23 On courtship political and amorous, see especially Arthur F. Marotti, "'Love is Not Love': Elizabethan Sonnet Sequences and the Social Order," *ELH* 49 (1982): 396–428. See also Ann Rosalind Jones and Peter Stallybrass, "The Politics of *Astrophil and Stella*," *Studies in English Literature* 24 (1984): 53–68; Louis Adrian Montrose, "Of Gentlemen and Shepherds: The Politics of Elizabethan Pastoral Form," *ELH* 50 (1983): 415–59; several of Montrose's other essays; and any number of more recent New-Historical studies.

24 From a somewhat different perspective, Joel Fineman touches on the process of how we identify ourselves by what we love, in *Shakespeare's Perjured Eye: The Invention of Poetic Subjectivity in the Sonnets* (Berkeley: University of California Press, 1986).

25 Of the Petrarch sonnet, Kalstone says, "Tempered by time, desire has disappeared" (p. 119).
26 *Petrarch's Lyric Poems*, trans. and ed. Robert M. Durling (Cambridge, MA: Harvard University Press, 1976), pp. 410–11. It is hard to read Petrarch's line (or sonnet) without finding in it more feelings of longing regret than of resigned submissiveness. On Petrarch, Laura, and death, see Renée Neu Watkins, "Petrarch and the Black Death: From Fear to Monuments," *Studies in the Renaissance* 19 (1972): 196–223. William Kerrigan and Gordon Braden retraverse the Petrarchan ground in *The Idea of the Renaissance* (Baltimore: Johns Hopkins University Press, 1989), pp. 157–89.
27 *The Poems of Sir Walter Ralegh*, ed. Agnes Latham (Cambridge, MA: Harvard University Press, 1951), *u* and *v* normalized. Marion Campbell, "Inscribing Imperfection: Sir Walter Ralegh and the Elizabethan Court," *English Literary Renaissance* 20 (1990): 233–53, suggests that Ralegh left the poem unfinished as a mark of his hopeless situation.
28 Robert E. Stillman, in "'Words cannot knytt': Language and Desire in Ralegh's *The Ocean to Cynthia*," *Studies in English Literature* 27 (1987): 35–51, writes: "Ralegh appears permanently trapped in history ... amidst the outworn conceits of a disabled symbolic order" (p. 49). With regard to Surrey's interpreting Troy as a lesson in faithful persistence, Shakespeare's *Troilus and Cressida* suggests how much difference a generation could make.
29 Lawrence Stone, *The Crisis of the Aristocracy*, 1588–1641 (Oxford: Clarendon Press, 1965).
30 And what did Sidney's contemporaries think of his love for Stella? Penelope Rich had her detractors, but John Buxton writes that "the poets, who were ever ready to acknowledge their debt to Sidney, and who accepted the model of his sonnets, were confederate in silence upon the love of Philip Sidney and Penelope Devereux. Tact so ubiquitous is scarcely within the scope of human frailty" (*Sir Philip Sidney and the English Renaissance* [London: Macmillan, 1966], p. 218). I think this "tact" is a measure both of their mixed feelings about that affair and of their continuing admiration for Sidney, which his infatuation for "Stella" did not lessen. It seems that *Astrophil and Stella* had on Sidney's friends precisely the effect he might have hoped for.

2 JOHN DONNE: "DEFECTS OF LONELINESSE"

1 On this mix of readers, see Frank Whigham, *Ambition and Privilege*: *The Social Tropes of Elizabethan Courtesy Theory* (Berkeley: University of California Press, 1984).

2 See introduction, note 7.

3 Or by Derridean transcendental signifiers – nothing but words – as David Schalkwyk suggests, in "A Lady's 'Verily' Is as Potent as a Lord's: Women, Word and Witchcraft in *The Winter's Tale*," *English Literary Renaissance* 22 (1992): 242–72.

4 Of course, *Epithalamion* captures love and marriage at their brief apogee. Long suffering went before; inevitable decline, perhaps even failure, will come after. See A. Kent Hieatt, *Short Time's Endless Monument* (New York: Columbia University Press, 1960); and Richard Neuse, "The Triumph over Hasty Accidents: A Note on the Symbolic Modes of the 'Epithalamion,'" *Modern Language Review* 61 (1966): 163–74.

5 Arthur F. Marotti, *John Donne, Coterie Poet* (Madison: University of Wisconsin Press, 1986).

6 All quotations from Donne's poetry are from *The Poems of John Donne*, ed. Herbert J. C. Grierson, 2 vols. (1912; rpt. London: Oxford University Press, 1951).

7 See Barbara L. Parker and J. Max Patrick, "Two Hollow Men: The Pretentious Wooer and the Wayward Bridegroom of Donne's 'Satyre I,'" *Seventeenth-Century News* 33 (1975): 10–14.

8 M. Thomas Hester, *Kinde Pitty and Brave Scorn: John Donne's Satyres* (Durham: Duke University Press, 1982).

9 On the bee and digestion metaphors and their significance see especially G. W. Pigman III, "Versions of Imitation in the Renaissance," *Renaissance Quarterly* 33 (1980): 1–32.

10 On the importance of rendering interpretation of dangerous issues problematic, see Annabel Patterson, *Censorship and Interpretation*: *The Conditions of Writing and Reading in Early Modern England* (Madison: University of Wisconsin Press, 1984).

11 See Arthur F. Marotti, "'Love Is Not Love': Elizabethan Sonnet Sequences and the Social Order," *ELH* 49 (1982): 396–428.

12 Anthony Esler, *The Aspiring Mind of the Elizabethan Younger Generation* (Durham: Duke University Press, 1966); Lawrence Stone, *The Crisis of the Aristocracy*: 1558–1641 (Oxford: Clarendon Press, 1965).

13 Richard Helgerson, *The Elizabethan Prodigals* (Berkeley: University of California Press, 1976), and *Self-Crowned Laureates: Spenser,*

Jonson, Milton and the Literary System (Berkeley: University of California Press, 1983).

14 Marotti, *John Donne, Coterie Poet*; Carey is quoted extensively and pertinently in Marotti's book; see especially his "The Ovidian Love Elegy in England," D. Phil. thesis, Oxford University, 1960.

15 For an argument that "Going to Bed" is covert criticism of British Protestant imperialism, see R. V. Young, "'O my America, my new-found land': Pornography and Imperial Politics in Donne's *Elegies*," *South Central Review* (1987):35–48.

16 On the social implications of the growing Renaissance interest in anatomizing and dissecting, see Devon L. Hodges, *Renaissance Fictions of Anatomy* (Amherst: University of Massachusetts Press, 1985).

17 So Judith Hertz, as Respondent, reminded me at an MLA session in 1986.

18 On Donne's similar, uncanny anticipation of Newton's concept of momentum, see Anthony Low, "The 'Turning Wheel': Carew, Jonson, Donne and the First Law of Motion," *John Donne Journal* 1 (1982): 69–80.

19 See Anthony Low, *The Georgic Revolution* (Princeton University Press, 1985), pp. 74–88.

20 See Arthur F. Marotti, "John Donne and the Rewards of Patronage," *Patronage in the Renaissance*, ed. Guy Fitch Lytle and Stephen Orgel (Princeton University Press, 1981). Suggestive studies of the pressures of patronage on poetry include Robert C. Evans, *Ben Jonson and the Poetics of Patronage* (Lewisburg: Bucknell University Press, 1989), and Michael C. Schoenfeldt, *Prayer and Power: George Herbert and Renaissance Courtship* (University of Chicago Press, 1991).

21 John Donne, *The Elegies and the Songs and Sonnets*, ed. Helen Gardner (Oxford: Clarendon Press, 1965).

22 Earl Miner, *The Metaphysical Mode from Donne to Cowley* (Princeton University Press, 1969). More recently, Heather Dubrow, *A Happier Eden: The Politics of Marriage in the Stuart Epithalamium* (Ithaca: Cornell University Press, 1990), remarks that "Donne's telling preoccupation with intrusion signals his predilection for seeing the community as a source of entrapment rather than support" (p. 153).

23 See Marotti, *John Donne, Coterie Poet*; John Carey, *John Donne: Life, Mind and Art* (New York: Oxford University Press, 1981); and Carey, "Ovidian Love Elegy in England."

24 Jonathan Goldberg, *James I and the Politics of Literature* (Baltimore: Johns Hopkins Press, 1983).

25 On this image and on Donne's attitude generally toward labor, see Low, *Georgic Revolution*, especially pp. 74–88.

26 This is the most economical explanation of Donne's curious ordering of the spheres in that poem, about which a number of critics vainly speculated until John T. Shawcross quietly solved the problem in his edition, *The Complete Poetry of John Donne* (New York: Doubleday, 1967), p. 296n.

27 Victor Turner, *The Ritual Process: Structure and Anti-Structure* (University of Chicago Press, 1969), and *Celebration: Studies in Festivity in Ritual*, ed. Turner (Washington, DC, 1982). Turner prefers the term "communitas"; but his ideas are now sufficiently familiar to allow us the English word. On carnivals, see Mikhail Bakhtin, *Rabelais and His World*, trans. Helene Iswolsky (Cambridge, MA: Harvard University Press, 1968).

28 Wayne A. Rebhorn, *Courtly Performances: Masking and Festivity in Castiglione's "Book of the Courtier"* (Detroit: Wayne State University Press, 1978).

29 Leah Sinanoglou Marcus, *Childhood and Cultural Despair: A Theme and Variations in Seventeenth-Century Literature* (University of Pittsburgh Press, 1978).

30 See Roslyn Richek, "Thomas Randolph's Salting (1627), Its Text, and John Milton's Sixth Prolusion as Another Salting," *English Literary Renaissance* 12 (1982): 102–31.

31 Theodore Redpath credits several colleagues with making the connection; see *The Songs and Sonets of John Donne*, ed. Redpath (London: Methuen, 1956), pp. 109–10.

32 On Donne's habit of crossing accepted lines of good taste, see William Kerrigan, "The Fearful Accomodations of John Donne," *English Literary Renaissance* 4 (1974): 337–63.

33 Marotti, *John Donne, Coterie Poet*, p. 147.

34 On the importance of friendship to the Cavaliers, see Earl Miner, *The Restoration Mode from Milton to Dryden* (Princeton University Press, 1974).

35 See Catullus V ("Vivamus, mea Lesbia, atque amemus"): "soles occidere et redire possunt: / nobis cum semel occidit brevis lux, / nox est perpetua una dormienda" (lines 4–6); in Thomas Campion's version: "heav'ns great lampes doe dive / Into their west, and strait againe revive, / But, soone as once set is our little light, / Then must we sleepe one ever-during night" ("My Sweetest Lesbia," lines 3–6).

36 This view runs through most of Burke's various books. See also R. P. Blackmur's important essay, "Language as Gesture," in his

collection of the same name (New York: Columbia University Press, 1952), pp. 3–24.

37 See J. C. A. Rathmell, "Jonson, Lord Lisle, and Penshurst," *English Literary Renaissance* 1 (1971): 250–60.

38 See Low, *Georgic Revolution*, pp. 98–117, 280–81, and Don E. Wayne, *Penshurst: The Semiotics of Place and the Poetics of History* (Madison: University of Wisconsin Press, 1984).

39 As the "subject" grows more Romantically subjective, the "object" becomes more scientifically objective. For a useful discussion of this two-sided process, which arises from long-term changes in perception but has significant real-world consequences, see Owen Barfield, *Saving the Appearances: A Study in Idolatry*, 2nd edition (Middlebury: Wesleyan University Press, 1988), pp. 11–106.

40 In her seminal article "The 'New Astronomy' and English Literary Imagination," *Studies in Philology* 32 (1935): 428–62, reprinted in *Science and Imagination* (Ithaca: Cornell University Press, 1956), pp. 30–57, Marjorie Nicolson argues that the *experience* of looking through the telescope, rather than the shift in theoretical ideas, most moved Donne and his contemporaries. Without disagreeing with her point about the immediacy of such visual and tactile experiences, I would argue that underlying shifts in *perception*, such as those we have been considering in this chapter, were equally important and must have been equally exciting to Donne and his contemporaries. Such shifts are not merely links in a chain of dead ideas found in books, but have intimate connections with matters basic to living experience – to one's sense of self and relation to others and to the world.

41 On the exertion of personal will to create a magical space see Kirby Farrell, *Shakespeare's Creation: The Language of Magic and Play* (Amherst: University of Massachusetts Press, 1976); and on the displacement of Christian inspiration by Romantic imagination, which relates to this process, see John Guillory, *Poetic Authority: Spenser, Milton, and Literary History* (New York: Columbia University Press, 1983), especially pp. 1–22.

42 A. J. Smith, "The Metaphysics of Love," *Review of English Studies* 9 (1958): 362–75. See also Smith's *The Metaphysics of Love* (Cambridge University Press, 1985).

43 Arnold, "To Marguerite – Continued" poem 5 of the "Switzerland" sequence), emphasis Arnold's.

3 JOHN DONNE: "THE *HOLY GHOST* IS AMOROUS IN HIS
METAPHORS"

1 Winfried Schleiner, *The Imagery of John Donne's Sermons* (Providence: Brown University Press, 1970), p. 158. Schleiner discusses this "field of imagery" only briefly (pp. 157–58).

2 *The Sermons of John Donne*, ed. Evelyn M. Simpson and George R. Potter, 10 vols. (Berkeley: University of California Press, 1953–62) 7:87–88. It is sometimes said that Protestants, or Anglicans, used the scriptural marriage-metaphor only of Christ and his Church, not of Christ and the individual soul; see, for example, Bruce Henricksen, "Donne's Orthodoxy," *Texas Studies in Literature and Language* 14 (1972): 5–16. This distinction is not correct; both usages are common. As this passage illustrates, Donne speaks of God marrying the soul – as did many other Protestant writers.

3 In the light of the whole sermon and of Donne's other writings, marriage without divorce probably does not imply irresistible election but confidence that God will never reject a soul arbitrarily. Luther uses quite a different trope for the divine-human relationship: "Thus the human will is like a beast of burden. If God rides it, it wills and goes whence God wills ... If Satan rides, it wills and goes where Satan wills. Nor may it choose ... But the riders themselves contend who shall have it and hold it" (Erasmus and Luther, *Discourse on Free Will*, trans. Ernst F. Winter [New York: Frederick Unger, 1961], p. 112).

4 See chapter 2, above.

5 For a reading which argues that "Show me deare Christ" "enacts Freud's thesis that religious 'ideology' is a form of sexual sublimation," see Robert Bagg, "The Electromagnet and the Shred of Platinum," *Arion* 8 (1969): 420. Wilbur Sanders writes: "In Donne's best religious poetry there is no shallow antithesis between the natural man and religious man, but a deep continuity" (*John Donne's Poetry* [Cambridge University Press, 1971], p. 110). Robert Nye argues for a "consistent" Donne whose secular and religious poetry alike concern "the problem of ... how to love well" ("The body is his book: the poetry of John Donne," *Critical Quarterly* 14 [1972]: 352). A. J. Smith argues that Donne was the last poet to hold together two areas of experience that later diverged: "After Donne, sexual love offered no way" to seek ultimate truths ("The Failure of Love: Love Lyrics after Donne," in *Metaphysical Poetry*, ed. Malcolm Bradbury and David Palmer, Stratford-Upon-Avon Studies 11 [London: Edward Arnold, 1970], pp. 52, 71). Robert S. Jackson, who finds continuity in

Donne's progress from proverbial Jack Donne to Dr. Donne, gives useful biblical sources for the marriage metaphor in "Show me deare Christ" (*John Donne's Christian Vocation* [Evanston: Northwestern University Press, 1970], pp. 146–78). Among numerous other studies, see A. L. French, "The Psychopathology of Donne's Holy Sonnets," *Critical Review* 13 (1970): 111–24; Lindsay A. Mann, "The Marriage Analogue of Letter and Spirit in Donne's Devotional Prose," *JEGP* 70 (1971): 607–16; Kitty Datta, "Love and Asceticism in Donne's Poetry: The Divine Analogy," *Critical Quarterly* 19 (1977): 5–25.

6 Helen C. White, *English Devotional Literature*, 1600–1640 (Madison: University of Wisconsin Press, 1931), p. 10. See also Debora Shuger's persuasive recent case for the centrality of religious attitudes in relation to politics and culture, in *Habits of Thought in the English Renaissance* (Berkeley: University of California Press, 1991). The many studies of such historians as Christopher Hill and Steven E. Ozment offer further cases in point.

7 I take Freud as the most representative and influential analytical figure of our century, but much the same might be said concerning the relation of the sacred, for example, to Lacan's "objet a" or to Winnicott's separation from the mother.

8 Robert Southwell, *Marie Magdalens Funeral Teares* (London, 1591), Preface. Cited by Louis Martz, *The Wit of Love* (University of Notre Dame Press, 1969), p. 141.

9 All quotations from the divine poems in this chapter are from *The Divine Poems of John Donne*, ed. Helen Gardner, 2nd edition (Oxford: Clarendon Press, 1978). The two quotations are from "Since she whome I lovd" (line 1) and "What if this present were the worlds last night?" (line 10).

10 Mario Praz, *Mnemosyne*: *The Parallel Between Literature and the Visual Arts*, Bollingen Series 35.16 (Princeton University Press, 1970), p. 97. Praz does not explain this passing comment apart from comparing the poems to Michelangelo's anteroom to the Laurentian Library and stressing dialectic reversal.

11 Carol Marks Sicherman, "Donne's Discoveries," *SEL* 11 (1971), p. 69 (author's abstract).

12 See chapter 2, above.

13 See Debora Shuger, *Habits of Thought in the English Renaissance*. She shows the importance of the father-king relationship in a number of writers, of whom Donne is decidedly the most extraordinary.

14 "Two shall be one": here Donne refers more immediately to Christian theology and canon law than to Neoplatonic mysticism.

See, for example, St. Thomas Aquinas, *Summa*, trans. Fathers of the English Dominican Province, 3 vols. (New York: Benziger Brothers, 1948) 3:2762–70 (Supplement, Q. 55); "carnal intercourse is the cause of affinity" (p. 2764; Q. 55, art. 3).

15 For general background, see Don Cameron Allen, *The Legend of Noah: Renaissance Rationalism in Art, Science, and Letters* (Urbana: University of Illinois Press, 1963); for concise background on the typological tradition, see David Shelley Berkeley, *Inwrought with Figures Dim: A Reading of Milton's "Lycidas"* (The Hague, Mouton, 1974), pp. 113–64. On individual typology, see Barbara Kiefer Lewalski, *Protestant Poetics and the Seventeenth-Century Religious Lyric* (Princeton University Press, 1979). Donne's "speaker imagines himself a new Noah about to experience a new Flood in a new Ark" (p. 280). I would only dispute Lewalski's view that this form of typology (foreshadowing the individual Christian's experience) is uniquely "Protestant." Application to self is also common in earlier Catholic and in Counter-reformation spirituality.

16 Female imagery for God is collected in many feminist studies which, however, sometimes implicate earlier writers in the struggle for dominance. For helpful comment see Caroline Walker Bynum, "The Body of Christ in the Later Middle Ages: A Reply to Leo Steinberg," *Renaissance Quarterly* 39 (1986): 399–439. Usually mother and nursing images emphasize God's tenderness and the soul's trusting reliance. A significant biblical source is Isaiah 49:15. I cite the previous verse to show how easily the image emerges from that of God as Israel's husband: "But Zion said, The Lord hath forsaken me, and my Lord hath forgotten me. Can a woman forget her sucking child, that she should not have compassion on the son of her womb? yea, they may forget, yet will I not forget thee."

17 See, for example, chapter 6 below.

18 As Debora Shuger points out in a letter to me, "although Donne has problems with submitting to a masculine God, he has less difficulty submitting to a punitive one" in such poems as "Spit in my face" and "Goodfriday."

19 Janel Mueller will argue that Donne's attitude toward lesbian eroticism is more positive than I find it, in an essay to appear in *Sexuality and Gender in Early Modern Europe: Institutions, Texts, Images*, ed. James G. Turner (Cambridge University Press, 1993).

20 For more on Donne's Pauline treatment of worldly shame in "To Mr. Tilman," see Anthony Low, *The Georgic Revolution* (Princeton University Press, 1985), pp. 182–83.

21 Although the relations implied by the Church as Mother and

Bride have dominated theology and tradition, Donne's images are not without precedent. Paul addresses his followers as "My little children, of whom I travail in birth again until Christ be formed in you" (Galatians 4:19). Also: "I write not these things to shame you, but as my beloved sons I warn you. For though ye have ten thousand instructors in Christ, yet have ye not many fathers: for in Christ Jesus I have begotten you through the gospel" (1 Corinthians 4:14–15).

4 GEORGE HERBERT: "THE BEST LOVE"

1 To document this comparative point would take far more space than I can devote to it here, for in recent years discussions of religion in English literature have almost entirely ignored the larger European context. Briefly, one might consider how in the Counter-Reformation St. Ignatius was complemented by St. Teresa; how much St. Francis de Sales was a spokesman for feminine spirituality (see chapter 5 below); and how among English Recusant exiles at Cambrai and Douai the priests were complemented by the nuns, Dom Augustine Baker by Dame Gertrude More. Nothing similar occurred, or could have occurred, in England at this time. For acute comment on the shift a century earlier to a more patriarchal religion, see Colin Richmond, "The English Gentry and Religion, *c.* 1500," in *Religious Belief and Ecclesiastical Careers in Late Medieval England*, ed. Christopher Harper-Bill (London: Boydell, 1990), pp. 121–50, especially pp. 140–43.

2 There are a number of studies on women and marriage in Protestant England; but little or nothing (beyond early polemic) to compare Protestant English practice with late-medieval and Renaissance continental Roman-Catholic practice. Among significant studies – generally biased, however, toward a Protestant outlook and dismissive of Catholic practice – are William and Malleville Haller, "The Puritan Art of Love," *Huntington Library Quarterly* 5 (1941): 235–72; and William Haller, "Hail Wedded Love," *ELH* 13 (1946): 79–97. Heather Dubrow, in *A Happier Eden*, pp. 1–41, shows that the simple Protestant/Catholic dichotomy often breaks down. On English Reformation women see *Silent but for the Word: Tudor Women as Patrons, Translators, and Writers of Religious Works*, ed. Margaret P. Hannay (Kent, OH: Kent State University Press, 1985). For women writers generally in the Renaissance, see bibliographies compiled by Elizabeth H. Hageman and Josephine A. Roberts in *English Literary Renaissance*

14 (1984): 409–439; and 18 (1988): 138–67. Studies of medieval marriage generally have not penetrated studies of marriage in the English Renaissance and seventeenth century. See especially Christopher N. L. Brooke, *The Medieval Idea of Marriage* (Oxford University Press, 1989); and, on the prevalence of love leading to marriage in medieval literature, Henry Ansgar Kelly, *Love and Marriage in the Age of Chaucer* (Ithaca: Cornell University Press, 1975).

3 See, for example, Joan Kelly, "Did Women Have a Renaissance?" in *Women, History, and Theory: The Essays of Joan Kelly* (University of Chicago Press, 1984), pp. 19–50.

4 See, for example, Guy Fitch Lytle, "Religion and the Lay Patron in Reformation England," in *Patronage in the Renaissance*, ed. Lytle and Stephen Orgel (Princeton University Press, 1981), pp. 65–114.

5 On this point generally, and on Donne's nostalgia for a lost Virgin Mary, see Maureen Sabine, *Feminine Engendered Faith: John Donne and Richard Crashaw* (London: Macmillan, 1992); and also chapter 5 below.

6 For a recent view of sexual love and gender roles in Herbert divergent from mine, see Michael C. Schoenfeldt, *Prayer and Power: George Herbert and Renaissance Courtship* (University of Chicago Press, 1991), pp. 230–70. Schoenfeldt usefully notes the misplaced squeamishness of some Herbert criticism. For a classic discussion of Herbert's sacred parody of secular love, on which I depend in general terms though not in detail, see Louis L. Martz, *The Poetry of Meditation* (New Haven: Yale University Press, 1954), pp. 184–97, 259–73.

7 Herbert was admitted to Trinity College, Cambridge, on 5 May 1609. As David Novarr, in *The Making of Walton's Lives* (Ithaca: Cornell University Press, 1958), has demonstrated, and many others have agreed, Walton cannot be unreservedly trusted. Still, we must rely on him as our only source for the text of the letter and sonnets and as our best contemporary authority for the circumstances of their composition. Supplementary biographical information is found in the introduction to *The Works of George Herbert*, ed. F. E. Hutchinson (1964; Oxford: Clarendon Press, 1941), from which all quotations from Herbert's works are taken; and in Amy M. Charles, *A Life of George Herbert* (Ithaca: Cornell University Press, 1977).

8 On *Outlandish Proverbs*, see Diana Benet, "The Magic Shoe," in *Like Season'd Timber: New Essays on George Herbert*, ed. Edmund Miller and Robert DiYanni (New York: Peter Lang, 1987), pp.

139–50. The proverbs are identified by Hutchinson's numbers (pp. 321–55).

9 The wedding took place 5 March 1629. *A Priest To the Temple*, first published in 1652, is dated "1632" at the conclusion of Herbert's preface, "The Author to the Reader."

10 The words do, however, separate Herbert from the more Puritan branch of his church, which preferred marriage to virginity.

11 *Aubrey's Brief Lives*, ed. Oliver Lawson Dick (Harmondsworth: Penguin, 1972), p. 218; cited in part (from the 1957 University of Michigan edition, p. 137), by Amy Charles, *Life of George Herbert*, (p. 143), who puts a mitigating construction on Aubrey's "waspish" words.

12 Walton adds that Herbert dispensed further alms himself, beyond Jane's tenth. Izaak Walton, *The Life of Mr. George Herbert* (1675), in *The Lives of John Donne, Sir Henry Wotton, Richard Hooker, George Herbert, and Robert Sanderson*, The World's Classics (1962; London: Oxford University Press, 1927), p. 306. On the nieces, see Walton's *Life*, Herbert's letter to his brother Sir Henry (Hutchinson, *Works*, pp. 375–76), and Herbert's will (*ibid.*, pp. 382–83).

13 On sacred parody of secular love poetry, important for discussing the relationship between the two, see Leah Jonas, "George Herbert, Richard Crashaw, and Henry Vaughan," in *The Divine Science: The Aesthetic of Some Representative Seventeenth-Century English Poets* (New York: Columbia University Press, 1940), pp. 211–27; Louis L. Martz, *The Poetry of Meditation* (New Haven: Yale University Press, 1954), pp. 184–93; Edward M. Wilson, "Spanish and English Poetry of the Seventeenth-Century," *Journal of Ecclesiastical History* 9 (1959): 38–53; Rosemary Freeman, "Parody as a Literary Form: George Herbert and Wilfred Owen," *Essays in Criticism* 13 (1963): 307–22; Frank J. Warnke, *Versions of Baroque: European Literature in the Seventeenth Century* (New Haven: Yale University Press, 1972), pp. 93–96, 130–33; Bruce W. Wardropper, "The Religious Conversion of Profane Poetry," in *Studies in the Continental Background of Renaissance English Literature: Essays Presented to John L. Lievsay*, ed. Dale B. J. Randall and George Walton Williams (Durham: Duke University Press, 1977), pp. 203–21; Thomas F. Merrill, "Sacred Parody and the Grammar of Devotion," *Criticism* 23 (1981): 195–210. A notable contrary view, which stresses "parody" as strictly the setting of sacred texts to secular music, is Rosemond Tuve, "Sacred Parody of Love Poetry, and Herbert," *Essays by Rosemond Tuve: Spenser, Herbert, Milton*, ed. Thomas P. Roche, Jr. (Princeton University Press, 1970), pp.

207–51. The greatest of sacred parodists was Herbert's near-contemporary, Lope de Vega (1562–1635).

14 Robert Southwell, *Marie Magdalens Funeral Teares* (London, 1591), preface; cited by Martz, *The Poetry of Meditation*, p. 141. For Southwell's words, see chapter 3 above.

15 On the emotional and philosophical import of the anatomy, see Devon L. Hodges, *Renaissance Fictions of Anatomy* (Amherst: University of Massachusetts Press, 1985).

16 See chapter 2, above.

17 Tuve, "Herbert and Caritas," in *Essays by Rosemond Tuve*, p. 168.

18 Since Herbert has recently been portrayed as something of a biblical fundamentalist by Richard Strier, *Love Known: Theology and Experience in George Herbert's Poetry* (University of Chicago Press, 1983), Chana Bloch, *Spelling the Word: George Herbert and the Bible* (Berkeley: University of California Press, 1985), and others, it may be useful to recall some of Herbert's own words: "The Countrey Parson is full of all knowledg. They say, it is an ill Mason that refuseth any stone … The Countrey Parson hath read the Fathers also, and the Schoolmen, and the later Writers, or a good proportion of all" (Hutchinson, *Works*, pp. 228–29).

19 A more recent authority, still useful on this subject, is Anders Nygren, *Agape and Eros*, trans. Philip S. Watson (1953; New York: Harper, 1969). Most critics who discuss Herbert necessarily discuss love, yet few have taken it as a main theme.

20 On the problem of reciprocation, see Diana Benet, *Secretary of Praise: The Poetic Vocation of George Herbert* (Columbia: University of Missouri Press, 1984).

21 She names Louis Martz, but only as the most "careful" and useful of critics who see a connection between sacred and secular love in Herbert (p. 204n). Presumably she is chiefly concerned to scotch any tendency to Freudianize or to confuse one kind of love with another. "For certainly never was a world more loveless (as Herbert defines love) than ours, nor confusion more rife as to the nature and connections of the many affections which we try unsuccessfully to denominate by that single word" (pp. 174–75).

22 *Sermons*, ed. Potter and Simpson, 1:183–84 (see chapter 3 above).

23 Tuve, "Herbert and Caritas," pp. 177–79.

24 On the Song of Songs, see Stanley Stewart, *The Enclosed Garden: The Tradition and the Image in Seventeenth-Century Poetry* (Madison: University of Wisconsin Press, 1966).

25 Francis Rous, *The Mysticall Marriage. Experimentall discoveries of the heavenly marriage betweene a soule and her Saviour* (London, 1631);

cited by Marc F. Bertonasco, *Crashaw and the Baroque* (University: University of Alabama Press, 1971), p. 49.

26 Is this, as Schoenfeldt seems delicately to lead his reader to infer (p. 239), a *double-entendre*? I think not. Sometimes, as Freud is said to have remarked, a cigar is just a cigar.

27 I say that marriage is a traditional "image" or metaphor since that is perhaps the best term for a Protestant poet. In the Catholic theological tradition, which Herbert may have accepted in part, it would be better to speak of a poetic image that is based on a central truth or mystery.

28 Marvell has been accused (even by his contemporaries) of lacking in mature, that is to say genital, sexuality; but no one has thought to bring this charge against Herbert.

29 See Anthony Low, "Herbert's 'Jordan (I)' and the Court Masque," *Criticism* 14 (1972): 109–18.

30 Schoenfeldt, *Prayer and Power*.

31 This acclamation is connected with an ancient, basic form of thanksgiving, which rejoices in the supremacy of God. Compare the phrase *Adonai Elohayna*, the Lord is our God, in the Hebrew prayer "Hear, oh Israel," or consider the royal psalms of praise.

32 See George Held, "Brother Poets: The Relation between George and Edward Herbert," in *Like Season'd Timber: New Essays on George Herbert*, ed. Edmund Miller and Robert DiYanni (New York: Peter Lang, 1987), pp. 19–35. For further psychological speculations – but with less than persuasive application to the poems – see E. Pearlman, "George Herbert's God," *English Literary Renaissance* 13 (1983): 88–112.

33 Debora K. Shuger, *Habits of Thought in the English Renaissance* (Berkeley: University of California Press, 1990).

34 On the theme of childhood, with some discussion of Herbert from another angle, see Leah Sinanoglou Marcus, *Childhood and Cultural Despair: A Theme and Variations in Seventeenth-Century Literature* (University of Pittsburgh Press, 1978).

35 For good examples of this kind of reaction – which in our time might often be characterized as a secular product of earlier Protestant attitudes – one need look no further than much twentieth-century criticism of Crashaw, cited below in chapter 5.

36 "Cultural conditioning has sponsored a wheyfaced Herbert." Russell Fraser, "George Herbert's Poetry," *Sewanee Review* 95 (1987): 581; cited by Schoenfeldt, *Prayer and Power*, p. 231. But, if in matters of religion later generations of English were far more priggish than Herbert, he may have helped lead the way.

5 RICHARD CRASHAW: "LOVE'S DELICIOUS FIRE"

1 See chapter 1 above, on Sir Philip Sidney.
2 Denis de Rougement, *Love in the Western World*, trans. Montgomery Belgion (New York: Pantheon, 1956); Mario Praz, *The Romantic Agony*, trans. Angus Davidson, 2nd edition (1933; London: Oxford University Press, 1970). A useful bibliography of secondary works on courtly love (with essays mounting a Robertsonian attack on this scholarship) is *The Meaning of Courtly Love*, ed. F. X. Newman (Albany: State University of New York Press, 1968).
3 *A Concordance to The English Poetry of Richard Crashaw*, compiled by Robert M. Cooper (Troy, NY: Whitston Publishing, 1981).
4 All quotations from Crashaw are from *The Poems English Latin and Greek of Richard Crashaw*, ed. L. C. Martin, 2nd edition (Oxford: Clarendon Press, 1957); I silently modernize *u*, *v*, *i*, and *j*, and expand contractions.
5 My count includes singular and plural and such variants on the root word as "lovely," "lover," and "loving."
6 His conversion was painful, because it involved the loss of his closest friends in England and permanent separation from his country; but there is no evidence that he doubted what course he should take. See his letter from Leyden to Ferrar Collet (Martin, *Poems*, pp. xxvii–xxxi).
7 *The Works of George Herbert*, ed. F. E. Hutchinson (1964; Oxford: Clarendon Press, 1941), p. 238 (italics removed).
8 On woman's free will see Diane Kelsey McColley, *Milton's Eve* (Urbana: University of Illinois Press, 1983).
9 Rosemond Tuve, *Elizabethan and Metaphysical Imagery: Renaissance Poetic and Twentieth-Century Critics* (University of Chicago Press, 1947), p. 307.
10 See especially Nancy Vickers, "Diana Described: Scattered Woman and Scattered Rhyme," *Critical Inquiry* 8 (1981): 265–81.
11 See Anthony Low, "Thomas Traherne: Mystical Hedonist," in *Love's Architecture: Devotional Modes in Seventeenth-Century English Poetry* (New York University Press, 1978), pp. 259–93.
12 "Crashawe: The Anagramme," lines 22–23, 37–38, in Martin, *Poems*, pp. 233–34. See this whole poem, especially lines 22–40, as evidence for Crashaw's ascetic style of life.
13 *Comus*, line 741. Milton undoubtedly approves of Comus' formula but not of his honesty, since (as elsewhere in the masque) the scene ironically belies his words. A typically aristocratic lover, Comus tries to force his unwanted and illegitimate desires on the

entrapped Lady. In context, the mutuality he evokes is illusory. In effect, he aspires to date-rape.

14 A suggestive analogue for his joyful tone in this context is the prenatal example of John the Baptist, familiar from the Christmas liturgy: "And it came to pass, that, when Elisabeth heard the salutation of Mary, the babe leaped in her womb" (Luke 1:41).

15 Milton's Nativity Ode is largely concerned with this question, which he resolves in the powerful phrase "But now begins" (line 167). Useful discussion of this debate among Reformers may be found in Richard A. Muller, "The Hermeneutic of Promise and Fulfillment in Calvin's Exegesis of the Old Testament Prophecies of the Kingdom," in *The Bible in the Sixteenth Century*, edited by David C. Steinmetz (Durham: Duke University Press, 1990), pp. 68–82. As a rule, Catholics put more stress than did Protestants on the efficacy of the Incarnation in transforming the material world and human history.

16 See Louis L. Martz, *The Wit of Love: Donne, Carew, Crashaw, Marvell* (University of Notre Dame Press, 1969), p. 131. "The Baroque tries, by multiplication of sensory impressions, to exhaust the sensory and to suggest the presence of the spiritual." Although I disagree on this point – I think the Baroque generally and Crashaw in particular put far more weight on the Incarnation and on the continuity of flesh and spirit than this view allows – Martz's essay remains seminal.

17 A useful discussion of the inter-temporal links between Christ's Comings is W. B. Hunter, "The War in Heaven: The Exaltation of the Son," in *Bright Essence: Studies in Milton's Theology*, ed. Hunter, C. A. Patrides, and J. H. Adamson (Salt Lake City: University of Utah Press, 1971), pp. 115–30.

18 On this background, see A. R. Cirillo, "Crashaw's 'Epiphany Hymn': The Dawn of Christian Time," *Studies in Philology* 67 (1970): 67–88.

19 Compare Dante's inscription over the gates of hell: "Fecemi la divina podestate, / La somma sapienza e 'l primo amore"; "The divine power made me, the supreme wisdom, and the primal love" (*Inferno* 1.3.5–6); and Milton's Satan: "whom hast thou then or what to accuse, / But Heav'ns free Love dealt equally to all? / Be then his Love accurst, since love or hate, / To me alike, it deals eternal woe" (*Paradise Lost* 4.67–70). See chapter 7 below; and further on the difficult issue of rejoicing over divine retributive justice, see Anthony Low, *The Blaze of Noon: A Reading of Samson Agonistes* (New York: Columbia University Press, 1974), pp. 185–205. The ending reverts to the text underlying the poem:

"Wherefore God also hath highly exalted him, and given him a name which is above every name: That at the name of Jesus every knee should bow, of things in heaven, and things in earth, and things under the earth; And that every tongue should confess that Jesus Christ is Lord" (Philippians 2:9–11).

20 Robert Southwell, *Marie Magdalens Funeral Teares* (London, 1591), Preface. Cited by Martz, *The Wit of Love*, p. 141.

21 See C. S. Lewis, *The Allegory of Love: A Study in Medieval Tradition* (London: Oxford University Press, 1936), especially pp. 297–360.

22 St. Francis de Sales, *A Treatise of the Love of God*, trans. Miles Car (Douai, 1630), p. 760 (12.2.1). The translator, a priest at Douai, also known as Thomas Carre or Miles Pinckney, was Crashaw's close friend in Paris and editor of *Carmen Deo Nostro*.

23 *Renaissance Dialectic and Renaissance Piety: Benet of Canfield's Rule of Perfection*, trans. Kent Emery, Jr. (Binghamton, NY: Medieval & Renaissance Texts & Studies, 1987), pp. 185–86 (The text is based on the Paris edition of 1610.)

24 Augustine Baker, *Sancta Sophia, or, Directions for the Prayer of Contemplation*, 2 vols. (Douai, 1657), 1:311–13 (2.2.2). For further background, see Anthony Low, *Augustine Baker* (New York: Twayne, 1970).

25 See Low, "Richard Crashaw: Sensible Affection," in *Love's Architecture*, pp. 116–59. On meditation as active and masculine, see also Louis L. Martz, "The Action of the Self: Devotional Poetry in the Seventeenth Century," in *Metaphysical Poetry*, edited by Malcolm Bradley and David Palmer, Stratford-upon-Avon Studies 11 (London: Edward Arnold, 1970), pp. 101–21. On meditation among English Protestants see Barbara Lewalski, *Protestant Poetics and the Seventeenth-Century Religious Lyric* (Princeton University Press, 1979).

26 Francis de Sales, *Treatise on the Love of God*, p. 332 (6.4.1). I have not located this particular remark of St. Thomas's; but see his *Summa Theologica*, Pt. 1, Q. 82, art. 3, "Whether the Will Is a Higher Power Than the Intellect": "When, therefore, the thing in which there is good is nobler than the soul itself, in which is the idea understood; by comparison with such a thing, the will is higher than the intellect. But when the thing which is good is less noble than the soul, then even in comparison with that thing the intellect is higher than the will. Wherefore the love of God is better than the knowledge of God; but, on the contrary, the knowledge of corporeal things is better than the love thereof" (trans. Fathers of the English Dominican Province, 3 vols. [New York: Benziger Brothers, 1947] 1: 415).

27 Similar thinking carries over into Erasmus' *Praise of Folly*.

28 *Treatise of the Love of God*, pp. 332–33 (6.4.2).

29 See Low, *Love's Architecture*, pp. 124–58; Augustine Baker, *Sancta Sophia*, 2:15–56, 136–45 (3.1.3–5, 3.3.1); St. Francis de Sales, *An Introduction to a Devoute Life*, trans. John Yakesley (Rouen, 1614), pp. 126–29; Jean Pierre Camus, *A Spirituall Combat*, trans. Thomas Carre (Douay, 1632), pp. 222–35. On the spiritual advisement of women, see also Sister M. St. Teresa Higgins, C. S. J., "Augustine Baker," diss. University of Wisconsin, 1963.

30 Baker, 2:123–25 (3.2.5.5–8).

31 Edited selections from her writings were published as *The Spiritual Exercises of the Most Vertuous and Religious D. Gertrude More*, ed. Fr. Francis Gascoigne (Paris, 1658). Her manuscript writings, collected by Baker under the title "Confessiones Amantes," remain unpublished. A modernized abridgement of her life and writings is *The Inner Life and the Writings of Dame Gertrude More*, ed. Dom Benedict Weld-Blundell, 2 vols. (London: R. & T. Washbourne, 1910–11).

32 These charges are so common as to constitute the received opinion of their time. For documentation and refutation see Marc F. Bertonasco, *Crashaw and the Baroque* (University: University of Alabama Press, 1971); Low, *Love's Architecture*, pp. 116–59; and Lorraine M. Roberts and John R. Roberts, "Crashavian Criticism: A Brief Interpretive History," in *New Perspectives*, ed. Roberts, pp. 1–29.

33 See Low, *Love's Architecture*; Paul A. Parrish, "The Feminizing of Power: Crashaw's Life and Art," in "*The Muses Common-Weale*": *Poetry and Politics in the Seventeenth Century*, ed. Claude J. Summers and Ted-Larry Pebworth (Columbia: University of Missouri Press, 1988), pp. 148–62; Parrish, "'O Sweet Contest': Gender and Value in 'The Weeper,'" in *New Perspectives on the Life and Art of Richard Crashaw*, ed. John R. Roberts (Columbia: University of Missouri Press, 1990); and Maureen Sabine, *Feminine Engendered Faith: John Donne and Richard Crashaw* (London: Macmillan, 1992).

34 A similar argument is forcefully advanced by Maureen Sabine, whose book (cited in note 33 above) I read in manuscript.

35 *The Complete Poetry of Richard Crashaw*, ed. George Walton Williams (New York: Doubleday, 1970), p. 65n.

36 R. V. Young, *Richard Crashaw and the Spanish Golden Age* (New Haven: Yale University Press, 1982), pp. 48–50. Young comments cogently on sacred parody: in general, in Crashaw, and among his Spanish predecessors (pp. 20–50).

37 Louise Schleiner, *The Living Lyre in English Verse from Elizabeth*

through the Restoration (Columbia: University of Missouri Press, 1984), pp. 91–93, discusses the song qualities of the poem and reprints the musical setting. Martin first noted the existence of this version and gave textual variants in revised printings of his edition, p. xciv. In the mid-twentieth century, the pun on "dying" was rather a favorite of New-Critical explicators and hunters of suggestive ambiguities.

38 St. Francis de Sales and Benet of Canfield; see notes 21 and 22 above.

39 For a contrasting kind of spiritual longing, out of absence and emptiness, see the chapter entitled "The Hungering Dark: Spiritual Psychology and the Failure of Participation," in Debora Shuger, *Habits of Thought in the English Renaissance* (Berkeley: University of California Press, 1990), pp. 69–90.

40 On Donne and Herbert, see chapters 3 and 4 above.

6 THOMAS CAREW: "FRESH INVENTION"

1 See chapter 2, above. On parodies of Petrarchism within the tradition, see Leonard Forster, *The Icy Fire: Five Studies in European Petrarchism* (Cambridge University Press, 1969).

2 On the Medieval agricultural revolution, see especially Georges Duby, *Rural Economy and Country Life in the Medieval West*, trans. Cynthia Postan (1962; Columbia: University of South Carolina Press, 1968); B. H. Slicher van Bath, *The Agricultural History of Western Europe, A. D. 500–1850*, trans. Olive Ordish (London: Edward Arnold, 1963).

3 Joyce Oldham Appleby, *Economic Thought and Ideology in Seventeenth-Century England* (Princeton University Press, 1978).

4 The tract still appears erroneously under Hartlib's name in the revised Wing *Short Title Catalogue*. It was Hartlib's habit to solicit information and collaborative writings from others of his circle on subjects of interest to him, without any of the parties being too concerned about the precise details of authorship. On *Macaria*, see Charles Webster, "The Authorship and Significance of *Macaria*, *Past and Present* 56 (1972), reprinted in *The Intellectual Revolution of the Seventeenth Century*, ed. Webster (London: Routledge & Kegan Paul, 1974), pp. 369–85; and Webster, *Utopian Planning and the Puritan Revolution: Gabriel Plattes, Samuel Hartlib and "Macaria"* (Oxford: Clarendon Press, 1979).

5 On the significance of the revaluation of labor based on this interpretation of Genesis 2:15, see Anthony Low, *The Georgic Revolution* (Princeton University Press, 1985), pp. 316–20.

6 I use the male gender in accordance with seventeenth-century practice. On the authority of Genesis, the curse of labor was said to have been imposed specifically on Adam, while Eve suffered her own distinctive curse, even though, in practice, agricultural labor was shared by women.

7 *The Poems of Thomas Carew*, ed. Rhodes Dunlap (1949; Oxford: Clarendon Press, 1964), pp. xvii–xviii. Further quotations from Carew are from this edition; contractions are expanded and the use of *u, v, i,* and *j* silently modernized.

8 Among recent discussions of the patronage system, see Guy Fitch Lytle and Stephen Orgel, eds., *Patronage in the Renaissance* (Princeton University Press, 1981); Robert C. Evans, *Ben Jonson and the Poetics of Patronage* (Lewisburgh: Bucknell University Press, 1989); Arthur Marotti, *John Donne, Coterie Poet* (Madison: University of Wisconsin Press, 1986).

9 Frank Whigham, "The Rhetoric of Elizabethan Suitors' Letters," *PMLA* 96 (1981): 864–82; see also his *Ambition and Privilege: The Social Tropes of Elizabethan Courtesy Theory* (Berkeley: University of California Press, 1984).

10 On the Villiers connection, see Rhodes Dunlap, *Poems*, pp. xxxiv–xxxv; and Michael P. Parker, "Carew, Kit Villiers, and the Character of Caroline Courtliness," *Renaissance Papers* (1983): 89–102. Arundel and Buckingham not only differed in character but were political foes; see Kevin Sharpe, "The Earl of Arundel, his Circle, and the Opposition to the Duke of Buckingham, 1621–8," in *Faction and Parliament: Essays on Early Stuart History*, ed. Sharpe (Oxford: Clarendon Press, 1978), pp. 209–244.

11 Sir Edward Herbert, later Lord Herbert of Cherbury, was in his middle years an epitome of vainglorious, aristocratic eccentricity, who appears to have chosen his companions in Paris chiefly for what Clarendon describes in Carew as "facetious Wit" (Dunlap, *Poems*, p. xxxiii). See also the amusing comments of George Held, "Brother Poets: The Relationship between Edward and George Herbert," in *Like Season'd Timber: New Essays on George Herbert*, ed. Edmund Miller and Robert DiYanni (New York: Peter Lang, 1987), pp. 19–35.

12 Parker, "Carew," p. 96.

13 See chapter 1 above.

14 On mutuality in "To A. L." and a view of its speaker convergent with mine, see Renée Hannaford, "Self-Presentation in Carew's 'To A. L. Perswasions to Love,'" *Studies in English Literature* 26 (1986): 97–106; for a divergent view, see Kevin Sharpe, *Criticism and Compliment: The Politics of Literature in the England of Charles I*

(Cambridge University Press, 1987), which interprets this poem (and others) more idealistically: "the poet/lover offers not merely the sexual gratification of the moment, but love for life" (p. 117). For another interpretation of biographical anecdote, see Joanne Altieri, "Responses to a Waning Mythology in Carew's Political Poetry," *Studies in English Literature* 26 (1986): 107–24; for suggestive comments on Carew's political stance as a poet, see Diana Benet, "Carew's Monarchy of Wit," in "*The Muses Commonweale*": *Poetry and Politics in the Seventeenth Century*, ed. Claude J. Summers and Ted-Larry Pebworth (Columbia: University of Missouri Press, 1988), pp. 80–91.

15 Carew also speaks of love as reaping in "Lips and Eyes" (where he inserts the metaphor into his translation of Marino) and in "Song: Perswasions to enjoy."

16 Low, *Georgic Revolution*, pp. 255–56. For comments on Bruno's *Lo Spaccio della Bestia Trionfante* and reform, see also pp. 135–40.

17 Recent feminist criticism has, of course, modified our sense of this idealization and elevation of the mistress, and emphasized the unequal power relationship between the masculine poet in a patriarchal society – the active subject who controls the poem – and his mistress, who is rendered a passive, fictionalized object. See, e.g., Nancy J. Vickers, "Diana Described: Scattered Woman and Scattered Rhyme," *Critical Inquiry* 8 (1981): 265–79; and Nona Fienberg, "The Emergence of Stella in *Astrophil and Stella*," *SEL* 25 (1985): 5–19. There is much of value in these insights; yet it remains true, I believe, that Petrarchan love lyrics usually elevate, idealize, and empower the mistress, however grudgingly.

7 JOHN MILTON: "BECAUSE WEE FREELY LOVE"

1 The best summary is Patrick Murray, *Milton: The Modern Phase, A Study of Twentieth-century Criticism* (London: Longmans, 1967). For brevity I take the most familiar critical animadversions in this and the following paragraph from Murray, who notes original sources.

2 This discussion has centered on *Samson Agonistes*. Earlier studies argue whether its spirit is more Hebraic than Greek, more recent ones whether it reveals Milton to be bigoted and vengeful, or whether he distances himself from his violent hero.

3 *Milton's God*, revised edition (London: Chatto & Windus, 1965), p. 10. See also his chapter on Milton in *Some Versions of Pastoral*, and Leavis's later comments in *The Common Pursuit*.

4 E. M. W. Tillyard, *Milton*, revised edition (London: Chatto & Windus, 1966), p. 283.

5 F. R. Leavis, "Milton's Verse," reprinted in *Revaluation: Tradition and Development in English Poetry* (London: George W. Steward, 1947; New York: Norton, 1963), p. 42.

6 Many would say Bush and Lewis were "conservative" – a slippery label. Since their deaths both have been often maligned. Bush was a Midwestern populist, liberal in politics. I remember his warm enthusiasm for Hubert Humphrey when I spoke with him toward the end of his life, and his disappointment that Humphrey had been coopted by Lyndon Johnson. Nor was C. S. Lewis really a "conservative."

7 "On Paradise Lost" (lines 7–10); *The Poems and Letters of Andrew Marvell*, ed. H. M. Margoliouth, 2 vols., 2nd edition (1967; Oxford: Clarendon Press, 1952), 1:131.

8 For an amusing account of the movement to make Donne into a modern, see Merritt Y. Hughes, "Kidnapping Donne," *University of California Publications in English* 4 (1934): 61–89.

9 This is such a large matter that one must either flatten the subtleties of critical opinion or spend a whole book distinguishing them. Among recent studies – many of which do not wholly approve of Milton's political violence, and some of which wholeheartedly deprecate it, yet seldom without some admiring ambivalence – might be numbered Stanley Fish, "Spectacle and Evidence in *Samson Agonistes*," *Critical Inquiry* 15 (1989): 556–86, which deprecates Samson's militancy but admires Milton's poetry for an essentially nihilistic destruction of customary pieties; David Loewenstein, *Milton and the Drama of History: Historical Vision, Iconoclasm, and the Literary Imagination* (Cambridge University Press, 1990), which at times is swept away by its powerful vision of Milton's iconclastic political destructiveness; and John Guillory, "The Father's House: *Samson Agonistes* in Its Historical Moment," in *Re-membering Milton: Essays on the Texts and Traditions*, ed. Mary Nyquist and Margaret W. Ferguson (London: Methuen, 1987), which treats Milton as a Marxist-Freudian demythologizer. Hundreds of other instances might be cited. Of course there are important dissenters who see Milton as an enemy of contemporary ideology, such as Sandra M. Gilbert, "Patriarchal Poetry and Women Readers: Reflections on Milton's Bogey," *PMLA* 93 (1978): 368–82; but for each dissenter many others are eager to coopt or recuperate Milton for political progress.

10 *The Works of John Milton*, ed. Frank Allen Patterson, *et al.*, 18 vols. plus index (New York: Columbia University Press, 1931–40). All quotations from Milton's poetry are from this edition and are cited by book and line number.

11 *St. Augustine's Enchiridion*: *Or Manual to Laurentius Concerning Faith, Hope, and Charity*, trans. Ernest Evans (London: S. P. C. K., 1953), p. 28. Also: "This is the true liberty, because of joy for the upright act; and no less is it pious servitude, because of obedience to the commandment."

12 On the remarkable pervasiveness of the idea of the historical Church as Antichrist in seventeenth-century England, see Christopher Hill, *Antichrist in Seventeenth-Century England* (London: Oxford University Press, 1971). On the immense significance of this view of history not only to the rise of religious Protestantism but to the nature of the modern West generally, see Anthony Kemp, *The Estrangement of the Past: A Study in the Origins of Modern Historical Consciousness* (Oxford University Press, 1991).

13 *Complete Prose Works of John Milton*, ed. Don Wolfe *et al.*, 8 vols. (New Haven: Yale University Press, 1953–82) 2:732. Quotations from Milton's English prose are cited from this edition by volume and page number.

14 *Sermons*, ed. Simpson and Potter, 7:87–88; see chapter 3 above. Indeed, Donne's rhetorical question imitates God's in scripture: "For when hee sayes, *Where is the Bill*, hee meanes there is no such *Bill.*" Although Donne here speaks of God's marriage with an individual soul, the principle applies in both cases.

15 Richard Hooker urges against Puritan reformers the orthodox Anglican view: "the stains and blemishes found in our state; which springing from the root of human frailty and corruption, not only are, but have always more or less, yea and (for any thing we know to the contrary) will be till the world's end complained of, what form of Government soever take place" ("A Preface" [3.7], *The Laws of Ecclesiastical Polity* [London: J. M. Dent, 1907] 1:98).

16 See Heinz Holeczek, *Humanistische Bibelphilologie als Reformproblem bis Erasmus von Rotterdam, Thomas More, und William Tyndale* (Leiden, 1975), pp. 331–42.

17 There are a few perfunctory exceptions in *The Reason of Church-Government*: "Christ, the head and husband of his Church" (1:749); "Certainly if God be the father of his family the Church ... Againe, if Christ be the Churches husband" (1:755); "Church-discipline ... is the worke of God as father, and of Christ as Husband of the Church" (1:756). See also *Martin Bucer* (2:464–65) and *Tetrachordon* (2:591, 607, 630, 682), where Milton cites Paul's comparison of marriage to Christ's love of the Church in much the same spirit as the passages I have previously quoted.

18 Although, as critics often point out, no topic other than divorce inspired him to such distortions of biblical texts.

19 The apocalyptic marriage of Christ and his Church was a part of the tradition, but only a part. As St. Bernard remarks, the Song of Songs comprises three aspects of the divine marriage: "the Creation of heaven and earth, the Reconciliation, and the Restoration"; *St. Bernard's Sermons on the Canticle of Canticles*, trans. by a Priest of Mt. Melleray, 2 vols. (Dublin: Browne & Nolan, 1920) 1:238. On connections between the Song of Songs and Revelation, which became more urgent in the seventeenth century especially among Puritan writers, see Stanley Stewart, *The Enclosed Garden: The Tradition and the Image in Seventeenth-Century Poetry* (Madison: University of Wisconsin Press, 1966), pp. 132–34; on the place of George Herbert's "Church Militant" in this tradition, see Raymond A. Anselment, "'The Church Militant': George Herbert and the Metamorphoses of Christian History," *Huntington Library Quarterly* 41 (1978): 299–316. Where Milton parts most from the tradition is in his approval only of the apocalyptic Bride.

20 "And there appeared a great wonder in heaven; a woman clothed with the sun, and the moon under her feet, and upon her head a crown of twelve stars: And she being with child ... [A]nd behold a great red dragon ... And his tail drew the third part of the stars of heaven, and did cast them to the earth: and the dragon stood before the woman which was ready to be delivered, for to devour her child as soon as it was born. And she brought forth a man child, who was to rule all nations with a rod of iron ... And the woman fled into the wilderness, where she hath a place prepared of God, that they should feed her there a thousand two hundred and threescore days" (Revelation 12:1–6).

21 Daniel Featley, "The Embleme of the Church Militant," *Clavis Mystica: A Key Opening Divers Difficult and Mysterious Texts of Holy Scripture* (London, 1636), p. 301; cited in Barbara Kiefer Lewalski, *Protestant Poetics and the Seventeenth-Century Religious Lyric* (Princeton University Press, 1979), p. 304.

    Featley's is, of course, a revision of the traditional Roman Catholic reading of the Woman Clothed with the Sun as Mary the Mother of Christ. For recent Catholic discussions of the nature of the Church, with considerable citation from tradition and from various Protestant views, see Henri de Lubac, *The Splendor of the Church*, trans. Michael Mason (1953; San Francisco: Ignatius Press, 1986); de Lubac, *The Motherhood of the Church*, trans. Sr. Sergia Englund (1971; San Francisco: Ignatius Press, 1982); Hans Urs von Balthasar, *The Office of Peter and the Structure of the Church*, trans. Andrée Emery (1974; San Francisco: Ignatius Press, 1986); Joseph Cardinal Ratzinger, *Principles of Catholic Theology*, trans. Sr.

Mary Frances McCarthy (1982; San Francisco: Ignatius Press, 1987); also Vatican II constitution *Lumen Gentium*.

22 The passage continues. On similar lines, see also *Of True Religion*: "Hence one of their own famous Writers found just cause to stile the Romish Church *Mother of Error, School of Heresie*" (8:421). According to Keith Stavely's note, Milton may misremember Petrarch's sonnet 107 (*Rime* 138), "scuola d'errori e templo d'eresia"; but Petrarch does not call the Church mother in that poem. Perhaps Milton conflated it with another on the Papal court of Avignon, *Rime* 114: "albergo di dolor, madre d'errori" (line 3).

23 Elsewhere Milton associates the corruption of the Church with the Donation of Constantine. But in *Paradise Lost* the process seems to occur much more quickly.

24 This is not to say that Milton had given up hope and become a political quietist. As *Samson Agonistes* reveals, he firmly believed in obedience to divine inspiration and in performance of righteous deeds, even should they issue in apparent failure. See, for example, M. A. N. Radzinowicz, "*Samson Agonistes* and Milton the Politician in Defeat," *Philological Quarterly* 44 (1965): 454–71, and Christopher Hill, *The Experience of Defeat: Milton and Some Contemporaries* (New York: Viking, 1984), pp. 297–328. As Achsah Guibbory argues in *The Map of Time* (Urbana: University of Illinois Press, 1986), p. 205, experience led Milton to shift "his faith in progress from the realm of history to the life of the individual."

25 It is as if the Church lasted just long enough to produce the Bible; then religion could be left to individuals and the Spirit. Indeed, as Milton points out elsewhere, the written record too has been corrupted by those who have transmitted it – though not in its essentials.

26 Milton was not a Calvinist in regard to grace and election. See *Paradise Lost* 3.183–97 (often, however, misinterpreted) and Dennis Richard Danielson, *Milton's Good God: A Study in Literary Theodicy* (Cambridge University Press, 1982).

27 By far the best criticism of the prose is that of Thomas Kranidas, in his early book *The Fierce Equation: A Study of Milton's Decorum* (The Hague: Mouton, 1965) and in recent articles, such as "Polarity and Structure in Milton's *Areopagitica*," *English Literary Renaissance* 14 (1984): 175–90.

28 William Prynne, *A Looking-Glasse* (1636), p. 103; cited 2:617n.

29 John Bunyan, *The Pilgrim's Progress*, ed. N. H. Keeble (Oxford University Press, 1984), p. 133.

30 For a discussion of the background to divine "hate" in Milton, see

Michael Lieb, "'Hate in Heav'n': Milton and the *Odium Dei*," *ELH* 53 (1986): 519–30; and on hate and love, see James G. Turner, *One Flesh* (Oxford: Clarendon Press, 1987), pp. 211–26.

31 Joseph H. Summers, *The Muse's Method: An Introduction to Paradise Lost* (London: Chatto & Windus, 1962), pp. 176–85, 180.

32 Arnold Stein, *Answerable Style: Essays on Paradise Lost* (Seattle: University of Washington Press, 1953), pp. 17–37.

33 John T. Shawcross, "The Balanced Structure of *Paradise Lost*," *Studies in Philology* 62 (1965): 696–718; and *Key-Indexed Study Guide to Milton's Paradise Lost* (Philadelphia: Educational Research Associates, 1966), p. 61. In the first edition of *Paradise Lost*, 5,275 lines precede and follow this line. On the importance of holy war, see Michael Lieb, *Poetics of the Holy: A Reading of Paradise Lost* (Chapel Hill: University of North Carolina Press, 1981).

34 "Milton's God: Authority in *Paradise Lost*," *Milton Studies* 4 (1972): 19–38. See especially 3.56–64.

35 Hell is the absence of God: a fundamental theological point. Milton's hell is "As far remov'd from God and light of Heav'n / As from the Center thrice to th' utmost Pole" (1.73–74). For the damned, who have rejected God's love (Satan tells Beelzebub) "fardest from him is best" (1.247).

36 Were the phrase not so debased, I might have said "meaningful relationships." "Heartfelt" is not quite adequate, since love was considered a matter of "will" as well as of "feeling," "emotion," and "affection." As we have seen (especially in chapter 3 above), "relation" had significant meaning for the seventeenth century as well as for ours.

37 Dante Alighieri, *The Divine Comedy*, trans. Charles S. Singleton, 6 vols. (Princeton University Press, 1970–75) 1:24–25 (1.3.1–9); I have reduced Singleton's translation to lower case.

38 Of course, the Enlightenment has an unacknowledged totalizing zeal of its own, as one can hardly fail to notice in reading, for example, Voltaire, whose views are summed up in his well-known phrase, *Ecrase l'infame*. See, for example, Theodor W. Adorno and Max Horkheimer, *The Dialectic of Enlightenment*, translated by John Cumming (New York: Herder and Herder, 1972).

39 Here again, Postmodernism is too diffuse to pin it down in less than a book. I speak of a major tendency in the area of Milton criticism. Herman Rapaport, *Milton and the Postmodern* (Lincoln: University of Nebraska Press, 1983), shows how easily Milton may be read by way of Nietzsche, Derrida, Kristeva, and some other icons of Postmodernism. But his outlook on Milton's violent divisiveness and on what he views as his Cartesian "instrumentalized reason"

is finally more regretful than approving. Indeed, especially when taken out of context, his judgments seem far more urgent than mine. Yet – as my argument might suggest – Rapaport's words are not without foundation in Milton's works: "Not only Descartes and Corneille but Milton as well were only too willing to underwrite such a cultural breakup ... The question is how we are to evaluate a political thinker who not only was a great writer of religious poetry, an extraordinarily brilliant classical scholar, fluent in ancient tongues even as a child, but who also writes tracts which look ahead to what in our day appears as the legitimation of storm troopers, death squads, and the other political apparatuses of terror, and all in the guise of instrumentalized reason?" (p. 171). In my view, misreadings of Milton by his successors – misreadings for which Milton admittedly provides some basis – chiefly make such tragic outcomes possible. But I may be too charitable to him.

40 Approaching the matter as a question of political liberty, Christopher Hill comments on the dilemma posed by Miltonic individualism: "Liberty and self-discipline are both *individual* virtues, self-regarding. Neither are communal virtues of the type which Winstanley wished to encourage. Nevertheless discipline is based on the consent of the congregation, and self-discipline is needed to make community life possible" (*Milton and the English Revolution* [New York: Viking, 1977], p. 257). By itself, "congregation" implies no more than a way station between the individual Christian and the credal *una ecclesia*, or the biblical "one fold, and one shepherd" (John 10:16) – whether governance and consent come chiefly from the top down or from the bottom up. On the need for a Church, as argued by a variety of authorities, see de Lubac, *The Motherhood of the Church*, pp. 8–18, and notably his quotation from Karl Barth (*Dogmatique*, 4.4.3.31): "The possibility of non-ecclesial Christianity, existing outside of worship rendered in common within the Church, could only have aroused supreme astonishment and total incomprehension in the New Testament community" (de Lubac, *Splendor*, p. 18). Denis Donoghue reminds me that Milton's millenarian repudiation of the Church may be traced back not only to Luther and Wyclif but to Joachim of Fiore (who urged that the age of the Holy Ghost had superseded those of the Father and the Son). See Norman Cohn's book, with its ominous subtitle, *The Pursuit of the Millenium: Revolutionary Messianism in Medieval and Reformation Europe and its Bearing on Modern Totalitarian Movements*, 2nd edition (New York: Harper & Brothers, 1961). For even earlier periods, see Ronald A. Knox, *Enthusiasm*

(Oxford University Press, 1950). And on the spread of religious individualism in the modern age see Harold Bloom, *The American Religion* (New York: Simon and Shuster, 1992). That Christianity without a Church is paradoxical is not at all obvious to the modern mind; in this, we are children of Milton and of the transformations he represents.

41 In *The Prophetic Milton* (Charlottesville: University Press of Virginia, 1974), William Kerrigan negotiates between admiration for the energies unleashed by Milton's confidence in divine inspiration and the contemporary assumption that such confidence cannot be objectively grounded.

42 Although I am concerned here mainly with Milton and divine love, many have also pointed out how *Paradise Lost*, *Areopagitica*, and the political tracts were increasingly influential in the Glorious Revolution of 1688, the Whig Movement, and the American Revolution.

8 JOHN MILTON: "HAILE WEDDED LOVE"

1 For admiring references to Milton and marriage, see Raymond D. Havens, *The Influence of Milton on English Poetry* (Cambridge, MA: Harvard University Press, 1922); Ann Gossman and G. W. Whiting, "Milton, Patron of Marriage," *Notes & Queries* 8 (1981): 180–81; Nancy Lee Riffe, "Milton in the 18th-Century Periodicals: 'Hail, Wedded Love,'" *Notes & Queries* 12 (1965): 18–19; and Dustin Griffin, *Regaining Paradise: Milton and the eighteenth century* (Cambridge University Press, 1986), pp. 124–33. For Milton and "companionate" marriage see Jean Hagstrum, *Sex and Sensibility: Ideal and Erotic Love from Milton to Mozart* (University of Chicago Press, 1980).

2 *Voltaire's Essay on Epic Poetry*, ed. F. D. White (Albany, 1915), p. 133; cited by Griffin, *Regaining Paradise*, p. 271, n. 93.

3 See Leo Miller, *John Milton Among the Polygamophiles* (New York: Loewenthal Press, 1974). For English responses to Milton's divorce tracts, see *Milton: A Bibliography for the Years 1624–1700*, compiled by John T. Shawcross (Binghamton: Medieval & Renaissance Texts & Studies, 1984), index, p. 401.

4 Robert Baillie, *A Dissuasive from the Errours Of the Time Wherein the Tenets of the principall Sects, especially of the Independents, are drawn together in one Map* (London, 1645), p. 116 for 112; cited in *Milton: The Critical Heritage*, ed. John T. Shawcross (London: Routledge & Kegan Paul, 1970), p. 12.

5 *The Correspondence of Samuel Richardson* (1804) 6:198; cited in *Milton*

1732–1801: *The Critical Heritage*, ed. John T. Shawcross (London: Routledge & Kegan Paul, 1972), p. 15.

6 *O. E. D.*, 1st edition, s.v. "Miltonist."

7 John T. Shawcross pointed me to an early use of "Miltonist" meaning divorcer in Christopher Wasse's poem "The Return," part of an epilogue to *Electra of Sophocles: Presented to Her Highnesse the Lady Elizabeth* (The Hague, 1649), sig. E8.

8 John G. Halkett, *Milton and the Idea of Matrimony: A Study of the Divorce Tracts and Paradise Lost* (New Haven: Yale University Press, 1970), p. 3. Because he treats the interface of marriage and divorce in Milton, I have found his work especially useful for my purposes. I should also mention here James Grantham Turner's powerful study, *One Flesh: Paradisal Marriage and Sexual Relations in the Age of Milton* (Oxford: Clarendon Press, 1987), from which I have learned much, although my interests (fortunately) are somewhat different from his. Turner focuses more directly on issues of sexuality than I do, probes the earlier traditions in greater detail, and focuses especially on the interpretive split in reading Adam and Eve's sexuality as either paradisal or sinful.

9 *Areopagitica*; *Complete Prose Works* 2:553. See chapter 7 above.

10 Jeremy Taylor, "The Marriage-Ring; or, the Mysteriousness and Duties of Marriage," in *The Whole Works*, ed. Reginald Heber (London, 1822) 5:258; cited by Halkett, p. 16. I am further indebted to Halkett for citing the passages on procreation and the Church that follow in the next two paragraphs.

11 William Guild, *Loves Entercours between The Lamb and his Bride, Christ and his Church* (London, 1658), pp. 1–2.

12 Parsons, *Boaz and Ruth Blessed Or A Sacred Contract Hounoured with a solemne Benediction* (Oxford, 1633), pp. 29–30. Contractions in this and other primary works are expanded. The primacy of procreation was not only a Christian position. Georges Duby argues that aristocratic lay practices that preceded the full establishment of Christian marriage doctrine likewise are based on the assumed primacy of procreation in marriage. See his *Medieval Marriage: Two Models from Twelfth-Century France*, trans. Elborg Forster (Baltimore: Johns Hopkins University Press, 1978), p. 92. As Duby also points out, it was the Church which, as early as the twelfth century, argued the importance of mutual consent and love in marriage, as against lay concern with parental arrangement and continuance of lineage. His evidence contradicts the common recent assumption that conjugal mutuality originated with Protestantism. See also Christopher N. L. Brooke, *The Medieval Idea of Marriage* (Oxford University Press, 1989), esp. pp. 128–29, and

John T. Noonan, "Marital Affection in the Canonists," *Studia Gratiana*, 12 (1967): 479–509, on the gradual transformation in meaning of the key term *maritalis affectio* from consent of the parties or heads of family in Roman law to consent of the couple in medieval papal decrees and ecclesiastical law and finally to mutually affectionate feelings. Consent of the parties is an objective fact, which implies affection or at least absence of antipathy.

13 William Perkins, "A Golden Chaine," in *Works* (Cambridge, 1603), p. 62, col. 2.

14 Samuel Hieron, "The Bridegroome," in *Sermons* (London: 1614–20), p. 469.

15 William Ames, *The Marrow of Sacred Divinity* (London, 1642), p. 323.

16 Richard Bernard, *Ruth's Recompence: or a Commentarie upon the Booke of Ruth* (London, 1628), p. 422.

17 Benjamin Needler, *Expository Notes, with Practical Observations, towards The opening of the five first Chapters of the first Book of Moses called Genesis* (London, 1655), p. 50.

18 *Sermons*, ed. Simpson and Potter, 3:245.

19 William Riley Parker, *Milton: A Biography*, 2 vols. (Oxford: Clarendon Press, 1968) 1:480. Milton's third marriage to Elizabeth Minshull, however, took place in Church (Parker, 1:583).

20 Marshall Grossman reminds me in a letter that the divorce tracts were written in the context of a parliamentary effort to control marriage through a Presbyterian state church. In the context of this debate, close relations between church and marriage were problematic. Milton was, however, free – as Royalists were differently free – to define "church" in terms other than those that the Presbyterian party were trying to enforce.

21 See Halkett, *Milton*, p. 100; and Marshall Grossman, *"Authors to Themselves": Milton and the Revelation of History* (Cambridge University Press, 1987): "The parody of the trinity provided by the Satanic family figures forth the entrapment of desire in the closed orbit of narcissism as the antithesis of the divine propagation of holy love in the emanation of desire for and through others" (p. 45).

22 The point is persuasively argued by A. G. George, *Milton and the Nature of Man* (London: Asia Publishing House, 1974), pp. 65–74.

23 Much discussion has passed to and fro on this issue; see especially Diane Kelsey McColley, *Milton's Eve* (Urbana: University of Illinois Press, 1983), who cites earlier studies and points out that "subordination is not inferiority" (p. 35) and is "an opportunity for the exercise of special virtues" (p. 27). See also Joseph

Wittreich, *Feminist Milton* (Ithaca: Cornell University Press, 1987); *Milton and the Idea of Woman*, ed. Julia M. Walker (Urbana: University of Illinois Press, 1988); and Anne Ferry, "Milton's Creation of Eve," *Studies in English Literature* 28 (1988): 113–32. Halkett's summary (*Milton*, pp. 103–38) remains convincing.

24 *Complete Prose Works* 2:596–97; on Milton's advocacy of alternating labor and relaxation see A. Low, *The Georgic Revolution* (Princeton University Press), pp. 304–06.

25 On this passage and on Augustine's view of sexuality see Peter A. Fiore, *Milton and Augustine: Patterns of Augustinian Thought in Paradise Lost* (University Park: Pennsylvania State University Press, 1981), pp. 32–33; see also Peter Lindenbaum, "Lovemaking in Milton's Paradise," *Milton Studies* 6 (1974):277–306.

26 See especially 4.344–417, 5.618–41, 7.594–634.

27 See especially Robert H. West, *Milton and the Angels* (Athens: University of Georgia Press, 1955). Milton's belief in material angels is a result of his monism, and therefore related to his mortalism, on which see Norman T. Burns, *Christian Mortalism from Tyndale to Milton* (Cambridge, MA: Harvard University Press, 1972). As to angelic procreation, some critics have found Satan's appearance as a "stripling Cherube" significant (3.636); but it is doubtful that too much can be drawn from this phrase.

28 See, for example, C. S. Lewis, *A Preface to Paradise Lost* (Oxford University Press, 1942), p. 127; Douglas Bush, *Paradise Lost in Our Time* (Ithaca: Cornell University Press, 1945), pp. 74–87; Anthony Low, *The Blaze of Noon: A Reading of Samson Agonistes* (New York: Columbia University Press, 1974), pp. 23–31.

29 Although the biblical text puts the union in physical terms, spiritual union is also understood by later interpreters. Milton did not distinguish body from spirit – which, although it does not make him a modern materialist, may again signal his unwitting availability for such future developments.

30 Lewis, *Preface to Paradise Lost*, p. 127.

31 Among the earliest proponents of this view is Dennis H. Burden, *The Logical Epic: A Study of the Argument of Paradise Lost* (London: Routledge & Kegan Paul, 1967), p. 170.

32 Strict Calvinists argued that each person is irresistibly elect or reprobate – but that no one but God can surely know the state of another person. In any case, Milton was not a Calvinist.

33 Halkett does not quite drive this point all the way home, but certainly raises it in connection with astrology (*Milton*, p. 49) and Platonism (*ibid.*, *pp.* 56–57).

34 John Selden, *Uxor Ebraica* (1646), 2:xx, pp. 471–73, translation

provided by Jason P. Rosenblatt, who called these passages to my attention. For his quotation from Claudius Ptolemy Selden cites *Tetrabiblos*, cap. Peri Sunarmogon.

35 Calvin, *Commentary on Genesis*, trans. John King (London, 1847), on Genesis 2:24; cited by Turner, *One Flesh*, p. 72. The reference to Plato is unusual for Calvin, who usually invokes even the Church Fathers by name only when disagreeing with them.

36 William Perkins, *Christian Oeconomie: or, a Short Survey of the Right Manner of Ordering a Familie according to the Scriptures* (London, 1609), pp. 23–24, 54–55, 57, 59, 62; cited by Halkett, *Milton*, p. 42.

37 "I am Alpha and Omega, the beginning and the end, the first and the last" (Revelation 22:13). On the deep structure of divorce and division as a habit of mind in Milton, see Sanford Budick, *The Dividing Muse: Images of Sacred Disjunction in Milton's Poetry* (New Haven: Yale University Press, 1985). Commenting on the method of the divorce tracts, Edward W. Tayler, in "Milton's Grim Laughter and Second Choices," in *Turning Points in the History of Poetic Knowledge*, ed. Roland Hagenbüchle and Laura Skandera, *Eichstäter Beiträge* 20 (1983): 76, remarks: "the radical exegete foreshadows the radical politician." Significantly, Milton reaches his theory of the primacy of divorce by a hermeneutics based on love; see Theodore L. Huguelet, "The Rule of Charity in Milton's Divorce Tracts," *Milton Studies* 6 (1974): 199–214.

38 In *Paradise Lost*, Satan speaks of "fate" as a way to avoid recognizing God's providence. Although Milton does not use the word in the divorce tracts, he approaches the principle.

39 Low, *Blaze of Noon*, pp. 144–58.

40 See, for example, Dayton Haskin, "Divorce as a Path to Union with God in *Samson Agonistes*," *ELH* 38 (1971): 358–76; Ricki Heller, "Opposites of Wifehood: Eve and Dalila," *Milton Studies* 24 (1989): 187–202.

41 John C. Ulreich, Jr., "'Incident to All our Sex': The Tragedy of Dalila," in *Milton and the Idea of Woman*, ed. Walker, pp. 185–210. I do not find Ulreich persuasive in arguing that Milton *meant* Samson and Dalila to be seen as equally culpable in failing to achieve a reconciliation. What is persuasive, however, is the fundamental contradiction that Ulreich exposes in Milton's views on Christian free will and divorce.

42 "Then came Peter to him, and said, Lord, how oft shall my brother sin against me, and I forgive him? till seven times? Jesus saith unto him, I say not unto thee, Until seven times: but, Until seventy times seven" (Matthew 18:21–22).

43 I have borrowed the word "abler" from Donne's "The Extasie,"

where he elaborates a theory concerning the power of mutual love to correct individual defects very similar to Adam's: "When love, with one another so / Interinanimates two soules, / That abler soule, which thence doth flow, / Defects of lonelinesse controules" (lines 41–44). Many recent studies, for example McColley's, have convincingly argued that Eve, like Adam, must be deemed "sufficient," fully capable of choice. But to further argue, as some critics have, that Eve did well to separate from Adam and consequently to face Satan alone is problematic. Milton is most doubtful about the powers of individual autonomy precisely with regard to marriage. For a useful discussion see, for example, Louis L. Martz, *Milton: Poet of Exile*, 2nd edition (New Haven: Yale University Press, 1986), pp. 127–36, and Joan S. Bennett, *Reviving Liberty: Radical Christian Humanism in Milton's Great Poems* (Cambridge, MA: Harvard University Press, 1989), pp. 94–118.

44 See Lewis, *Preface to Paradise Lost*, pp. 116–21; about Eve, the "inferior" member of the pair, he says: "You must not think but that if you and I could enter Milton's Eden and meet her we should very quickly be taught what it is to speak to the 'universal dame'" (p. 120). In effect, Lewis puts his hero, Ransom, and the reader into Eve's company in *Perelandra*, with just the humbling and distancing effect he anticipates here. Fiore is helpful on the "preternatural life" of Adam and Eve before their fall (*Milton and Augustine*, pp. 23–41). But, as numerous recent studies suggest (for example, Barbara Lewalski, "Milton on Women – Yet Once More," *Milton Studies* 6 [1975]: 3–19), unfallen life in *Paradise Lost* more closely resembles fallen life than one might expect. And as Turner notes, many readers have found the Eden story "insufferably remote and uncomfortably present" (*One Flesh*, p. 5).

45 Freud drew heavily on Milton when creating his theories. See Paul C. Vitz, *Sigmund Freud's Christian Unconscious* (New York: Guilford Press, 1988); and Perry Meisel, introduction to *Freud: A Collection of Critical Essays* (Englewood Cliffs, NJ: Prentice-Hall, 1981). Together with Moses, as Meisel remarks, Milton was one of the two fatherly authority figures with whom Freud felt a particular need to struggle – a need to fear and depose him. The origins of feminism are elsewhere, but wrestling with Shakespeare and Milton has helped to define it.

46 As many readers will know, Griswold finds in the Constitution a right to privacy in the married relationship with respect to contraception; Roe v. Wade finds a right to privacy of the woman (here not the couple) with respect to abortion.

47 See *Urbane Milton: The Latin Poetry*, ed. James A. Freeman and

Anthony Low (Pittsburgh University Press, 1984); and Anna K. Nardo, *Milton's Sonnets and the Ideal Community* (Lincoln: University of Nebraska Press, 1979).

48 See John M. Steadman, *Milton and the Renaissance Hero* (Oxford: Clarendon Press, 1967), pp. 108–36; and Low, *Blaze of Noon*, pp. 26–31. It is noticeable, too, how little Patricia A. Parker's discussion of Milton in *Inescapable Romance* (Princeton University Press, 1979), pp. 114–58, touches on deferral of desire. The romance of *Paradise Lost* is of another kind.

49 Kerrigan and Braden, *The Idea of the Renaissance*, pp. 26–31.

CONCLUSION

1 *Religio Medici* (1.31), in *The Prose of Sir Thomas Browne*, ed. Norman J. Endicott (New York: Doubleday, 1967), p. 39.

2 Burton, *The Anatomy of Melancholy* (3.2.1.2), ed. Holbrook Jackson, 3 vols. (London: J. M. Dent & Sons, 1932) 3:54–55.

3 Burton, *Anatomy* (3.2.1.2), 3:53; Holbrook's translations in square brackets. For information of a more sociological nature that the Middle Ages anticipated the Renaissance in *maritalis affectio* (if it is not already obvious) see, for example, recent studies by Barbara Hanawalt and Shulamith Shahar. Pre-publication publicity indicates that Jean H. Hagstrum's forthcoming *Esteem Enlivened by Desire: The Couple from Homer to Shakespeare* (Chicago University Press, 1992) – which I have not seen – will argue that love leading to marriage is ancient.

4 *The Workes of T. Becon*, 3 vols (1564), 1 (1560): sig. QQqiii-iv; cited by Heather Dubrow, *A Happier Eden: The Politics of Marriage in the Stuart Epithalamium* (Ithaca: Cornell University Press, 1990), p. 22.

Index